CAPTAIN DREYFUS

THE STORY OF A MASS HYSTERIA

BY

NICHOLAS HALASZ

GROVE PRESS, INC.   NEW YORK

EVERGREEN BOOKS LTD. LONDON

TO

KARL POLANYI

FRIEND AND GUIDE

ACKNOWLEDGMENTS

THE *admiration of Professor Hans Zeisel of the University of Chicago Law School for the Dreyfusard intellectuals whose protest against a judicial error became a high-water mark of Western civilization gave rise to this book at this particular time. Mr. Joseph Barnes made valuable criticisms and suggestions in the formative stage. Dr. and Mrs. Paul Erdos helped with sympathetic comment. Ilona Duczynska's insight into the author's true intentions organized the manuscript. The inspired editing of Ira Wolfert gave the book its final shape.*

The author is deeply indebted to them for their friendly assistance.

The technical completion of the manuscript owes all to Mrs. Grace Carter's perseverance.

N. H.

CONTENTS

"THOU SHALT NOT FOLLOW A MULTITUDE TO DO EVIL"
—Exodus XXIII, 2

Part One

THE TRAITOR

I

ON JULY 20, 1894, a visitor was announced to Colonel Max von Schwarzkoppen, military attaché of the German Embassy in Paris. The colonel descended the few steps from his office into the lobby—a tall, cool, intelligent-looking officer, not arrogant, but bearing himself in accordance with the iron-necked standards of a Prussian nobleman.

Facing him was a slightly built gentleman with drawn features, deep-seated small black eyes and a large mustache that hid a drooping chin. He was in his early forties. The red ribbon of the Legion of Honor ornamented the buttonhole of his black overcoat, and he carried himself with a standardized manner of his own. He was unmistakably a French officer in mufti.

The exact dialogue that then ensued was never recorded, but Colonel von Schwarzkoppen's utter astonishment has been. It was the kind of scene in which the director would make the actor pop his monocle. The French officer volunteered his services as a spy. He explained that financial difficulties, aggravated by his wife's illness, had forced him to this expedient. He had served in Algiers and on the Italian frontier; worked in the intelligence department of the Ministry of War; had good connections with the head of that department, Colonel Jean Sandherr; was a schoolmate of the President of the Republic, Jean Casimir-Périer. Thus he made clear that he was in a position to render valuable services. To prove it he reached into his pocket and offered to hand over a secret document.

Recovered from his astonishment, the Prussian colonel raised his hand in a gesture of refusal. He would not even look at the document.

3

He would not help an officer betray his country. He earnestly counseled the man to find some other way out of his financial difficulties. There was suicide, the officer in mufti suggested; that was the only other way. The colonel brushed the suggestion aside. He exhorted him once more against so fateful a step as treason, and then withdrew to his office deeply disturbed, leaving the pale, slight, mustachioed Frenchman to find his way out alone.

The year before, France had concluded an alliance with Russia. It had made it necessary for the French General Staff to reorient the strategy for coping with the cardinal enemy, Germany. New comprehensive plans for mobilization were drawn up. Mobilization plans are vast matters, reaching into the farthest corners of a nation. It is not only a question of calling up men but also of weapons. New guns were being designed and tested in that year 1894—new explosives. The Germans took it for granted that such would be the case, and their spies flocked to the scene.

Colonel von Schwarzkoppen himself had succeeded a military attaché whose name had been connected with espionage and who therefore had had to withdraw from France. In the excitement of the scandal, the German Ambassador Count Münster, a diplomat of the old school, gave his word of honor that he would not tolerate any connection between his personnel and espionage. The gentlemanly old count did not know that his new military attaché had received secret instructions in Berlin before leaving for Paris, placing him under direct orders from the German General Staff.

Thus it had not been for moral but for practical reasons that Colonel von Schwarzkoppen had rejected the services of the officer in mufti. Who can trust a man, however desperate, who comes unknown from the streets to canvass at one's front door with such goods? Who is to say he was not an *agent provocateur* sent by the French?

However, the colonel was a soldier and did not have to make decisions on his own. He reported the strange visit to Berlin. The reply came back swiftly: Negotiate.

The colonel had no way of locating the French officer, but he did not have long to wait to activate his orders. Two days after his first visit, the desperate figure in mufti walked in the front door for a second time. The conversation did not take place in the lobby. He was conducted into the colonel's office. This time he gave his name: Major Count Ferdinand Walsin-Esterhazy, commander of a battalion of the

French Army stationed at Rouen. He brought with him his own most recent mobilization orders as an earnest of the work he could do and asked to be put on the payroll at a salary of 2,000 francs a month—about $400 at that time.

Schwarzkoppen advised him to get in touch with Berlin. This the French battalion commander refused to do. He put his mobilization orders on the desk and left. The colonel took the next train to Berlin. Those who deal with spies know that they are seedy men, of the class of sneak thieves, and prefer to pay them in that way, in the way fences pay for stolen goods. In Berlin, Schwarzkoppen was instructed not to commit himself to any regular salary but to pay cash on delivery according to what the stuff was worth.

So began a morality play that was to achieve a grandeur unparalleled in the history of the modern state and make France examine in fire and in fear the bedrock upon which democracy is founded. The sanctity of the individual, yes. A noble ideal, no doubt. But as a practical matter, should the whole be sacrificed for the minutest part? Is the moral vindication of one Frenchman worth jeopardizing the security of all Frenchmen?

In facing the question France, the nation of reason, went out of her mind. Normal life stopped. Only a handful of men retained faith in the ability of democracy to provide security for all. The rest had faith only in the State and its Army, and went into paroxysms over any act that reflected on it. In the words of a contemporary writer, "Heroism was needed even to utter the word justice. To protest against the violation of right was made out a crime, and to doubt the infallibility of a military court was considered treason."

Governments fell. Eventually no court, not even the highest, was trusted. The Chamber of Deputies passed a law to prevent France's highest criminal court from considering the matter further. With courts unable to rule in law, the nation came to the brink of anarchy. The fact that the truth was discovered very soon after the nation had accepted the lie made no difference. The lie had to continue to be accepted. To reject it was to reject the material force of the Army as a shield against Germany and embrace instead an abstract ideal as a refuge from brutal violence. The nation refused to do it. It sided with the lie and declared it the only truth.

Even the German Emperor, who knew that the spy he had paid was named Esterhazy and not Dreyfus, as the French insisted, believed that Dreyfus must be a spy and that the French had erred only in the nation which benefited from his treason.

Finally a prince of a small country neighboring on France undertook a confidential journey among the ruling sovereigns of Europe to discover whether the lie had any basis in fact, whether Dreyfus had betrayed France to any nation. Last on his list was the President of the French Republic. They spent a pleasant afternoon together. The prince had a delicate tongue and was skilled in diplomacy. He approached the revelation of his proofs of Dreyfus' innocence with the utmost tact. But he might have spared himself the effort. Tact was not enough, nor were facts and proofs. Nothing would convince the President that the lie was not true and the truth was not a lie. The pleasant afternoon ended in mutual resentment.

That night the President suffered a heart attack and before morning he was dead. He had been known to have an ailing heart, but first Paris and then France seethed with the belief that the visiting prince had killed him with a poisoned cigarette.

The handful of men who fought for the truth and thus for the restoration of the human ideal as a fortress stronger than any army were defamed, cursed, despised, physically attacked, despoiled of their honors, their offices, jailed, driven into exile. But giants of the mind and spirit led the fight. They attracted to themselves men such as the young, high-ranking Army officer who unfolded before the world a noble and serenely beautiful character, insisting in the face of captivity, of threats to his life and the contempt of the entire corps of his brother officers that the truth was true and that only in it was there security for all.

In the end they forced their will on a nation that had become an anarchic mob and returned it to the rule of law. But memorable years of horror and grandeur separated them from that consummation.

2

THE INTELLIGENCE DEPARTMENT of the French General Staff was called the Second Bureau and counter-espionage was handled by the Second Bureau's "Section of Statistics," under the command of Colonel Jean Sandherr.

In all armies opportunities for glory or for imaginative, creative work are scantiest in Intelligence, and thus its jobs tend to fall into the hands of men who have lost out in the more competitive fields of operations, communications and supply. But in casting about for a scapegoat to explain to itself the defeat in 1870 by the Germans, the French—not altogether without reason—had settled on treason, and therefore the Army's Second Bureau had become well equipped with funds and with energy if not quite so well equipped with brains and character.

At the time Count Esterhazy began his negotiations with Colonel von Schwarzkoppen, the Second Bureau was well aware that the Germans were busy trying to ferret out what changes the Russian alliance was precipitating in French war plans and preparations, and Colonel Sandherr's statistical section had scored a counter-espionage coup. It had discovered that Schwarzkoppen in Paris was directing an espionage system with agents in Brussels, Strasbourg and Switzerland.

Contact had been made with the Brussels agent, Richard Cuers. A French agent named Lajoux was feeding Cuers with "secret" documents supplied by the Second Bureau itself. These documents, of course, were carefully prepared. The inconsequential ones were genuine, the important ones deliberately misleading—naturally enough, since it was even better to have the Germans relying on false information than receiving no information at all.

Similar successes had been made in Strasbourg and Switzerland, and when the Germans realized it they had to fire their agents and start building anew.

But, as always happens in the field of espionage, neither were the French able to place any reliance on their own agents. Several of them operating in Germany had been arrested. They reported to the Second Bureau that they had managed to avoid imprisonment by agreeing to act for Germany within the French service. Their agreement was a lie, they insisted; but to whom had the lie been told—to the Germans with their threat of punishment, or to the French with their promise of reward? And, in general, what was to prevent any spy—even one who had not been trapped—from serving two masters, taking money from France as an agent and from Germany as a counter-agent?

This is an eternal dilemma of intelligence departments, and, to solve it, the Second Bureau had a brainstorm. It dispatched confidential instructions to various of its agents, telling them what truths and half-truths and outright lies to let slip to the Germans and also feeding them a melange of concocted "secrets" that were to be kept entirely from the Germans. It followed this up with queries to other of its agents in Berlin as to what was getting through to the Germans. So one set of spies was put to work checking on another set of spies.

In these operations, the files of the Second Bureau became a veritable jungle of forgeries and falsifications. It was common for intelligence officers to tell one another at this time that the day would come when no one would be able to tell the real from the faked. Nor has it ever been satisfactorily established who fooled whom. French military writers are still skeptical of the value of the work done by the Second Bureau, while Germans accuse their General Staff of having been misled by clumsy forgeries.

Yet an occasional German spy was caught. One, Thomas, a technician working at Bourges on the new explosive, melanite, was arrested in connection with German efforts to get hold of a sample. Another German spy, Greiner, was discovered working as a clerk in the French Admiralty. The librarian at the Church of St. Thomas Aquinas, a man named Boutonnet, was found to be serving as a liaison between the German Embassy and the agents in its pay.

The public followed these cases with lively trepidation, and the extreme left and the extreme right strove to make political capital of them. They attacked the Government mercilessly, centering their fire on the Minister of War, who, at this crucial moment, was General August Mercier. The general was made to order for the cartoonists: a figure erect and thin as a blade, the eyes mere slits looking out distrustfully at all comers, the bloodless upper lip closed on the lower lip in a sharp, straight line—the mouth of a barracuda, as it were, and a personality not entirely dissimilar. There was no flair for politics in him. He had risen to his eminence in the hard, honorable way that so often unfits a man for it, or at least fails to prepare him. His school had been the battlefield. Although a Catholic, he kept aloof from the clerical and royalist circles that dominated the right. They had no use for him anyway, his wife being English and Protestant.

The spy cases were extremely involved, and some never have been entirely cleared up. As an example of one of the simpler ones, the Germans were known to have acquired the formula for certain explosives. Tracking back, the Second Bureau's bloodhounds came to the laboratory where the formula had been invented. An assistant proved very patriotic. He cast suspicion on the inventor himself, Turpin.

Turpin was arrested, tried and convicted. But later it was discovered that the patriotic assistant had been the actual spy and that Turpin was entirely innocent.

The innocent victim of an even more involved spying case was still hanging around the Second Bureau. His name: Bruecker.

Bruecker had succeeded in acquiring an invaluable helper for the so-called statistical section of the Second Bureau. This was Mme. Bastian, one of the charladies at the German Embassy. Mme. Bastian made a career out of giving an impression of stupidity. She acted the part so perfectly that it never occurred to the German personnel to suspect her. Countess Mary von Münster, the daughter of the Ambassador, took advantage of this to employ Mme. Bastian discreetly in carrying messages to and from various amorous young men. Mme. Bastian took advantage of it to carry messages to the French General Staff's counter-espionage agent. Her errands for the young countess gave the dull-looking charlady the freedom of the Ambassador's apartment as well as the embassy offices in the building, and she emptied the wastebaskets regularly and delivered their contents to Bruecker.

Suddenly the Second Bureau was informed that Bruecker would bear watching, that he was no patriot but a businessman willing to spy for the highest bidder. The information came from a girl known to history only by the assumed name of Millescamp. She was having a love affair with Bruecker and he, she swore, had confided his avarice to her during their intimate moments.

Bruecker must have known that an agent's interest in money would come as no surprise to an intelligence bureau. But he flew into a passion anyway. Perhaps it was connected with his preoccupation as a lover rather than his occupation as a spy. At any rate he denounced the girl as having stolen secret documents from him and selling them to the Germans. He produced evidence. She was arrested, convicted and sentenced to five years.

But Bruecker's sacrifice of his love life did not impress French Army officers as much as it might have ballad writers. Mme. Bastian was instructed to stop delivering her stolen German wastepaper to Bruecker and to hand it over instead directly to a staff officer of the Second Bureau—a Major Hubert Henry, a man whose loyalty to the French Army was unquestionable and, in fact, never faltered throughout.

What is loyalty to an army? Is it loyalty to its ideals or to its commands, to what its commands should in all honor be or to what in fact they are? Major Henry gave the simple answer to the question. He was not a man of ideals, but of hard, practical facts. He was loyal to the Army. That was enough. It gave him a position in life, and preserved it. He had given evidence on the battlefield of his willingness to die for the Army. He was willing all his life to die for it—and, in the end, when he found that loyalty to the Army was not enough to preserve his position, he did die for it. He was unwilling to go on living in a world that was too complicated for him, that demanded loyalty to an ideal rather than to an institution entrusted with the task of fulfilling it.

But, in the meantime, in July of 1894, that was the situation when Major Count Ferdinand Walsin-Esterhazy left on the desk of Colonel von Schwarzkoppen his battalion's orders in the event of mobilization. If the papers found their way into Schwarzkoppen's wastebasket, they would come under Mme. Bastian's apron. She would bring them to any one of a number of Paris churches that had been selected as contact points and there place them in the hands of Major Hubert Henry.

3

BUT THE ESTERHAZY PAPERS had not gone into Schwarzkoppen's wastebasket. The colonel instead had carried them to Berlin.

Three weeks later, on August 13, Esterhazy appeared for the third time at the German Embassy. He was affable and at ease now, a salesman building up a customer to expect delivery of an important shipment. On August 15, he made the delivery in person: general orders for the artillery in the event of mobilization. Its value appeared unquestionable. Schwarzkoppen handed over 1,000 francs ($200) in cash.

On September 1, Esterhazy delivered a bundle of documents; he also meant to deliver with them, written out in his own hand, a *bordereau,* or itemized list of the kind careful clerks prepare to make sure that all items enclosed with it or sent under separate cover may be checked and accounted for by the recipient. Von Schwarzkoppen received all the documents but not the itemized list. The *bordereau* was to become world famous. It was written on both sides of a cream-colored slip of lightweight paper, perhaps graph paper since it was stamped with squares. It read:

I have no news to indicate that you wish to see me; however, I am sending you some interesting information.

1. A note on the hydraulic brake of the 120 mm. gun and on the way it was found to work.
2. A note on the supporting troops. Some modifications will be introduced by the new plan.
3. A note on the modification of artillery formations.
4. A note concerning Madagascar.
5. The provisional Firing Manual for Field Artillery [March 14, 1894].

This last document is extraordinarily difficult to procure, and I have it at my disposal only for a very few days. The Minister of War has issued a limited number to the corps, and the corps are responsible for them. Each officer who has a copy has to send it back after the maneuvers. If, therefore, you will take notes of whatever is of interest to you, and hold it at my disposal, I shall take it back. That is, unless you want me to have it copied in full and send you the copy. I am just off to the maneuvers.

Neither did these documents nor the *bordereau* itemizing them go into Schwarzkoppen's wastebasket. But it was at this point in the drama that the agent Bruecker, wounded and enfeebled in his career by his love passage with Mlle. Millescamp, made a desperate effort to re-establish himself in the eyes of the Second Bureau. He chose a propitious moment.

As far back as three years before, the Second Bureau had become aware that the German Embassy had an agent with access to material in the possession of the French General Staff. New military maps of regions along the German and Italian frontiers were disappearing mysteriously. Major Hubert Henry had undertaken to find out how.

A brave soldier in the wars on the continent of Europe as well as in the colonies, Major Henry was the only officer on the General Staff to have risen from the ranks. A Minister of War had selected him for his first tour in this exalted circle as a concession to the idea of democracy in the Army—an idea which had lain rather fallow since the days of the first Napoleon when every soldier was said to be carrying a marshal's baton in his knapsack. Of course, Major Henry was assigned only to Intelligence. Still, it was the General Staff.

When the Government had fallen, the Minister of War who had

made the gesture of appeasement to democracy had toppled with it. Intelligence then had rid itself promptly of Major Henry. It had ordered him to a tour of duty in Africa. But the major took it with a soldier's grace. He worked hard and uncomplainingly and, his African tour completed, had been able to bring excellent recommendations to the Chief of the General Staff, General de Boisdeffre. Perhaps it pleased the general that Henry, in the face of his raw deal, had loyally played his politics to secure advancement in the Army rather than "outside" among politicians. At any rate, he reassigned the major to the General Staff—again only to the Second Bureau.

Henry was a large, powerfully built man who towered over the average Frenchman. He carried with him into officers' country something of the sergeant-major: a martial mustache, a blunt, almost brutal purposefulness, and a fierce devotion to superiors that tempered their well-bred distaste for his lack of breeding. But his faithful dog's eyes could of a sudden take on the shrewd glance of the peasant who knows that he cannot get ahead among the gentry and stay straight. They will rely on him to do their dirty work.

The major was under the direct command of Colonel Jean Sandherr and his deputy, Lieutenant Colonel Albert Cordier, who ran the Second Bureau's counter-espionage arm. Neither lowered himself to associate in any but a business way with the peasant from the ranks. Being uneducated and unversed in any foreign language, Henry had to depend heavily on two other officers—Captain Jules-Maximilien Lauth, and the archivist Félix Gribelin. They were inferior to him in rank but superior in social standing, and Henry became very conscious of the fact that he was surrounded by invisible walls whose chilling gates there was no way for him to unlock except by getting born all over again in different circumstances. Everybody was comradely enough during working hours, but when they left the office they disappeared into a world where Henry was never invited to accompany them.

Major Henry did not flatten his nose against this world as a child might flatten his against a window full of goodies. But when Major Count Ferdinand Walsin-Esterhazy set himself to make a friend in the Second Bureau he found Henry a pushover.

Esterhazy was exactly the opposite of Henry—of superior birth where Henry's was inferior, a ne'er-do-well where Henry was an ever-do-well. Esterhazy came from the high aristocracy of Hungary. He had been born in Paris. His father had commanded a French division that had seen active service in the Crimean War. The boy had been orphaned at an early age, and had spent his childhood and youth at military boarding schools in Austria.

His military record was varied and distinguished. He had fought in the Austrian Army against the Prussians in 1866. Later he had served in the Papal Army. In 1870 he was a French officer, at the throat of the Prussians again, and decorated for valor. But he was a nearly unmitigated scoundrel. He married into the French aristocracy. Within a short time he had squandered his wife's very substantial dowry. For the rest of his life he was never to be out of financial difficulties and he spent his time leaping from Scylla to Charybdis and back again. He would turn up now as director of a dubious finance corporation, now as shareholder in a fashionable house of prostitution.

In the early and prosperous days of the anti-Semitic newspaper, *La Libre Parole,* he was often seen in conference with its bearded editor, Edouard Drumont. But when Drumont accepted a challenge to a duel from a Jewish officer, Esterhazy acted as second to the Jewish officer and then proceeded to cash in on it. Duels in those days were symbolic actions that seldom involved bloodshed unless the participants were too excited to take the proper precautions against hitting their opponents, or unless—as sometimes happened—one or the other of them forgot his manners and decided that getting even was preferable to acting gallantly. But after the harmless duel he seconded against Drumont, Esterhazy wrote to Baron de Rothschild, pointing out his own pro-Jewishness and his need to overcome a temporary financial embarrassment. He wrote in a similar vein to the chief rabbi of Paris, Zadoc Kahn, and he and the bearded, violent, preposterous Drumont continued to remain good friends—or as good friends as such self-centered men can be. Drumont appeared to believe that any crook who swindled Jews was worthy of cultivation.

Esterhazy's squalid financial practices were by no means unknown to his fellow officers. But Major Henry was blind to everything Esterhazy lacked and seemed to see only what he had. The count spoke seven languages. He knew German affairs thoroughly, and had considerable background on Austrian and Italian affairs as well. For an international illiterate like Henry, the count's help in translations and in background information was invaluable. It enabled him to get along without the snooty Captain Lauth and to become one up on the archivist, Gribelin. The count wined and dined Henry and put himself out to fascinate him with his wit and savoir-faire and a display of lavish extravagance. The extravagance went so far that the count almost forced a considerable loan on Henry.

For Esterhazy had a purpose in view. This was before he had begun to sell himself to Schwarzkoppen. He was maneuvering for an assignment to the Second Bureau. He knew that no other officer on the General Staff would support his application for such an assignment, but he hoped that this one would. Henry, of course, felt puffed up at the prospect of sponsoring a count and a true Esterhazy. The count was a good soldier. But life in a Rouen garrison bored him. Anyone could understand this in a man with a cosmopolitan background such as Esterhazy's. His knowledge of people and languages and his international family ties made him just the man for counter-espionage under Henry.

However, Colonel Jean Sandherr was more than Major Henry could manage. Being from Lorraine, he generally distrusted foreigners and nursed a savage hatred for all things German. His hatred was so deep that, although he had been a Protestant, he became converted to Catholicism. Protestantism brought him too close to Prussian Germany. It is not known whether Esterhazy's squalid financial dealings awakened any distaste in Colonel Sandherr, but it is known that the count's ancestry was far too international to please him. However, the colonel was a sick man and it looked as though Esterhazy would not have to wait long for him to retire or die. So, despite Henry's initial failure, Esterhazy did not discard him. He introduced Henry to his good friend, Drumont of *La Libre Parole*.

As might have been expected, anti-Semitism attracted him. But he was crafty and cautious, no more willing to take chances than any other peasant who had risen to petit-bourgeoisdom, and he did not cultivate Drumont openly. However, he kept in close touch through Esterhazy.

No suspicion of Esterhazy's dealings with the Germans crossed Henry's mind. With his customary ardor to please his superiors, Henry had worked mightily to uncover the German avenue into the General Staff. Schwarzkoppen's mail was intercepted, his every step followed.

It developed that Schwarzkoppen was working very closely with the Italian military attaché, Lieutenant Colonel Panizzardi. But it was very difficult to determine who was doing what, since all their communications to each other were signed with the same alias and, to complicate it further, the alias was changed from time to time. Only by getting samples of the handwriting of each from the French Ministry of Foreign Affairs and comparing both with the letters that were intercepted could the Second Bureau tell whether Panizzardi or Schwarzkoppen had written them.

There was no Mme. Bastian in the Italian Embassy to rifle Panizzardi's wastebasket as Schwarzkoppen's was being rifled, but the Second Bureau had a finger on his secrets anyway—a French agent named Corninge who had succeeded in persuading the Italian military attaché that his spurious offer to spy for him was genuine.

An apartment across the road from the German Embassy attracted the attention of the Second Bureau. Embassy personnel had rented it to get away from office pressures, for a change of pace in the course of a busy day, for an occasional gossipy stretch of intellectual legs or a brief snooze. Microphones had been perfected by that time, following hard on the heels of the telephone, and the Second Bureau managed to install one in the fireplace of this apartment. The apartment above was then rented and a man placed in it to monitor the conversations taking place below.

In this manner the Second Bureau discovered the ultimate resting places of the frontier maps that had been disappearing. Both Schwarzkoppen and Panizzardi were after them. On December 29, 1893, more than six months before Esterhazy appeared on the scene to threaten suicide, Schwarzkoppen left Paris for a visit to Berlin. Before boarding the train, he left a message for his second in command, instructing him to pay 300 francs to "the man of the Meuse forts," or to the man's mother, against further delivery of frontier maps. The Second Bureau got hold of that message and of later correspondence that proved these other maps had not been delivered.

Three hundred francs. "The man of the Meuse forts" and his obliging mother were obviously small fry. Nevertheless, it was treason, and when the Minister of War, the barracuda-mouthed General Mercier, was informed of it he became greatly excited. Either the German Ambassador had deliberately lied when he had promised he would not tolerate espionage activities by embassy personnel, or his orders were not being respected.

However, it was not anything General Mercier felt he could take open action against. There were his enemies of the right and the left in the Chamber of Deputies. Should they discover that documents had been stolen from the offices of the General Staff, it was conceivable that they would succeed in making the Government fall. In any case, it was certain he would be ruined. He urged Colonel Sandherr to make every effort to catch the traitor. A brilliant solution to the crime arrived at before the crime became known would stifle any uproar over the fact that the crime had been committed in the first place.

So Henry continued zealously to intercept messages. Panizzardi and Schwarzkoppen were signing them with the name "Alexandrine" now. One signed "Alexandrine" read as follows:

Enclosed are twelve detail maps of Nice that the Scoundrel D—— left with me for you. I told him that you had no intention of taking up relations with him again. He said that there was a misunderstanding, and that he will do his best to satisfy you. He said he had been stubborn and you should not be angry. I replied he was silly and that I did not believe you would take up relations with him again.

An examination of the handwriting proved that the "Alexandrine" of this note was Schwarzkoppen. Of course, it occurred to Henry that the initial D had been used to refer to "the Scoundrel" because it had no connection with his real name. But this was all he had to go on, and the Second Bureau was ransacked to find the man. A clerk at the Cartographic Institute, where the frontier maps were drawn, was suspected because his name was Dubois and he had a mother, but no other evidence could be found.

On Christmas Day, 1893, four days before departing from Paris, Schwarzkoppen received a telegram from Berlin. It came mutilated into the hands of the Second Bureau and all the staff could make out of it were the words: "Concerning . . . no sign of General Staff." A few days later Mme. Bastian's humble fingers grubbed up torn slips of paper in Schwarzkoppen's handwriting. Put together in the most logical sequence, they read:

Doubt . . . proof . . . Officer . . . Dangerous situation for me with a French officer . . . Not to negotiate personally . . . Bring what he was . . . Absolute Ge . . . Bureau of Intelligence . . . No relation to troops . . . Only if important . . . coming from Ministry . . . Already elsewhere.

The Second Bureau was baffled. Its best deduction was that it was the draft of a reply to the mutilated telegram. But it did not fill in the blank spaces in that telegram, nor did it give any clue to what it itself was all about. However, it related clearly to espionage and to no measly "man of the Meuse forts," the "Scoundrel D———." Obviously Schwarzkoppen was dealing with an officer he deemed to be of importance.

An around-the-clock watch was kept on the German Embassy. No doubt Esterhazy was seen walking in and out six months later. But the fact that a Frenchman, even a French officer, visited the embassy was no evidence of treason and did not even offer grounds for suspicion. Germany had annexed the French provinces of Alsace and Lorraine after the war of 1870. Even Colonel Sandherr, when he wished to visit his relatives there, had to call at the embassy to obtain a pass.

Still, nothing availed. The German contact in the General Staff remained hidden. But the fact that this contact existed could not be kept entirely secret over such a prolonged period, no matter how politically desirable complete secrecy might seem to General Mercier. Even a former military attaché of the Spanish Embassy in Paris, a somewhat shady character, the Marquis Val Carlos, learned of it. "There's a wolf or two in the sheepfold," he told an agent of the Second Bureau named François Guénée.

Possibly it was in this way that the news trickled out to Bruecker. It reached him very late in the game, three months after Esterhazy had established his relationship with Schwarzkoppen. But the situation— involving, as it did, frustration on the highest level through Major Henry to Colonel Sandherr and up into the stratosphere where jittered and fumed General Mercier himself—was made to order for a man wounded in a love battle and anxious to reassert himself.

Bruecker performed a desperate deed. There was no use appealing to Mme. Bastian. She took her orders from Major Henry. Bruecker did it himself, walking into the lobby of the German Embassy, reaching into Schwarzkoppen's incoming mail, grabbing therefrom a single document and then walking out.

The document was the *bordereau* Esterhazy had written in his own handwriting to itemize the material he was delivering to Schwarzkoppen. How it had got among his mail has never been learned. Esterhazy in his elation may have forgotten to hand over the *bordereau*. When he discovered it in his pocket he may have returned and dropped it into the military attaché's mail. Anyhow, there it was, and the supremely elated Bruecker turned it over to the statistical section of the Second Bureau on September 26.

Major Henry was away on leave at the time and in his absence the document went directly to his chief, Colonel Sandherr. Appalled, he summoned his colleagues, Lieutenant Colonel Cordier, Captain Lauth and Gribelin. They agreed, as a first step, that before showing the paper to anyone outside the Second Bureau, the fact that it had been stolen outright should be concealed. They tore it up into little pieces and then carefully pasted it together again. In that way it could be made to seem to have come "in the regular way"—as Mme. Bastian's wastepaper pilferings were officially described.

It was apparent that the author of the *bordereau* must be on, or closely connected with someone on, the General Staff. How else could he get secret information about such different activities of the Army— a new field piece, the organization of infantry support for it, a report on its tests, a firing manual, modifications in the ways of deploying artillery, knowledge of an expedition to Madagascar? Here, Colonel Sandherr decided, was the ghost that had been haunting them—the "Scoundrel D——" who turned out not to be Dubois, and the officer of importance in Von Schwarzkoppen's puzzling notes.

Sandherr took the document to the Fourth Bureau, in charge of military transportation. True, the *bordereau* was undated, but it was obvious that it must have been sent recently since the man had written "I am just off to the maneuvers." By the time Sandherr reached the office of Colonel Pierre-Élie Fabre, chief of the Fourth Bureau, he was convinced that the traitor must be on the General Staff itself.

Colonel Fabre at once accepted that view. After all, Sandherr was an expert. Fabre scrutinized the *bordereau* with his deputy, Colonel Albert D'Aboville. D'Aboville decided its author must be an artillery-man with contacts in other branches of the service. "A probationer!" he cried, dazzled by the brilliance of his solution.

Breathlessly, they got out the file of probationers—the young officers who were not yet attached to any one bureau of the General Staff but were shifted on temporary assignment from one office to the other. They went down the *D*s and came to a halt at the name of Dreyfus.

In their immense relief, they found no words. Each read the other's thought: "It was the Jew!"

4

THE DEVASTATING IMPACT of politics on the individual life had first been brought home to Alfred Dreyfus in 1870 when he was eleven years old. He also learned then for the first time that it was possible for injustice to prevail.

For that was the year when the French lost a lightning war to Germany. The Dreyfus family lived in Mulhouse in Alsace, near the German border. Alfred's father, Raphael, operated a thriving textile mill and the family lived in the comfortable fashion of the bourgeoisie in an eminently respectable house in the old Alsatian city. They fled before the invading German troops, crowding into the home of Alfred's eldest sister, Henriette, and her husband in Carpentras.

After the peace, the Dreyfus family returned to Mulhouse. But Alsace was now German, and Raphael Dreyfus was French. All the Dreyfuses were French. They could not feel at home in a German city. Jacques, the eldest son, was entrusted with the management of the factory and the rest of the family moved to France. The father gave up business. In conquering France, Germany had conquered his life.

Alfred remained in the care of his sister, Henriette. It marked the resumption of a relationship that had been interrupted by her marriage and removal to her own home in Carpentras. He had been born late in his mother's life and she had been in poor health since his coming. It had been Henriette, energetic, intelligent and womanly, who took the place of mother to Alfred. The taciturn boy opened his heart to his eldest sister and told her of his most cherished ambition. He wanted to become an Army officer.

Perhaps it would have happened anyway. Alfred was a stubborn boy who kept to himself and went his own way. But Henriette approved, and so it happened more easily than it might have. Even so he had to make a fight against his own family. He was graduated from high school at Grenoble and then went to the Collège Sainte Barbe, where his older brothers had completed their studies. He was keen to learn and to excel. His sharp mind and his zeal brought him recognition, but he was uncommunicative and made no friends. Instead, he suffered greatly from homesickness. In fact, although in his writings he seems unaware of it, he may very well have been one of those characters familiar in literature since the early Greeks and their bloody gods and kings and princes—a man who within his own most private being remains without a home in the world until he accomplishes the mission to which he has dedicated himself.

By this time the very human process of live-and-let-live had had its effect in both Alsace and Lorraine. Enough of the Germanism and Francophilia had worn out so that Frenchmen could live there as French citizens. Alfred's brothers had done that, returning to Mulhouse to help Jacques run the family business. Now they brought Alfred back. By this time they were aware of his ambitions for a military career and they hoped to dissuade him.

But the Germans seemed to have become aware of Alfred's ambitions, too. They refused him permission to remain in Mulhouse. He returned to his sister's home in Carpentras and then went back to the Collège in Paris to prepare for the entrance examination to the Ecole Polytechnique—that famous institution which had launched so many young men on military careers.

He was nineteen then. There was nothing about his appearance to catch the eye of the passer-by except perhaps his light-blue eyes and a curious breathless expression of eagerness frozen into his taut lower lip. He was not popular with his classmates. He had too much zeal for his studies and an excessive reverence for his teachers. He was considered a bore, but no one knew whether he minded. Only points of scholarship could prick him out of his habitually cold reserve.

At the time he entered the Ecole Polytechnique, in 1878, he was comfortably off financially. His father had distributed the business among the family. The three oldest sons—Jacques, Mathieu and Léon—ran it, but Alfred and his three sisters shared in it. The three girls and Alfred had interests in the business capitalized at $60,000 apiece, which brought Alfred $5,000 a year.

This income did not make him better liked by his fellow students. They were for the most part sons of the old nobility or of civil servants. Those who were not poor had been brought up to think of their wealth as of small consequence. The great majority of them came from the Jesuit school that specialized in preparing students for the Ecole Polytechnique. They formed a closely knit group—obvious candidates for preferment in the Army and promotion to the General Staff.

Such advancement depended on a committee of officers who were under the influence of a clique in the Army known as "Postards" because they had been graduated from the Jesuit preparatory school in the Rue des Postes. The head of the Jesuit order was Father du Lac, father-confessor to General Le Mouton de Boisdeffre, Chief of the General Staff. Incidentally, it had been General de Boisdeffre who had been selected to persuade the Tsar of Russia in a personal interview of the effectiveness of the French Army and of the effectiveness of France as an ally against German aspirations. It was the outstanding success of his mission that had precipitated, among numerous other things, that outburst of espionage and counter-espionage.

The general never neglected seeing Father du Lac before undertaking anything of importance, and the Jesuit father liked to hold him up as an example to other officers of lesser rank who thus learned quickly which way was up on the Army ladder. As for those who were not Postards because their families were Protestant or Jewish or had neglected to place them in that particular preparatory school, their hope of advancement lay only in their behavior and record in scholarship. The Postards do not seem to have discriminated among Protestants, Jews and Catholic "outsiders." They classed them together as not of the clan and rarely stepped out of the clique to make friends. But there were no overt acts. They were all young gentlemen who had brought good manners with them from home, and besides, the official policy discouraged giving offense. When an outsider stepped inside —into, say, a group of Postards—no door was slammed in his face. No silence, no cessation of activity greeted him. But he was not invited to come again.

There were a few other Jewish students at the Ecole besides Alfred. French Jews of that day believed that the cure for anti-Semitism lay in assimilation. The argument went that as long as a trait of the stranger remained, the community could not be expected to take no note of it.

Assimilation was progressing famously. France had been first among the nations of Europe to make its Jews full citizens. The nineteenth century was marked by a growing indifference to religion and a breakdown in the capacity of religious institutions to organize society. This made it easier for Catholics, Protestants and Jews to mix. But it stopped at the front door, where the women stood guard. Women were not so much affected by the shift in power in the outside world. Their domain was the home and its children. Even the daughters of prominent anti-clericals and professed atheists continued to go to first

Communion and to insist on being married in church. The traditionalism of the women did not alter the course of the industrial revolution; it did not restore the Church to its medieval power over the outer world. But for Catholics, Jews and Protestants alike, it maintained the dividing lines in the inner world. These dividing lines were most noticeable when it came to marriage, where the French, whatever their religion, always prefer to be guided by reason rather than sentiment. But the lines were to become drawn in red when the Dreyfus affair struck the nation in full fury.

Three years before Alfred entered the Ecole, the French Chamber of Deputies (the equivalent of our House of Representatives) had replaced the monarchy formally and legally by adopting a new Constitution. It was passed by a single vote and in the draft the word "republic" did not occur until a last-minute amendment described the head of the state as President of the Republic. The saying went that the Republic had been created but not declared.

However, in the first election under the new Constitution, the people made the declaration. A republican majority was returned and the so-called Third Republic was on its way; it did not halt until 1945. In those early days, however, high army officers remained royalist—more steadfastly than vocally. The teaching staff of the Ecole, dependent as they were on government appropriations, made it a point of discipline to put up with the Republic. Political partisanship was discouraged on the basis that the Army was above the parties. For those who were not Postards the change even provided some protection against favoritism in promotions—as witness the first short-lived tour of duty of Major Henry with the General Staff.

These were turbulent years politically, but Alfred Dreyfus' career ran its course more smoothly than it might have in quieter times. He earned a reputation as a daring horseman and was considered good at fencing. He was engrossed in his uniform and the life it required of him—a youth not to be accosted easily except by those unafraid of a rebuff. There were those in civilian life who regarded him as a very caricature of the Army caste, and they shook their heads because it had happened to him when he was so young.

In 1880 he was graduated from the Ecole Polytechnique and was sent to the artillery school at Fontainebleau as a second lieutenant. Two years later he was promoted to lieutenant of artillery and joined a regiment at Mans.

A year later he was awarded the plum of service with a regiment garrisoned in Paris. But it was no such plum to him as to another man. The Army was his world and he was as indifferent to what surrounded it as a confirmed city dweller is to the countryside. He enjoyed Paris, but only because it was the capital of the French Army. His brother Mathieu, who traveled for the family firm, visited Paris often and would try unsuccessfully to show Alfred some nighttime sights—concerts, theaters, cabarets. Mathieu was an amiable and good-humored man, handsome, with fine, regular features and kindly brown eyes, his intelligent face framed in gray whiskers. He pitied his young brother, whose ambitions seemed to him to leave no room for the good life.

By 1889 Alfred Dreyfus was a captain and was serving in the Central School of Explosives at Bourges. He applied for admission to the Ecole de Guerre, which was open only to those recommended by their commanding officers as suitable material for the General Staff.

Dreyfus was thirty then. At Bourges he had made the acquaintance of Lucie Hadamard. It had been the doing of the amiable Mathieu. Mathieu knew an old friend of the Hadamards, a distinguished family of French Jews that had given the world two great mathematicians, and he liked to talk about his brilliant young brother. The friend arranged a meeting between the young couple. They were believed to be a perfect match.

As a little girl, Lucie had been what the French call *trop sage*—too obedient, too easily commanded by adults, the type of child for whom sensible adults feel pity. She was a wealthy girl, the daughter of a jeweler in a fashionable district of Paris. She was expected to enjoy social life and felt it her duty to do so. She was a small, slight woman and her large black eyes and thin, arched nose made her face seem as pert and warming as a bird's. The first impression one had of her was of meekness and almost oriental submissiveness. But, as the world was to discover, there was iron in her. It could be seen even then around her mouth. An early recognition of what definitely was right and what definitely was wrong, and no nonsense about it, pressed her thin lips tightly together.

The two serious young people—one serious about her social joys, the other about his work—understood each other quickly and became engaged to be married. But the death of Alfred's mother, whom he could never remember having seen in good health, made them postpone their marriage for almost a year. It was not until April 21, 1890, that they were married. On the same day Alfred was officially notified he had been accepted at the Ecole de Guerre. The union could not have begun with a happier omen.

After the honeymoon, Alfred and Lucie settled down to a life of military scholarship, taking up residence on Paris' Avenue du Trocadéro in the fashionable district of Passy.

The Ecole de Guerre, a postgraduate school, was housed within France's West Point, the Ecole Militaire, on the Champ de Mars, near the Eiffel Tower. Each morning Dreyfus turned out for an early ride in the Bois de Boulogne. He looked to the exercise to keep his body fit and make his mind alert for the day's work. Lucie, at breakfast, would listen attentively as he drew up his program of action for the day. Then, as he walked up the Avenue du Trocadéro, his eyes would wander over the Champ de Mars and come to rest on the scene of his private battlefield—the buildings of the Ecole Militaire. Around him was the great city of light still half asleep in the morning mists, and as he walked he customarily wore the expression of one called on to shield and protect her.

The classroom was indeed a battlefield for him. In a class of eighty-one, he was admitted as No. 67—a rather poor showing. Advancement to the General Staff by graduates of the Ecole de Guerre was not automatic, and unless he improved his standing Dreyfus had little chance. He was not a Postard. He had to compete on unequal terms with the pick of the Army, the brightest officers of his generation, the majority of them buttressed by the general good will from on high which goes with family connections and the old school tie. Dreyfus had nothing to buttress him but his mind and his formidable capacity for enduring grueling work. But the Postards at the Ecole were no less brilliant, and they had the advantage of expressing their talents with ease and charm. Their ambitions may have been just as intense as Dreyfus' but they were not so devouring. They had room for what Mathieu thought of as the good life.

An embodiment of this type was Marie-Georges Picquart, who, at the time Dreyfus first met him, was an instructor at the Ecole and the youngest major in the Army. The Jesuits who had groomed Picquart for his career had high hopes for him. He was a slender man, a brainy dreamer of a type much more common among artists than soldiers. He loved music, spoke German, English and Spanish with equal fluency, and excelled in mathematics and the military arts. Dreyfus tried to engage the youthful major's interest but had no success. Picquart seemed to share the common opinion of Dreyfus: the man was a grind and therefore a bore. Picquart, unlike the other instructors, was not even impressed with Dreyfus' intelligence. Yet curiously it was to Picquart, and only Picquart among the vast concourse of his brother officers, that Dreyfus was to owe his life, Picquart destroying his own in the process of saving Dreyfus'. Greater love hath no man than this, that a man lay down his life for his friend. But it was for the idea that Picquart laid down his life, since Picquart refused to have Dreyfus as a friend.

Dreyfus liked to discuss his problems at home with his bride. Lucie soon began to realize what was lacking in her husband's approach to his life: outgoingness to humanity. He seemed to know little about the personalities of his teachers and colleagues, and to care less. His interest was confined to subject matter. His comrades appeared in his conversation only as minds that had been correct or incorrect, ingenious or dull in solving a problem or coping with a task or in responding to his own mind.

But Lucie was not the woman to seek to change her husband. Instead she concentrated on making him comfortable. It seemed to her wisest. She was deeply devoted to his ambitions, and Alfred's success in his career to date encouraged her to believe that it was better to rely on what one had than to strain after what one lacked. The girl who had been so serious about her social joys now sought seclusion from society. It was a way to ease her husband's heart. People meant so little to Alfred, seemed such an unhappy waste of time.

In 1891 a boy, Pierre, was born to the young couple and in 1893 a girl, Jeanne. Now two people had come into the world who had meaning for Alfred. His brother Mathieu noted with satisfaction that the little family eased Alfred's tenseness. Life seemed more of a smiling matter, and the face that had been locked at "Attention!" now came warmly to "At ease."

But that was in the home. His papers on military matters—one on the financial aspects of mobilization, another on the fallacy of numbers —won him high praise. But in the oral arguments on his theses his teachers continued to be put off by his self-containment. However, one could not affect Dreyfus by disliking him, only by disliking a product of his mind.

On one occasion the Ecole staged a field day. The mission was to observe artillery positions at maneuvers in the vicinity of Charmes. A conference followed at which the students were invited to offer comment and criticism and make suggestions. The conference was in full swing when the Chief of the General Staff, General Le Mouton de Boisdeffre himself, made a surprise appearance.

When it was Dreyfus' turn to speak, Boisdeffre listened with mounting interest. Lunch was taken in the open. The Chief of Staff called the young captain to his side and put further questions to him. Later he took Dreyfus all by himself for a walk toward the bridge on the Moselle, letting the captain elaborate on his ideas. Students and instructors watched in awe and envy.

It was a personal success so unexpected and incisive that it touched the man underneath the manner. Dreyfus never forgot it. His gratitude toward the highest, most honored soldier of the day never faded. Not even in the abyss of his subsequent torment did he falter in his faith that General de Boisdeffre would save him.

When all is said, Dreyfus—like so many who feel they have no home among their fellow men—was an unworldly, simple soul.

It was while Dreyfus was still at the Ecole de Guerre that Edouard Drumont, the friend of Count Esterhazy and, through him, the friend of Major Hubert Henry, issued the first edition of his new newspaper, *La Libre Parole*. It struck a note of outspoken anti-Semitism far more violent than any that had ever been printed in France before.

This shocking paper enjoyed the open support of such men as the prominent Catholic, the Marquis de Morès. Rumor had it that its publisher had been supplied with funds by the Jesuits, who, it may be remembered, were the guiding influence of the Army's Postards. What was not rumor but fact was the impact on the populace. Disturbingly, it bought *La Libre Parole* in large quantities, a first warning that a profound change had taken place out of sight and hitherto out of knowledge in the consciousness of many Frenchmen. Throughout the century, the frame of reference for that consciousness had been democracy which makes all men equal in rights. Now in the closing decade of the century the frame seemed to have shrunk for an astonishingly large number of people.

Drumont's first campaign was a fierce attack on Jewish officers in the Army. A feature column kept the subject warm.

Some articles appeared over the signature Lamase. Others were unsigned. Allegedly they were all written by the Marquis de Morès himself, a former Army officer and a man who dreamed adventurously of restoring to its power over society the spirit of the pre-industrial Christian community when the Church was at the top and each man had his place on the ladder and did not devote his life to climbing up it.

La Libre Parole published the names of the Jewish officers in the Army as potential traitors. A rash of duels broke out. A Jewish captain of dragoons, Crémieux-Foa, challenged publisher-editor Drumont. One of the Jewish officer's seconds was the ineffable Major Esterhazy, who thought it quite proper to resent with one's life an imputation of treason. Honor was satisfied without bloodshed.

Then Captain Crémieux-Foa challenged the journalist Lamase whose name was signed to the articles the Marquis de Morès is believed to have written. Secrecy was agreed on between the seconds— the Marquis de Morès for Lamase, another Jewish Army captain, Armand Meyer, for Crémieux-Foa.

La Libre Parole, being so close to the marquis, of course observed the pledge of secrecy. But Major Esterhazy leaked the news to a friend on the editorial staff of *Le Matin*, and this large Parisian daily published it. The marquis promptly accused Captain Meyer of a breach of his word of honor. Thereupon a third duel followed. This one did result in bloodshed. The marquis did not observe the amiable, unwritten code, and Captain Meyer was fatally wounded.

His death provoked a flare-up of comment. The Chamber of Deputies itself protested against the indignity of anti-Semitism and its violence. *La Libre Parole* seemed discredited and even was expected to go out of business. Instead, business boomed. Overnight it became one of the most widely read newspapers in France.

It was painful for Dreyfus to see his fellow officers read *La Libre Parole* openly without drawing any comment from the instructors. In addition to Dreyfus, there had been one other Jewish officer admitted to the course. General Bonnefond, one of their instructors, gave them both inferior grades. When they expressed their disappointment, General Bonnefond remarked calmly before the assembled form that he did not want to see Jews on the General Staff. The Commission of Examinations demurred, but nothing happened.

It amounted to losing points on the final grading on which their subsequent careers depended, and this was more than Dreyfus would tolerate. Although his colleague thought it was wiser to shrug it all

off, he protested to the director of the school. General Lebelin de
Dionne investigated, admitted that the marks were unfair and expressed regret. But again nothing happened. The marks remained unchanged.

Like all Alsatians, Alfred's brothers Mathieu and Jacques were
more French than the French. They smarted under the attack of the
anti-Semites. Once more they made a serious effort to induce Alfred
to leave the Army. But he refused. He had made a fine record. In spite
of the unfair marks in the subject taught by General Bonnefond, he
had risen from sixty-seventh in the class at the beginning to ninth
at the end. The way to the General Staff was open to him and he would
not let himself be deterred by the day's fashion in politics.

In 1893, a year after *La Libre Parole* had begun publication, a year
before Esterhazy wrote the meticulous if indiscreet *bordereau,* Captain
Dreyfus was appointed to the General Staff as a probationer. The
presence of a Jew in this inner sanctum came as a shock to the staff
officers, the overwhelming majority of them Postards.

A last-minute effort was made to fend off Dreyfus. Colonel Jean
Sandherr, head of counter-espionage at the Second Bureau, entered
a formal protest. He described the appointment as a security risk. Outside the General Staff such a description would have struck too many
as outrageous, and the head of the Second Bureau, General Charles-
Arthur Gonse, did not forward the protest to the Minister of War,
General Mercier. However, he talked the matter over with Major
Georges Picquart. The young major was now in charge of probationers
at the General Staff. General Gonse suggested that Dreyfus be assigned to the First Bureau, where his work involved maneuvers. Not
only were no top-level military secrets available there, but the general
in charge was known to be least prejudiced against Jews.

There was nothing the anti-Semites and those who truckled to them
could do. The fitness reports on Captain Dreyfus throughout his military career testified to his abilities and high standards of professional
conduct. Only one of his superiors, Colonel Pierre-Elie Fabre, had
entered a derogatory comment. This was to the effect that Dreyfus was
rather self-assured and a prig. It was not enough to hang a man, and
so Dreyfus was on the General Staff when Esterhazy's *bordereau* ex-
ploded on Colonel Sandherr's desk and ignited the mind of Colonel
Fabre, who was now head of the General Staff's Fourth Bureau.

5

THE JEW, THE JEW. The word sped back to Colonel Sandherr's office on the ardent legs of Colonel Fabre and his deputy, Colonel D'Aboville.

Of course. Colonel Sandherr wondered why he had not suspected Dreyfus from the start. After all, had he or had he not meant it a year before when he had described Jews as security risks? Still, there was the matter of evidence.

"Did you compare the handwritings?" he asked. Fabre and D'Aboville had been so overwhelmed by the brilliance of their deduction that they had overlooked this detail. Dreyfus' file was now brought and placed side by side with the *bordereau* that was in Major Esterhazy's handwriting. The three officers pored over it, comparing the two handwritings. They noted a similarity, but they were not men who needed much convincing. Sandherr went to report to General Charles Gonse, who had by now become Deputy Chief of the General Staff. Rumor ran before him: it was the Jew, the Jew.

The insufferable pressure of the last months gave way to silent exhilaration. Peculiar type, this Dreyfus, D'Aboville recalled, inquisitive and indiscreet. Colonel Fabre remembered with pride that he alone of all Dreyfus' commanding officers had not had the wool pulled over his eyes. Hadn't he made a derogatory observation in a fitness report, calling Dreyfus self-assured and a prig?

Before reporting to General de Boisdeffre, his chief, General Gonse decided to have the handwritings compared by an expert. To this end he summoned the Marquis Mercier du Paty de Clam, a major on the General Staff—not the first nor the last but certainly one of the more unusual of the many unusual characters who played a part in the Dreyfus affair.

The Marquis du Paty de Clam was a descendant of a family distinguished in French history, but he was a strange nut to grow from such a tree. The little marquis came to General Gonse's office bemonocled. A nearsighted handwriting "expert" he was—the kind of "expert" who tells fortunes and character—so nearsighted that he walked awkwardly without eyeglasses, but he was too vain to wear them. He dropped his monocle and raised two papers close to his eyes

—one the *bordereau* written by Major Esterhazy, the other a sample of Dreyfus' writing. He compared the two and announced they were of the same type but showed dissimilarities.

He was then warned that this concerned a very grave case. The marquis hesitated. He asked for more time to compare the two handwritings.

General Gonse decided he could not keep his superiors out of it any longer. He reported to General de Boisdeffre, his chief, who passed on the news to the Minister of War, General Mercier.

To Mercier, bedeviled by the right and the left, in torment over the fear that the politicians would get on to the fact that his General Staff had been letting a spy operate under its lofty nose, the news that a lead to the culprit had been discovered came as a godsend. He hastened to impart the tidings to President Jean Casimir-Périer. He then closeted himself for a long talk with the Premier, Charles Dupuy.

Both these men were aware that they were handling dynamite. The fate of the Government was involved. To announce publicly that a spy had been caught inevitably would reveal that spying had been done. They must make very sure of the criminal before letting the political opposition learn of the crime. Premier Dupuy and General Mercier agreed that all must be kept secret until the case was airtight and that only those cabinet ministers who might be required to take action should be informed of developments to date.

One of these was the Foreign Minister, Gabriel Hanotaux. Hanotaux was opposed to any judicial procedure that involved placing in the record the *bordereau*—thus far the only evidence available. He argued that to disclose the fact that the French had stolen a document from a foreign legation, even in "the ordinary way," would touch off an international uproar and might lead to a diplomatic rupture with Germany, even to war. The case, he insisted, should be suppressed unless less compromising evidence could be found.

But Mercier knew how impossible it would be to prevent a leak if the case were quashed. A leak even to the friendly press would be his end. The right-wing papers had been taking him to task lately for his lack of organizing and executive abilities. If it were learned that he had acceded to letting treason go unpunished, he might even be suspected of having been an accessory. He was determined to proceed.

Back at his office, General Mercier found that things had moved rapidly. Anyone who has worked in an office will understand why. Careers hung in the balance. The boss wanted results. Those who could not give them to him would not be demonstrating efficiency. Of course, the result had to stand up, but speed was important, too.

While Du Paty de Clam was thinking it over, General Gonse had called in the handwriting expert of the Banque de France, Alfred Gobert. M. Gobert was a solemn and precise man. He was not permitted to know the identity of the person whose handwriting he had been asked to compare with the handwriting on the *bordereau*. This seemed highly irregular to him. Also he resented being rushed. Finally he stated his conclusion in the precise, pedantic language of the kind of expert a bank trusts: the *bordereau* could have been written by a person other than the writer of the samples submitted to him for comparison. General Gonse classed this opinion—which, in America, would automatically have acquitted Dreyfus—as "noncommittal."

He then called in Alphonse Bertillon, a statistician who was then head of the so-called anthropometric department of the police, a department based on Bertillon's method of identifying criminals. Bertillon measured and classified these men according to 222 bones of the human skeleton, proving mathematically to his satisfaction not only that no two human beings are alike but that there are eleven principal skeletal characteristics which do not change no matter how the human being waxes and wanes between the ages of twenty and sixty.

Not long before this time the police department had begun to photograph arrested persons. Their files were bulging, but since photographs discriminate sharply only between the clean-shaven and the bearded, between the fat-faced and the lean, there was no way to tell from them whether a suspect had ever been arrested before. To conceal his record, a criminal had only to grow a beard or develop a squint or put on or lose weight, or just let a few years pass between exposures to the police camera.

However, Bertillon's system provided a way—foolproof, he announced—and it made him world-famous. When fingerprinting was advanced as a surer, less cumbersome method of identification, he dismissed it, and such was his prestige that fingerprinting did not make much headway among the police for almost twenty years. Then a curious thing happened at Leavenworth Prison in Kansas, in the United States. A prisoner being admitted was photographed in the regular way and put through the routine Bertillon anthropometric measurements. His name was William West. The Bertillon files at the prison disclosed that he had previously been convicted of murder. He denied this stubbornly and when confronted with the fact that seven of the eleven Bertillon characteristics were identical with those of the William West who had been convicted of murder, and the remaining four differed only minutely, he continued to deny his guilt. He was not believed until somebody thought of searching the inmate files. There it was discovered that the William West who had been convicted of murder had been serving time for it in Leavenworth itself for the last ten years.

This was a blow from which anthropometry never fully recovered. But Bertillon did, by the simple process of switching to fingerprints. His system is still used by police in their rogues' galleries, but only to provide leads where fingerprints are unavailable or useless.

However, in 1894 he was at the height of his fame. The first William West had not even committed murder yet, and his anthropometrical twin was an innocent in a perambulator. Bertillon was a strange detective. His father and his older brother were very able statisticians. He himself had been the black sheep of the family and was a confirmed anti-Semite. But he had the family's passion for numbers, and confidence that the world marched as numbers do. He was very dubious of the approved handwriting expertise of the day—not enough numbers in it. He himself had worked out a theory of handwriting identification which was so rife with numbers that nobody but he could cope with it. Courts listened respectfully but did not pretend to understand.

Du Paty de Clam, who knew everybody, of course knew Bertillon. He took the precaution of tipping Bertillon off in confidence that there was crushing evidence of the guilt of the person who had written the *bordereau*. Bertillon went into his measurements and emerged from them to pronounce his opinion: "If the hypothesis is discarded that the author of the *bordereau* forged another's handwriting while preparing it, it appears to be manifest that the identical person wrote both the samples and the incriminating document."

The officers of the Second Bureau were utterly at a loss in following Bertillon's steps as he explained how he had come to his conclusion. But it was the opinion they wanted. It was accepted as proof of Dreyfus' guilt, and War Minister Mercier moved swiftly into action. He himself was about to leave with Boisdeffre for the annual maneuvers.

He turned over the investigation to Du Paty de Clam, summoned a police officer named Cochefort, signed a warrant for the arrest of Dreyfus and informed Major Ferdinand Forzinetti, director of the Cherche-Midi prison, that a high officer would visit him on a top-secret mission.

The handwriting was not proof; it was only evidence. But it was almost taken for granted, so powerful was the wave of wishful thinking that swept the General Staff, that the investigation would disclose enough evidence to amount to proof. By arresting a man from their own midst the cloud of suspicion under which all had lived would lift, and the fact that the man was a Jew would keep an unfavorable light from being cast on the General Staff, for the Jew was an outsider even within the fold. Yes, it was a consummation devoutly to be wished, and men anxious to give the boss those results for which he would be so grateful began to feel less than fastidious about how the consummation could be arrived at.

There was a patent inconsistency in the sole piece of evidence thus far adduced. The author of the *bordereau* had described himself in it as being "off to the maneuvers," and the staff's probationers had been informed as early as May that they would not take part in the maneuvers that year. Esterhazy had sent the *bordereau* to Schwarzkoppen on September 1. The maneuvers had been about to begin then. It had been September 26 before Colonel Sandherr had got hold of the document and carefully torn it into little pieces. All this time Captain Dreyfus had not stirred from Paris and, in fact, as the orders for the investigation and arrest were being issued, was at home with Lucie and their two children.

However, the *bordereau* was undated and Colonel Fabre explained the inconsistency away in this manner: Dreyfus had accompanied him on an inspection tour in June. That was probably what he meant by being "off to the maneuvers." Du Paty later offered another explanation: the *bordereau* might have been written before May, when the probationers were informed they would have no duty at the maneuvers. Why a man should write before May that he was "off" to maneuvers which would not begin until September Du Paty did not explain. Nor did anyone concern himself about the *bordereau's* Germanisms, which stuck out so obviously in the French text. Dreyfus spoke and wrote a French which was flawlessly French.

At the height of the excitement, Major Henry returned from his leave. Did he recognize the handwriting of his friend, Esterhazy, when he studied the *bordereau*? If so, he gave no voice to his recognition. As always, the peasant's son was given the dirty job. His orders were to take Dreyfus to jail.

Colonel D'Aboville was the high officer who called on Major Forzinetti at the Cherche-Midi prison. He personally selected a cell he deemed appropriate for Dreyfus and warned the prison director that he was to keep the identity of the man who would be incarcerated in it secret even from his superior, the military commandant of Paris. Secrecy, of course, was a political necessity until the investigation proved the guilt that had been so quickly assumed. It would be unforgivable, a towering blunder, to reveal the crime by making known an arrest and then have to reveal that the wrong man had been arrested. It would be stupidity squared, and further investigation would have to be conducted in the din of a pack of opposition politicians yowling for the blood of the investigators. But D'Aboville did not communicate to Forzinetti the sensible reason for desiring secrecy. Instead, he said that a leak of the news would complicate the prison director's duties. "The Jews will leave no stone unturned to find out where Dreyfus is," he warned. Forzinetti objected to the secrecy. He objected, too, to the interference from on high in what was after all his command. But D'Aboville was communicating orders directly from the War Minister.

In the meantime Major du Paty de Clam had been given congenial orders and was carrying them out *con molte*. He devised a scheme to make the arrest proceed without incident. General Gonse signed an order directing Captain Dreyfus to appear at an inspection of General Staff probationers at the office of the Chief of Staff. The time: October 15, 9:00 P.M. Civilian attire.

Dreyfus arrived punctually. He was astonished to discover only Major du Paty present and three men in civilian attire who obviously were not staff officers. The three stood about feigning indifference. One was the police officer, Cochefort, the two others his aides. But the little bemonocled marquis did not explain their presence. He told Dreyfus that General Gonse would arrive soon and asked Dreyfus if he would be kind enough to write a letter for him in the meantime. He had injured his finger, the marquis explained, and could hold a pen only with difficulty.

Dreyfus sat down at a small desk by the window and Du Paty began to dictate. He dictated an ordinary letter, but it was loaded with phrases from the *bordereau*. According to his own description of the scene, when he had dictated the words "a note on the hydraulic brake of the 120 mm. gun," he halted abruptly. "What's the matter with you?" he cried. "You are trembling." "Am I?" replied Dreyfus. "Perhaps my fingers are cold."

It seemed to Du Paty a flippant response to an attempt to open the way to the man for a breakdown and confession. He scowled at Dreyfus. "Watch out," he warned. "This is very serious."

He resumed dictating and Dreyfus resumed writing. The blackguard, it seemed to Du Paty, had no nerves. Phrase after phrase from the *bordereau* peppered him, yet his writing remained calm and businesslike. Du Paty gave it up in midstream. "I arrest you in the name of the law," he shouted. "You are accused of high treason," he continued at the top of his voice.

Cochefort moved to stand over Dreyfus. The captain jumped to his feet. "Here are my keys," he said to Cochefort. "Search my home. I am innocent." Suddenly the blood rushed to his head and he turned to Major du Paty. "Show me the proof of the infamy you pretend I committed," he cried out in terrible anger.

"The proofs are overwhelming," Du Paty replied curtly. He took a pistol from his pocket and put it on the table before Dreyfus. Then he stared silently.

Dreyfus stared, too. It was an appalling moment, the first indication Dreyfus had had of the extent to which his superiors were convinced of his guilt. "I am innocent," he said at last. "I won't kill myself. I want to live to prove my innocence. This outrage must be repaired."

Major Henry had been waiting in an adjoining office. He entered, robust and vulgar. In the cab in which he took Dreyfus to the Cherche-Midi prison, Henry pretended cunningly to be ignorant of the matter and asked what it was all about. "I haven't the slightest idea," Dreyfus replied.

Du Paty and the archivist Gribelin meanwhile had hastened to the Avenue du Trocadéro to take Lucie Dreyfus by surprise. Two other officers were dispatched to search the home of Dreyfus' father-in-law, the jeweler Hadamard.

Mme. Dreyfus sensed disaster instantly. Du Paty was courteous but grave. "I am afraid I bring bad news," he said. Lucie paled. "Is he dead?" Du Paty shook his head. "Has he fallen from his horse?" Again Du Paty shook his head. "It is much worse," he said at last. "He is in jail."

The small, slender woman straightened. She gave the two officers a look of hostility that both remembered for a long time. Her husband could have done no wrong. She was certain there had been a misunderstanding. "Where is he?" she demanded. "I want to be taken to him immediately."

Oh no, replied Du Paty. If you want to help your husband, he warned her, you must not see him and you must not try to find out where he is; you must keep everything secret and tell no one anything. He appealed to her on patriotic grounds. A slip of the tongue, he said, and war might break out. Perhaps Lucie believed him. Perhaps she understood that, once the arrest of her husband became known, it would be politically imperative on the part of his superiors to secure a conviction. At any rate, she did not inform even his brothers in Mulhouse of Alfred's arrest. This was a mistake, as it turned out. For, at this juncture, before further evidence could be forged, the chances were that an energetic intervention would have set Dreyfus free. The honor of the Army had not yet been committed, only the efficiency of its highest command, and there were politicians who would have rallied public opinion to his support.

Du Paty produced a search warrant. "What are you looking for?" asked Lucie. "For what we will find," replied Du Paty. But they did not find it. The two officers searched for two hours. They ransacked every drawer, closet, bookshelf, and examined minutely every slip of paper. Who knew what might or might not be in code? They took away the household ledger and the love letters Alfred and Lucie had written during their engagement. But they turned up no incriminating documents nor a piece of that flimsy cream-colored graph paper with the small blue squares on which the *bordereau* had been written and which was what they had been looking for. The search party at the Hadamard home was equally unsuccessful.

It is not necessary to imagine how Dreyfus felt when he was left alone in his cell. The facts have been recorded. He went berserk. A volcano erupted in this cold, inhibited man. He smashed at stone and iron. A tornado blew from his frothing lips. He screamed his rage to heaven. The guards became alarmed and summoned the prison director. Major Forzinetti made repeated efforts to calm his prisoner, but they were to no avail. A lifetime of suppression had burst its dams and was on the loose. Forzinetti sent a report to the Minister of War. He was concerned for Dreyfus' sanity.

General Mercier summoned the major to his office to discuss the matter orally. General de Boisdeffre listened in on the conference. The secret investigation had developed no evidence thus far. For a moment hope had flared. Paris' network of stool pigeons had produced a report that Dreyfus frequented suspicious cafés and was a gambler. But it had turned out to be another Dreyfus, a Max Dreyfus, a man with a police record. Police Chief Louis Lépine himself had checked and discovered that Alfred Dreyfus, a wealthy man, restricted his social contacts to a few close friends and kept to his home and family. There was no apparent motive for the crime. It was all very discouraging.

Boisdeffre listened in silence to Major Forzinetti's fears for Dreyfus' sanity. He leaned forward. After all, Forzinetti had seen thousands of accused men. He should have a sense of whether a man was guilty or innocent. What was his conclusion about Dreyfus?

"I would not have presumed to volunteer it," Major Forzinetti answered. "But since you ask me, I tell you that this man is as innocent as I am."

The two generals allowed Major Forzinetti to go without a word.

Perhaps it was Du Paty who enabled Dreyfus to regain hold of himself. The marquis was in a fever of activity. He went to the Cherche-Midi and asked for a flashlight. He had devised some complicated game for catching Dreyfus off-guard. Major Forzinetti would have none of it. But Du Paty was insuppressible. While the police scoured Paris and pawed inch by inch over Dreyfus' entire path through life from his cradle in Mulhouse, and French espionage agents pried in every way possible in all the countries for evidence, any evidence, a grain even of suspicion of his perfidy, the marquis spent hours in Dreyfus' cell.

He made Dreyfus write out the text of the *bordereau* in various postures. It appeared that Du Paty was not satisfied with Bertillon's opinion. He was aware that when Bertillon began explaining the labyrinth of numbers on which his handwriting expertise was based, the judges would be lost in the maze. So Du Paty had called in three other handwriting experts. Each carefully examined the *bordereau* written by Esterhazy and a sample of writing by Dreyfus. He informed each under the rose that other proofs of Dreyfus' guilt existed. But even so, the expert opinion was less than convincing. The first of the experts, Pierre Teysonnières, declared without reservation that the handwritings came from the same man. The second, Etienne Charavay, made some reservations but in the main agreed with Teysonnières. The third, Pelletier, did not feel that the writing on the *bordereau* could be attributed to Dreyfus. But even the two who did noted that dissimilarities existed. Hence the postures Dreyfus had to assume while writing the text of the *bordereau* over and over at Du Paty's request. Dreyfus wrote sitting, he wrote standing, he wrote leaning against a wall, crouched over the floor, sitting erect, sitting hunched over, standing erect, standing hunched over. He wrote in every way except under water, and Du Paty was convinced he must discover in the end the position which would make Dreyfus' handwriting identical with that on the *bordereau.*

It didn't happen, but the game kept on, and Dreyfus made no protest. It stopped his screaming. It gave him something besides a black stillness to fight. Du Paty had photostatic copies of the *bordereau* made and cut them into minute shreds. He did the same with samples of Dreyfus' writing, and brought all the shreds to Dreyfus in his cap, telling the captain to pick them out and identify which were in his handwriting and which were not. Dreyfus made not a single mistake. Each shred of scribble that he identified as his own was in fact his own and each shred that he said was not his own was not his own.

A week had gone by, and now another was going. Dreyfus still had no knowledge of the case against himself, and demanded ceaselessly to be told. Du Paty would reveal only that it involved selling military secrets to a foreign power. Dreyfus tried to convince Du Paty that it must be a case of mistaken identity and the marquis, craftily, assured him he had an open mind. Was not he the Marquis du Paty de Clam, the grandson of that great champion of justice, Mercier du Paty, who a hundred years before had made a public stand for the innocence of three men, innocent victims of a miscarriage of justice? Mercier du Paty's brief in their defense had been publicly burned. Yet the old marquis' stand had been vindicated later when the innocence of the three now dead had become established.

Trust me, Du Paty kept telling Dreyfus, trust my heritage, confide the truth to me. Dreyfus told the marquis the truth and the marquis listened with a disbelieving mind. But the police investigation was equally fruitless. No evidence was developed to support the highly assailable evidence of the similar-dissimilar handwriting on the *bordereau*. It seemed as if Dreyfus must be released with the Scottish verdict of "not proven."

Then, on October 28, Drumont at *La Libre Parole* received a note: "Dreyfus is at Cherche-Midi. He is supposed to be on a trip. Quite untrue. They want to quash the case. Israel is up in arms." The note was signed "Henry."

The next day the following appeared in the columns of the popular anti-Semitic sheet: "Is it a fact that on orders from the military a very important arrest has been made? The prisoner is accused of high treason. If this news is true, why the silence? An answer is urgently requested."

The dreaded leak had occurred. Henry had pulled the plug, but had he done it on his own, or had he been manipulated into it by his friend Esterhazy? By the accident of things having started during his leave, Henry had been pushed to the periphery of the great event. Du Paty stood in the center, along with Sandherr, Fabre, D'Aboville, Gonse. Now if the "result" was obtained, it would not be Henry to whom Mercier and Boisdeffre would feel indebted. On the other hand, Esterhazy had every reason to maneuver Henry into doing it. What could he lose if the issue against Dreyfus were forced? The least he could gain would be the shouts and alarums which might permanently obfuscate his own guilt. There might even be a conviction of Dreyfus.

Whether Henry pulled the plug on his own or was prodded by Esterhazy, the fact was that it had now been done and a conviction by a court had become a matter of the utmost importance. Du Paty closed the barren investigation without committing himself one way or the other, and passed the file on to the Minister of War. The Cabinet met and General Mercier issued a communiqué through the official news agency:

Serious accusations have led to the temporary confinement under arrest of an officer of the Army. He is suspected of having communicated to foreigners some documents which, though of slight importance, were nevertheless confidential. The investigation is being pursued with the discretion that is required in such matters. The conclusion may be expected in the near future.

La Libre Parole promptly went over to the attack: The truth was that the material Esterhazy had delivered to Schwarzkoppen was of very minor significance, but the truth has always been a red rag for the deranged. It is a force pressing them back into the rational world from whose terrors they had escaped in the first place by embracing lies. It was Mercier's statement that the documents were of slight importance that *La Libre Parole* pounced on. There's a Minister of War for you, it cried editorially. He who ought to be the guardian and true depository of patriotism, what is he making of his office? A cesspool, worse than the Augean stables, for no Hercules has been found to clean this up. In any other country such a minister would be taken by the scruff of the neck and kicked out for making common cause with a traitor by whittling down his crime.

But the other papers, too, were on to a big news story. *L'Intransigeant* reported a conversation with an aide in the War Ministry who said that General Mercier's ambiguous attitude to the case of Captain Dreyfus was putting the entire personnel on his staff in an impossible situation. *L'Eclair,* usually inspired by the General Staff, came to the edge of the facts. It hinted that an insider had tipped off the press in order to force the hands of those in the ministry whose one concern had been to avoid a scandal.

In the light of these developments, the Cabinet held another meeting. It was decided that the Government could not survive a quashing of the case against Dreyfus. He must have his day in court.

A mixture of rumor and denunciation began boiling on the front burners of the nation's press. *La Libre Parole* reported that Foreign Minister Hanotaux had called on the German Ambassador, Count Münster. Was a deal in progress? The paper demanded a trial of Dreyfus that would be open to the public. It feared that, in an effort to avoid complications, the indictment would be restricted to a mere trifle and Dreyfus would escape with prison instead of death.

The next day the same newspaper continued: There was conclusive proof of Dreyfus' guilt, coming from sources connected with a "Great Power." The French Government consisted of a bunch of cowards. Soon it was screaming that the main incriminating document had disappeared from the files. But, by great good luck, there existed a photostatic copy of it. Three days later it took back surreptitiously its story of the disappearance, and at the same time managed to imply that the Jews had been responsible for the disappearance. It accomplished this feat of legerdemain in two sentences. The first reported great excitement in "Jewish circles" over the fact that General Mercier possessed a photostatic copy of the document. For now, whether the document disappeared or not, it was certain the press would be able to reproduce it.

Thus obliquely it intimated for the first time that perhaps the document had not disappeared after all. But there had been a sudden change in attitude toward Mercier. No doubt Drumont had learned through Major Henry that it was Mercier who had pressed for prosecution in the cabinet meeting. Congratulations to Mercier, it concluded. The Jews, at last, have met their man. Throughout those feverish days *La Libre Parole* drew a portrait of events that was so contradictory to the facts as to seem laughable. It saw the Jews conspiring to free a guilty Dreyfus and Mercier battling single-handed against them. But, of course, very few knew the truth then, and none who did was a journalist.

In the meantime *Le Matin*, the daily with the largest circulation in Paris, now launched an attack on the German Embassy in Paris. It described it as a center of espionage, with Schwarzkoppen the leader. Count Münster promptly called on the President of France and the Prime Minister, asking them to take steps to counter the campaign against his embassy and his military attaché. The French Government issued a short communiqué to the effect that it had no intention of discontinuing its permission to foreign embassies to have military attachés on their staffs and that the article in a certain newspaper on the activities of a certain military attaché was in error on several points.

This sidling defense satisfied neither the German Ambassador nor his Government. Count Münster protested again, this time more heatedly. This brought a declaration from the French Government to the effect that there was no truth in the press reports implicating foreign embassies in the current espionage case.

But the irrepressible press continued on its merry way. *Le Figaro*, a respectable daily, printed what purported to be an interview with General Mercier. It quoted the War Minister as saying there was proof Dreyfus had had connections for three years with a foreign government, neither the Italian nor the Austrian. However, he had not done it for money. The next day *Le Temps* printed the general's denial that he had granted any such interview to *Le Figaro*. That newspaper, however, insisted that Mercier had. The Catholic daily *La Croix,* presumably reflecting the opinion of the Postards on the General Staff, wrote that if the trial were held in public, facts might come to light that would lead to war.

When her husband's name had been made public, Lucie Dreyfus had sent a telegram to Mulhouse to her brother-in-law Mathieu, who had been closest to Alfred. He hastened to Paris. On the train the Paris newspaper accounts of Alfred made the trip a waking nightmare. By the time he reached Paris he was beside himself. He implored Major du Paty and Gribelin to let him visit his brother's cell. The major might hide behind a curtain or a door so that he could see Alfred's every gesture, hear every word with which Alfred would answer Mathieu's questions. Mathieu gave his word of honor that should his brother confess that in a moment of insanity or for any reason whatsoever he had committed treason, then he, Mathieu, would hand his own brother a revolver and demand that he kill himself then and there.

"To me he will tell the truth no matter what," Mathieu said, weeping. Du Paty and Gribelin rejected the prayer. They wanted no more tests of whether Dreyfus was innocent or guilty. The case against the captain was in trouble enough already.

On December 4, the prosecutor Bexon D'Ormeschville—in France more accurately described as Investigator for the Court—drew up his case. It consisted of the *bordereau*. This still remained the sole piece of evidence in the file, but it pointed firmly only to the fact that treason had been committed, and waveringly indeed to Dreyfus as the traitor.

To this day the examination of forged and disguised handwriting remains one of the most treacherous problems in police science. In that day even comparison of handwritings was treacherous. Experts relied exclusively on the calligraphic method—the comparison of the outer shapes of the letters. It would be a decade and longer before such men as Albert Osborn and Hans Schneickert would put the handwriting expert on firmer ground. No expert today would have the least difficulty in distinguishing between Esterhazy's writing and Dreyfus', or, since a sample of Esterhazy's writing had not been consulted, in deciding that Dreyfus could not have written the *bordereau*. An astonishing number of lay persons are blind to small differences in forms, but those who are not would have no difficulty in telling one from the other. However, the prosecutor had five handwriting experts to rely on, and those who had come to a firm conclusion were in the minority. Not only that. The firm opinions contradicted one another.

D'Ormeschville rested his case on a bucket of eels when he rested on the "experts." For the remainder, he decided to rely on argument. He would attribute the dissimilarities between Dreyfus' writing and the writing on the *bordereau* to the fact that Dreyfus was a careful traitor who had taken the precaution to disguise his hand when indulging in criminal penmanship. That the intensive investigation, including the search of Dreyfus' home and the probing of his entire career, had been barren of results he would attribute to Dreyfus' veritable genius for being careful. That Dreyfus had made no slip in the course of exhaustive questioning he would cite as proof that Dreyfus not only was clever but had a supercriminal's mental equipment—that is, he was a moral imbecile who lacked the conscience that undid lesser criminals when confronted with police questioning.

The chances are D'Ormeschville was not very happy about his case. He was even unhappier about another piece of documentary evidence that had come into the hands of the Second Bureau. The counter-espionage agents, in their effort to find some link between Dreyfus and the men they were spying on, had got hold of it. But all it proved was that there had been no link.

It seemed that when the Italian military attaché, Lieutenant Colonel Panizzardi, had read in the newspapers of Dreyfus' arrest, he had called on Schwarzkoppen at the German Embassy to find out whether Dreyfus had been employed there. He was understandably concerned. After all, he and Schwarzkoppen were both named "Alexandrine" in their messages to each other and had worked together very closely in espionage. Schwarzkoppen denied emphatically any knowledge of Dreyfus, and Panizzardi returned to the Italian Embassy and sent a cable in code to Rome: "If Captain D. had no relations with you, a denial would be welcome to avoid press comment."

This was on November 2. It was decoded in the French Foreign Office, and Major du Paty made a "free translation" of it for the Second Bureau's files: "D. arrested. Precautions taken. Emissary warned."

The major was no precisionist to render a dull text in a dull way. But the prosecutor knew his French penal code. Article 101 reads: "All documents that might serve to convict the defendant must be shown to him, and he must be asked whether he recognizes them." How long could Du Paty's "free translation" stand up under the scrutiny of a defense lawyer who would demand and have every right under law to see the original? Besides, the presentation of such evidence would disclose not only that the French had had access to Panizzardi's office but that they had broken the code. Would the Government consider it worth while to make such a costly disclosure for the sake of a piece of evidence that would inevitably blow up in its face?

But the pressure was on. The press had been given a free hand to inflate the case to monstrous proportions. *Le Petit Journal,* which usually did not take sides in politics and on that account, perhaps, had three million readers, declared: "Had war broken out, Dreyfus would have been a trusted man of the Ministry. He might have sent his comrades to their death in traps set with his connivance."

A newspaper as conservative as *L'Echo de Paris* reported without qualification that Dreyfus had also sold to the enemy information on the scale and timing and concentration areas of mobilization. "To rewrite the timetable alone will take three years," it stated.

All unsolved treasons of the recent past were charged to Dreyfus. The captain had never visited Russia, but one newspaper reported that he had been seen in St. Petersburg in the company of German aristocrats. It even gave the name of the hotel and the number of the room in which he had been "known" to stay.

The important dailies *Le Temps* and *Le Matin* joined in unearthing a love interest. Dreyfus, according to them, had a sweetheart at Nice, an Italian beauty of noble birth. It was she who had seduced him into committing treason, they announced.

"Dreyfus is an agent of international Jewry," wrote the Catholic paper, *La Croix,* "which has decided to ruin the French people and to acquire the territory of France." *La Libre Parole, La Cocarde* and *La Patrie* united in demanding that Dreyfus be put to death.

It was obvious to the General Staff what would follow a failure to convict Dreyfus. Mercier would be out, probably the Government, too. A new War Minister must dismiss the personnel of the Second Bureau for incompetence in having blundered in discovering the traitor. Possibly the entire General Staff would be replaced. After all, the traitor must be considered to be still among them.

In this crisis a proposition was put forward by Colonel Sandherr of the Second Bureau. It had come to him from Major du Paty. This was simply to confront the court with the file the Second Bureau had prepared on the case and classify it "secret," thus preventing the defense from examining it and tearing it to pieces.

The officers of the Second Bureau were schooled in skirting the edge of crime. *Agents provocateurs,* nameless and faceless human trappers, were weapons they were accustomed to rely on. Their activities were safe from interference by the law. The hush-hush of national security sheltered them. But this was a direct and open violation of the law.

General Mercier hesitated for a long time. That Dreyfus was actually guilty he never doubted, nor did any other officers on the staff with the possible exception of Major Henry and Major du Paty. Henry unquestionably suspected more than he has ever told. But Esterhazy was not only a man to whom he was grateful; Henry was deeply involved with the count. His own career must suffer should Esterhazy be exposed. Du Paty was a horse of quite another color. For him the unexpected was always the desirable. He took a perverse delight in bringing about chaotic situations, in concocting absurdities that he ended by believing in passionately. The one mortal sin to him was boredom. As for Colonel Sandherr, he could hardly be expected to doubt the Jew was guilty. Once at a parade he had seen tears come into the eyes of an Alsatian Jew when the French tricolor had been hoisted. "How I detest these hypocrites!" he had said in a loud, jarring tone.

But a War Minister cannot ignore the law without incurring grave risks. A cabinet officer has both rivals and enemies. His friends shift with the political winds, and political winds are made by whispers. Rumors become accusations—if not today when he is secure, tomorrow when he is not so secure, and when a cabinet officer is not so secure he has no friends. He has only ex-friends rushing to get out from under his fall. To set aside Article 101 in the present temper of affairs would be regarded as an act of patriotism. What would it be regarded as tomorrow and the day after when the present temper changed? Mercier must worry about it. Overruling a law of the land was not an action that would be quickly forgotten. It would be his indelible mark on political affairs for the rest of his life, waiting to be put forward for public inspection again and again whenever his opposition thought it advantageous.

He told Sandherr that he must have time to think about it. Three days passed without word from him.

On December 15, Drumont, through his pipeline to the General Staff, announced triumphantly in *La Libre Parole*: "Dreyfus is committed for trial by court martial on December 20. Mercier with the brutal bluntness of his patriotism has prevailed over his enemies who conspired in the dark."

Even if the date were wrong, the die was cast. The ideal of government by law and not by men was committed to its ordeal.

6

IN CASTING ABOUT for a lawyer to defend Alfred, the Dreyfus family had settled on Edgar Demange. Demange, of high repute in criminal law, was a man of advanced age and a devout Catholic. It was obvious he would not be attracted by a fee however substantial. It was equally obvious that he would not face the withering publicity just to get his name in the papers. His name had been in the papers. Abraham Lincoln once parsed a career in law as follows: on, onner, onnest. First the lawyer gets on. Then he gets honor. Then he gets honest. It was apparent to the dullest that Demange had reached the age and position in life when his honesty could not be doubted.

There was no nonsense in Demange about the benefit of the doubt going to the defendant—at least there was none in this case. "Should I find the least reason to doubt his innocence," he told the Dreyfus family, "I will refuse to defend him. This will be known and commented on. In effect, I shall be his first judge."

The family accepted the risk. Demange studied the family's evidence on Dreyfus' career and then called for the Government's evidence under Article 101. He was provided with D'Ormeschville's file. He was thunderstruck. Was this all, the *bordereau*, a dispute among handwriting experts, a prosecutor's petit-point of suppositions and theories? It was all. The decision to use the Second Bureau's file had not yet been taken.

The old man went to see Dreyfus in his cell. "I am convinced of your innocence," he said. "I will defend you."

The decision to go to trial taken, Dreyfus was permitted to write his wife. "My judges are loyal and honest soldiers like myself," he wrote. "They will recognize the error that has been committed. . . . They will listen to me attentively and the matter will be cleared up."

On December 18 he wrote Lucie: "Tomorrow I shall stand before my judges upright and at peace with myself. I have nothing to fear."

7

TRIAL BEGAN DECEMBER 19, 1894, in an eighteenth-century palace on the Rue Cherche-Midi, near the prison. The ancient palace had been converted into a military courthouse.

The courtroom was large and gloomy, illuminated by yellow gaslight. Its tiny windows were cut into thick stone walls. They gave on the prison yard.

The press had never made up its mind whether the court-martial would open its proceedings to the public or hold them behind closed doors. As a result, few of the public attended. *La Libre Parole* wrote that "people with crooked noses were to be seen among the audience." But it was alone in stating that. Other newspapers reported that the Jews were conspicuously absent, refusing to involve themselves with a traitor even if he were a fellow Jew. In any case, the public provided only a minor background at the trial.

Seven officers had been selected to serve the court-martial as judges. Their family backgrounds varied enough to represent a cross-section of France. The lowest rank among the judges was captain, the highest, and therefore the judge presiding, a colonel named Maurel. Three deputy judges sat behind the long table with the judges. Although there was extensive mention in the *bordereau* of artillery secrets having been delivered, no artilleryman was among the judges or deputies.

There were three handwriting experts summoned by the prosecution, with Alphonse Bertillon the heavy gun among them. Major du Paty basked in the presence of General Gonse and twittered about as if he were the producer of a play whose actors he was responsible for. Major Henry beetled at the audience like a police chief. The audience consisted chiefly of the press. But the chief of police himself, Louis Lépine, was present, as was Major Georges Picquart. Dreyfus' former instructor at the war college and now his chief as commander of probationers of the General Staff had been appointed by General Mercier to represent the Ministry of War as observer.

Colonel Maurel, the presiding judge, ordered the accused to be escorted in. Captain Dreyfus entered rigidly. The thin-haired, bespectacled man, a small mustache under his sharp nose, his skin drawn and shining, had attired himself in the gala full-dress uniform of an officer of the General Staff. He glanced around stiffly and felt reassured. A gathering of officers looked down on him. He was among his own, among a diversity of types he knew so well and had seen molded in the same form in which he had been molded. But he answered the first formal questions about his name, address and rank in a voice that, while firm and carefully emotionless, yet had an artificial intonation. This had always happened when he was fighting for control of himself. He had long known it made a bad impression. But that only made it more difficult to change.

The attorney for the Republic, Captain Brisset, rose and the proceedings officially began. They began with an argument over whether the trial should be public. The Republic wanted the trial held *in camera*. The defense, naturally, wanted the public present.

After all, while Demange knew that there was only one incriminating document and that this document did not incriminate Dreyfus, the public had been informed by the press that there was overwhelming evidence. In fact, the press had already condemned Dreyfus in public and had begun a campaign to restore capital punishment for high treason. The public had been told that Dreyfus would escape the guillotine only because the law providing for such an end for traitors had been repealed.

Demange's tactic was to take advantage of the opening argument, while the trial was not yet declared secret, to inform the public through the press of the fact that there was only one piece of evidence in the file, the *bordereau*, and to have this fact put on the official record. But the prosecution was prepared for him. The president of the court interrupted him before he could get the precious words out. The attorney for the Republic interrupted him. A stormy debate ensued, in which the old man could hardly get a word finished. In the end, the trial was declared secret.

It was defeat, and Demange knew it. But to him the court was hallowed ground. It was a moment at which he could have made a sensation by resigning and forcing the trial to suspend. Then he could have explained why he was resigning. But he would never use a trial as a rostrum to appeal to the public over the heads of the judges. He had no faith in mob passions and absolute faith in legal process for setting right such injustices as human frailty allowed to happen. So he submitted only a legal protest against the court's ruling.

Dreyfus, too, although no lawyer, sensed the significance of the defeat. The public prosecutor's ominous argument still rang in the suddenly hushed room: "There are other interests involved in this case than those of the defense or of the prosecution." There was the question of the embarrassment of great foreign powers. Dreyfus, of course, would have to yield to that. Did this mean that he would be acquitted behind sealed doors? But what comfort would that be, with his reputation ruined on the front pages? The blood rushed to Dreyfus' head. He flushed a deep red. His two brothers, Mathieu and Jacques, left grudgingly and anxiously. Only witnesses and experts, the chief of police and Major Picquart were permitted to remain. The court cleared the room of all others.

The early nervousness left Dreyfus when he began his testimony. He went over the various items listed in the *bordereau* as having been delivered in a matter-of-fact, almost discursive tone of voice. He explained why it was impossible for him to have been in possession of information about the 120 mm. gun and its supporting troops, or on the Madagascar expedition, and why he could not have written "I'm off to the maneuvers." But at the end his voice rose and then broke. Why should he have become a traitor, he who had renounced wealth and comfort for a life in the barracks, had risen through spartan denials to the highest schools and won the chance of a military lifetime, had open before him a brilliant career and was completely happy in his family life? It all burst out of him abruptly as in a fit and the unnatural intonation returned to his voice, the unpleasant nasality.

Another witness staged an outburst—Major du Paty de Clam. The bemonocled little man, flawlessly attired, arrogant in manner, related how Dreyfus had trembled when he had dictated to him a letter containing phrases from the *bordereau*. At which phrase had the witness begun to tremble? asked Demange. Would the marquis point it out? In a supreme example of his arrogance, the marquis decided the lawyer was mocking him. He refused to comply with the request, and sat down seething.

Then he popped up again without requesting permission of the court. He said he had discovered how Dreyfus might have been rewarded by the Germans for his treason. A part of the family factory in Mulhouse had burned down. It had been insured with a German company. Perhaps the payment had been in excess of the damage. Had it been in excess? Du Paty did not know, but it was an idea. The idea seemed farfetched and the marquis sat down seething again.

Except for his one outburst, Dreyfus continued to give precise answers in a precise tone. His memory never failed him, and he did not hesitate unduly over his answers. Such hesitation as there was seemed due to his anxiety to inform the court completely and concisely rather than to concern over what he might inadvertently reveal.

The taking of his testimony ended with the termination of the court's first session. Captain Dreyfus had made a very good impression. So Major Picquart reported to General Mercier. The official observer declared to the War Minister that it seemed quite likely the court would acquit.

This report made for a busy night in the War Ministry. The lights in high places burned late. General Mercier had previously ordered Du Paty to write a commentary on what the Second Bureau's investigation had turned up on Dreyfus. Du Paty had written a kind of criminal biography of the captain, beginning with his ambitions to get into the French Army, and seeing in his zeal and studious grinding throughout his career a German-inspired desire to learn far more about the Army in all its branches than he was required by his duties to know. He had deftly worked in the evidence developed in previously unsolved espionage cases—the "man of the Meuse forts" and his obliging mother, even though Dreyfus' mother had been dead more than four years at the time Schwarzkoppen's reference had made the Second Bureau aware of the existence, if not the identity, of this piquant and forever mysterious personality: the man with the initial "D" who had turned out not to be Dubois. He had included the theft of the formula for melanite from Bourges and, while mentioning the fact that Dreyfus had served at Bourges, had omitted mentioning that Dreyfus' tour of duty there had not begun until after the formula had come into the hands of the Germans.

There was other material, all from the Second Bureau's file. It seemed too windy and complicated to General Mercier. He conferred that night with Colonel Sandherr, then decided to write his own commentary on Dreyfus in two short pages.

Together General Mercier and Colonel Sandherr sifted through the Second Bureau's file, seeking documentary evidence to attach to the War Minister's commentary. When they were satisfied, they sealed it in an envelope, placed the sealed envelope in a larger envelope along with a note to the court, then sealed that envelope, too, and gave it to Du Paty to deliver to the court when the taking of testimony concluded and the judges were about to retire for their deliberations.

On the second day Dreyfus' fellow officers began testifying. Those must have been harrowing hours for Dreyfus. When he was in jail two kindhearted strangers—Major Forzinetti and the lawyer Demange—had showed pity for the awkward soul who was so incapable of expressing his pain in a free flow, and the awkward soul had expressed his pain, writing to Lucie: "My haughty reserve, the freedom of my word and judgment, my lack of leniency torment me now most. I was not born a supple or clever flatterer. We kept to ourselves and away from people. We stayed entrenched in our home, content to be alone in our happiness."

Now for the first time Dreyfus had brought home to him the extent of the animosity that had surrounded him without his ever having noticed it, much less done anything about it. Fellow officers swore that they had long been suspicious of him because of his eagerness to learn. Some of them dished up stories of petty jealousies concerning girls. Dreyfus had been unfair in competition for their favors, they complained, and had not scrupled to use his financial advantages. There were a few who stuck to the truth about Dreyfus, but they were very few. After all, who rushes forward to confess that a spy pulled the wool over his eyes and is still doing it?

But painful though it was, Dreyfus must have realized that the testimony was not hurting him, was in fact exposing the Government's case for what it was—a fusillade of popcorn. The handwriting experts stuck to their equivocal opinions. Bertillon entangled the court in a highly "scientific" explanation of why the dissimilarities between Dreyfus' handwriting and the handwriting on the *bordereau* proved that Dreyfus had been disguising his handwriting. No one could follow it, and after a while everyone gave up trying.

Then Major Henry, his mind as usual a vulgar muscle, stepped in to do his bit. One of the judges was an acquaintance of his. He suggested that the judge call him as a witness and ask him whether he had had any advance warning that Dreyfus was a spy.

The major was called and the question was answered in a thunderous, barracks-room voice. An unimpeachable gentleman had warned Major Henry as early as the previous March that there was a traitor in the Ministry of War. The same man had repeated his warning in June.

At this point the huge witness paused. Suddenly he turned to the accused, raised his arm and made as if to impale Dreyfus on a pointing finger. "And there is the traitor," he roared.

Dreyfus jumped indignantly to his feet. So did his counsel. They demanded that Henry name the person who gave the warning. Henry refused. They insisted that under Article 101 and under various other articles the accused had the right to be faced with his accuser. Finally Henry touched his uniform hat. "There are secrets in the head of an officer that are kept even from his képi," he said.

The presiding judge intervened. "You do not have to name the person," he told Henry. "It will suffice if you affirm on your honor that this person told you the traitor was Dreyfus." Major Henry lifted his hand to the crucifix and in a voice that shook the courtroom cried: "I swear."

Still, an accusation is not proof, not even in a court-martial, and the nameless and indeed nonexistent informer had provided Major Henry with no evidence to support his accusation. On the fourth day of the trial, December 22, the presentation of evidence concluded.

There was a stir and rustle as the judges prepared to retire to deliberate over their verdict. Attachés and aides jumped up. Men leaned to whisper in one another's ears. Major du Paty sauntered toward the judges. He slipped the presiding judge, Colonel Maurel, the envelope from General Mercier. It was done so casually that it seemed no more than a routine matter. Colonel Maurel opened the envelope and saw the smaller envelope in it, to which was attached a note. The War Minister's note requested Colonel Maurel to read the contents of the smaller envelope to the judges during their deliberations and then seal it again and return it to the officer messenger. Colonel Maurel took the envelope with him to the chamber to which the judges had adjourned and there read its contents to his associates.

The envelope General Mercier had prepared with the help of the chief of the Second Bureau, Colonel Sandherr, contained the following:

1. The biography of Dreyfus as compiled by Du Paty and revised by General Mercier. It stated flatly that, while at Bourges, Dreyfus had sold the secret of the melanite shell to the Germans and did not reveal the information in the possession of the Second Bureau that the Germans had obtained the formula before Dreyfus had arrived at Bourges.

It also declared that Dreyfus, while at the War College, had divulged the details of a confidential lecture on mobilization.

2. The "Alexandrine" letter from Schwarzkoppen to Panizzardi, referring to the detail maps of Nice and the "Scoundrel D———" who admitted he had been "stubborn" and was declared to be "silly."

3. The confused and confusing mélange of words on torn slips of paper stolen by Mme. Bastian from Schwarzkoppen's wastebasket at the end of December 1893—the words the Second Bureau had been unable to make head or tail of and whose only significance was that they referred to a "French officer."

4. A letter from Panizzardi to Schwarzkoppen in January 1894: "I have written to Davignon again, and thus if you have to take up this matter again with your friend, please do it privately so that Davignon knows nothing about it." [Lieutenant Colonel Davignon was the Second Bureau's official spokesman to foreign military attachés, giving them such information as was permissible. This letter was included in the envelope only for its reference to the unnamed "friend."]

5. The Panizzardi telegram to his Government inquiring about Dreyfus and suggesting an official denial of any relations with him. The original was not included, only Du Paty's "free translation" reading: "D. arrested. Precautions taken. Emissary warned."

6. A memorandum on the verbal observation of the former Spanish military attaché: "There is a wolf or two in your sheepfold."

With these documents was enclosed a terse note. It read:

1. The officer (or person) who handed over the Nice maps may have belonged to the Fortifications Section, since the maps were there.

2. The traitor's name begins with a D.

3. The person at the time was out of Von Schwarzkoppen's favor. He was trying to resume relations.

General inference: the above facts may be applied to Dreyfus. In that case Von Schwarzkoppen's contact in Davignon's office, the D. who betrayed the Nice maps, the writer of the *bordereau* and Captain Dreyfus can only be one and the same person.

Whatever the note's conclusion lacked in logic it made up for in authority. It was signed by General Mercier. It would not have taken a very clever lawyer to make hash of it, but no lawyer was present— only General Mercier's subordinates. After an hour they called court into session again to hear the final pleas.

Demange spoke for three hours. He concentrated on the *bordereau*. After all, it was all the Republic had produced in evidence. The prosecutor's speech was very brief. He suggested that the judges take a magnifying glass and examine the *bordereau* themselves. Then Dreyfus rose. "I am innocent," he said simply.

The court withdrew and Dreyfus was led out. The accused was not allowed to be present at the reading of the verdict. The doors were thrown open to the public. A handful entered and seated themselves. When order was restored, the judges returned to the courtroom.

Colonel Maurel read the verdict. It was unanimous. Dreyfus was found guilty of treason and condemned to dishonorable discharge from the Army, to deportation from France and exile for life in a fortified place.

In the courtroom the only broken heart was Demange's. The old man wept aloud.

8

IT WAS LATE in the day when Dreyfus himself was informed. He was led out of his cell and brought under guard to the deserted courtroom. The guard presented arms. A candelabrum had been lighted. The clerk of the court read out the sentence by its light.

Dreyfus stood at attention. He listened stiffly, made a smart about-face and returned to his cell. But when he was alone, he decided to kill himself. He ran against the wall head first to shatter his skull. Forzinetti was sent for. The prison director came running. He persuaded Dreyfus that suicide would only confirm his guilt in the eyes of the world and leave an ineradicable stain on his family. Later Lucie visited him. She spoke hopefully of the future.

In the meantime, the presiding judge had returned to Major du Paty the fatal envelope and its contents. The marquis dispatched it to General Mercier. The general ordered his commentary destroyed and told Colonel Sandherr to disperse the documents in the files in the original folders from which they had been taken. It was no longer to be a Dreyfus file. The original headings under which the documents had been filed were to be maintained.

It was plain to Colonel Sandherr what the general was up to. The general was wiping out all trace of the part he himself had played in the violation of the penal code. War ministers come and war ministers go, but staff officers remain—or hope to, and may if they are shrewd. Colonel Sandherr conferred with Major Henry. They decided to be shrewd. They were not going to stick their necks out for a mere War Minister. A secret file was made up. General Mercier's commentary was not destroyed. It went into the secret file. Along with it went the original of Du Paty's biography of Dreyfus plus the intercept of the telegram the Italian military attaché had sent his government. But Du Paty's mistranslation was not included. Instead, they attached an accurate one. The whole was sealed, marked "Secret File" by Major Henry and locked up in a safe. The net effect was to play down the Second Bureau's part in the violation of the law and preserve the evidence of the part played by General Mercier and the Marquis du Paty.

Even after the court's verdict had been announced, General Mercier still yearned for proof that it was a just one. He sent for Major du Paty and commissioned him to see Dreyfus privately in his cell and make the following proposition to him: There were many ways in which his life in exile could be made supportable. The place chosen need not be a blistering rock in a desolate sea. It could be a garden spot. His family might be permitted to join him. There could be other privileges. Dreyfus had only to confess. He need not admit deliberate treason. It would suffice if he pleaded a moment of mental aberration, perhaps only criminal carelessness.

Du Paty made the offer of privileges and Dreyfus replied to them instantly in a letter to General Mercier. The only privilege he wanted was that the search for the traitor be continued and pressed to a successful conclusion.

General Mercier introduced into the Chamber of Deputies a bill removing treason from the list of political crimes and making it a crime against the people punishable by death.

It was in character that the day Dreyfus dreaded above all others in the grim years that lay ahead was the day on which he would be publicly drummed out of the Army. On January 4 he wrote Lucie: "Tomorrow I am going to suffer the supreme ordeal for your sake and for the sake of our children." And on that morrow, January 5, great crowds began pressing toward the Champ de Mars, where the punishment would be carried out on the parade grounds of the Ecole Militaire.

The crowd was a mob. It was in a lynching mood. "Death to the Jew" was heard from all sides. But a heavy military cordon kept them at bay. A double line of guards had been thrown around the outside of the iron railing which fenced in the quadrangle where the proceedings —formal as an execution—were to take place. They confined the mob to looking on over their shoulders.

Each regiment of the Paris garrison had sent a unit to represent it. A trumpet sounded, commands were barked and a small door was thrown open. From it stepped a giant sergeant of the Republican Guard. He led four soldiers with drawn swords in whose midst walked Captain Dreyfus. They marched up to General Darras, who sat waiting for them on horseback.

The vast crowd hemming in the quadrangle densely on all four sides was so silent that the heels of the little group of men could be heard thudding. They ground to a halt before General Darras. The general drew his sword. In a voice that sounded tiny in that huge, silent space he cried: "Alfred Dreyfus, you are unworthy of carrying arms. We herewith degrade you in the name of the people of France."

Dreyfus stirred. He had been standing at attention. Now he lifted up his head. "Soldiers!" he shouted. "An innocent is dishonored. Long live France!" His voice, too, sounded tiny in that huge silent space, but it carried to the crowd outside. A great rumbling roar came from them: Death to the Jew! It rocked the air.

The giant sergeant rushed at Dreyfus. He tore the epaulets from the captain's shoulders and then tore the red stripes, marking him as a General Staff officer, from the captain's trousers. Finally he took the captain's sword and broke it in two. He threw the pieces on the ground. With the epaulets and the red stripes it made a little pile of refuse.

Dreyfus was then marched past the soldiers ranked column after column in lines of parade dress. He walked with the unbending precision of a staff officer on inspection. The effect was ghastly. His uniform seemed suddenly naked. At regular intervals, he threw up his arms and with a face that was nearly maniacal in its effort to conceal its suffering cried: "I am innocent. Long live France!"

The soldiers remained silent. They were stiff in their ranks. "Death to the Jew!" roared the crowd, but the voices of rage had become fewer. The rigid man, his arms pulled up mechanically, his voice pulled out of him by despair as a manikin might be pulled by a string, was having an effect. At the conclusion of the devastating ceremony, Dreyfus halted and stared transfixed at the little pile of refuse that had once formed so securely the boundaries of his high place in the world. A sneer twisted the lips of Major Georges Picquart. The major's mission as an observer for the Ministry of War included observing the death. "Just like a Jew," he remarked. "Even now he is calculating how much money he lost when he went to the tailor."

But the crowd went home more quietly than it had come. "The performance of January 5," declared *L'Avenir Militaire,* "produced an effect diametrically contrary to the intentions of those who ordered it. Its grievous consequences will soon manifest themselves with no possibility of a remedy for them." Said the conservative *L'Echo de Paris*: "Lynching would have been more to the purpose than the dismal and futile performance we owe to General Darras. . . . Dreyfus succeeded in instilling doubts in some wavering souls. He had his vengeance!"

But the royalist Léon Daudet, son of the world-famous author Alphonse, wrote: "Suffering means nothing to this wretch [Dreyfus]. We were more tormented by it than he was." The Catholic *La Croix* said: "His cry of 'Long live France!' was the kiss of Judas Iscariot." And *La Libre Parole*: "It was not an individual who was degraded here for an individual crime. The shame of an entire race was bared in its nakedness."

But the fog of pity, the sense of the futility that is inseparable from all human judgments seemed to linger. For the press suddenly discovered that the secrecy in which the trial had been held was a mistake. They blamed the quick dissipation of the crowd's blood-hunger on that. It was a German plot, declared both *La Libre Parole* and *L'Intransigeant*. "Mercier wanted the death sentence imposed, but the German Ambassador pointed to the Military Code which provides deportation for life as the maximum penalty for high treason. When he insisted on it, he ostentatiously held his passport in his hand."

Suddenly a rumor swept Paris. Dreyfus had confessed. A captain of the Republican Guard that had stood watch over Dreyfus prior to the ceremony of degradation originated it. It reached the General Staff with lightning speed. Mercier knew better, but the Chief of Staff, General de Boisdeffre, didn't. Mercier had kept to himself the letter in which Dreyfus had rejected all inducements. He did not want it generally known that he felt the need for a confession to buttress the judgment of the court. However, Boisdeffre issued orders to trace the rumor to its source and have its author brought to him. The guard captain was found and brought into the presence of the Chief of Staff, the President of the Republic and the Minister of War. He must have been frightened out of his wits by the presence of so much brass. They would not have taken time out from their crowded schedules had not they hoped passionately for an end to their own doubts about the justice of the verdict. But the captain offered them no solace. He had to admit he had drunk too many drinks and had only been bragging.

The rumor that Dreyfus had confessed was circulated so widely that an official denial had to be issued. But the official denial was not believed. What was believed was that the denial had been issued to placate the Germans, and again Count Münster's embassy came under press fire.

This time the fire was so hot that the Kaiser took note of it personally. He ordered the German Chancellor to instruct Count Münster to see the President of the Republic and tell him that His Imperial Majesty expected the French Government to confirm publicly the fact, should such a fact be ascertained, that the German Embassy was not implicated in the Dreyfus case. Unless this was done, the inventions concocted and circulated by the press must inevitably compromise the position of His Imperial Highness' representative in Paris.

When Count Münster made this demand of Casimir-Périer, the President decided for the first time to become frank. He told the German Ambassador of the existence of the *bordereau*. Count Münster was startled. Of course, Périer assured him, the embassy could not be held responsible for communications directed to it. Count Münster was even more startled when he returned to his embassy. Von Schwarzkoppen had no knowledge of any *bordereau*. This was indeed true. The *bordereau* had been stolen before the military attaché had seen it. But there was no doubting the President's assurance that the *bordereau* existed.

Count Münster regarded the subject as having been exhausted. The French press began to feel the same. Demange continued to be convinced of Dreyfus' innocence and did not hesitate to express himself in private conversations. Warned *Le Petit Journal*: Demange should be content with the handsome fee he has pocketed and let that be his justification for having volunteered to defend a traitor. To continue to defend him after sentence has been passed would be little short of making him an accessory after the fact. . . .

It was a last tired grumble before the long stillness that was to descend.

In the meantime, Dreyfus had been writing, too. To his beloved sister Henriette and her husband in Carpentras:

MY DEAR FRIENDS,

I am shattered by grief. To be innocent and overwhelmed by misfortune is perhaps too much for me to bear. If my force and courage abandon me . . .

Love my wife, please. She deserves it. She has been worthy of admiration in her courage and heroism. Make her your friend. I am, my dear Henriette, always the one you knew—good, brave and honest. But fate prevailed over me, pursues me; there are moral blows that are difficult to take, such pains break a man's resistance. You know that I am courageous in the face of physical suffering, but to see my name branded as a traitor—this is too much for me. No matter what happens, should I live or die, do not stop searching, restore to me my name of honest man. I hope that sooner or later you will find the guilty one. I embrace you as I love you.

That was written immediately after the verdict, while Dreyfus was still torn with the desire to commit suicide. On January 10, 1895, five days after the formal funeral staged for his sword and insignia of rank, he wrote Lucie:

Who is the monster who came to drop misfortune and dishonor into an honest family? . . . But my courage does not weaken. I strengthen myself by thinking of the future. It is impossible that the truth should not come to light. It must. The will is a powerful lever. You know that I have always been proud and worthy, that I have put duty before everything else. . . . You can thus imagine how much I suffer. And this is why I want to live, I want to shout to the world my innocence, to shout it every day, to my last breath, to the last drop of my blood. . . .

He had his opportunity soon thereafter. He was kept at the Cherche-Midi prison until the courts had sentenced enough deportees to make up a trainload. Then he was taken to the freight yards at night, put on board and rushed to La Rochelle, where he was to be ferried to the Ile de Ré to await the prison ship to Devil's Island. The train arrived at La Rochelle in the early morning, and what happened there is best described in Dreyfus' own words: "Our departure from Paris had not been disclosed and if, on arriving, the authorities had embarked me at once for the Ile de Ré, I should have passed unrecognized."

There were the usual station loafers, in greater number at La Rochelle perhaps than at other railway stations because of the piquant entertainment provided by the spectacle of convicts arriving. Wrote Dreyfus:

My guards thought it best to wait until the onlookers had gone. But every few moments the chief guard was called away from the cars by the deputy of the Minister of the Interior. On his return he would give mysterious orders to the other guards who would go out, each in his turn, and then come bustling back to close now one grating, now another, and keep up a constant whispering. It was clear that this singular maneuvering would end by attracting the attention of the curious who would understand that there must be an important prisoner in the car, and, as he had not been taken out, they would wait to see him.

Then all at once the guards and deputy lost their heads. It seemed that someone had been indiscreet and pronounced my name. The news spread abroad, and the crowd rapidly increased. I had to remain in the car all afternoon cramped in the same cell, listening to the crowd outside which became more turbulent as time went on.

Finally at nightfall, I was taken from the car. As soon as I appeared, the clamor redoubled. The throng made a sudden and angry rush at me and blows fell on and around me. I stood impassive in the midst of this mob for a moment, almost undefended. I was ready to deliver up my body to it. But my soul was my own, and I understood only too well the outraged feelings of this poor, misguided people. I cried out to them the pitiful error they were making. I motioned away the guards who came to my assistance, but they replied that they were responsible for me. . . . I longed to escape from the guards, to present my naked breast to those for whom I was a natural object and say: Don't insult me. The heart you cannot penetrate is pure and free from all defilement. But, if you believe me guilty, here, take my body. I give it to you without regret.

This is what he wrote later in his memoirs. But it was no fancy recollected in tranquillity. He was a soldier to the core. The people's trust in their Army was a sacred charge to him. He understood it and sympathized with it. "I was transported as the vile scoundrel whom I represent deserves to be," he wrote Lucie at the time. "As long as I represent such a miserable creature I cannot but approve."

The crowd was beaten back and he was got safely to the Ile de Ré, an hour's ferry ride from La Rochelle. That was on January 12. His wife and relatives were allowed to visit him, but iron bars were kept between them. Not even Lucie was allowed to reach through the bars to touch him. Even so, he was stripped of all clothing after each visit and searched thoroughly.

On the night of February 21, 1895, without warning, while he was awaiting another visit from his wife, he was whisked to the *St. Nazaire* for the long voyage to the tropical waters of the Guiana coast and debarkation on Devil's Island. He was chained to the seat of his cell. Preparations were made to defend the ship in the event of attack on the high seas.

Did they think Jews had a navy of their own? History is silent on this point. It records only that Dreyfus' jailers took no chances.

9

"I HAVE a soldier's courage, but not a martyr's soul," Alfred wrote to Lucie.

"At last I have received your dear letters. . . . It is such a sweet sensation to see your beloved handwriting again," Lucie wrote to Alfred. She goes on:

I was proud to be your wife. . . . When I feel too lonely to bear it any longer, when our separation becomes unbearably cruel, I call up memories especially dear to me. I remember those few years in which you made me the happiest of women, and I remind myself that if no one has suffered as we have yet few have known such perfect, serene joy as was our lot until this terrible misfortune assailed us. It depends on us whether that life will once more be renewed, and the only way to ensure it is to shed light upon this whole dreadful mystery. . . . My confidence is absolute. My faith is complete.

Her faith came from her knowledge of Alfred, her confidence from a few words dropped here and there. "Have patience," Demange kept telling Mme. Dreyfus and Alfred's brother Mathieu. "Perhaps a year or two from now when the wave of anti-Semitism subsides——" Occasionally somebody would come rushing to tell Lucie or Mathieu that yet another person doubted Dreyfus' guilt. They went to see each doubter. They kept a record of each casually uttered word.

She asked to be allowed to join her husband in exile. It was a favor the law accorded to wives of deportees. The request was rejected in her case. Her written pleas to Du Paty and to the Minister of War went unanswered. Patience. Patience. It was the only word of consolation given her.

"I no longer have the slightest doubt but that we shall succeed [in exposing the real traitor]," wrote Lucie to Alfred.

Later, Dreyfus wrote his own description of his place of incarceration on Devil's Island:

The Iles de Salut form a group made up of three islands: the Ile Royale, where the commander-in-chief of the prisons has his headquarters and dwellings, the Ile Saint-Joseph and Devil's Island.

. . . The hut designated for my use was built of stone and covered about seventeen square yards. The windows were grated. The door was of latticework with simple iron bars. This door led to a little anteroom six feet square, at the other end of which was a solid wooden door. In this anteroom a guard was always on duty. He was relieved every two hours. The guard was not to lose sight of me day and night. Five men were detailed to this duty.

At night the outer door was locked inside and out, so that every two hours when the guard was changed there was an infernal clatter of keys and iron bars and grates.

It was an island that had been abandoned as a place of deportation because of its inhuman conditions. For a time after that lepers had been kept there in isolation. Yet even they had been taken off. The intense, unbroken heat desiccated the body, slowed down its metabolism, made it difficult to feed on the food that was being digested.

Dreyfus requested that work be assigned to him. The request was turned down. In France the name of Dreyfus was never mentioned in public. In the Chamber a deputy asked the Minister of the Interior whether he would not deem it appropriate in the interests of the security of the nation to concentrate the Jews in the center of the country. The intelligent Jews themselves would understand that France could not afford to tolerate security risks near the frontiers. On Devil's Island, Dreyfus was never allowed to sit facing the sea. It was feared he might signal there to someone or something in that blinding glitter.

No letter containing any allusion to his case was allowed to reach him. When he was taken for a walk on the shadeless strip of rock adjoining his hut, no one was allowed to talk to him. His guards were not permitted to answer his questions. He maintained his rigid bearing and his military composure. But violent neuralgias began to rack his head. When storms stirred up the sea and the waves thundered against the rock, he took advantage of the sound to give vent to shrieks of despair. He waited for storms because he did not want anyone to hear him.

No one heard. He and his case were entombed in silence.

Then Dreyfus had to cease mingling his shrieks with the tumult of the storms.

"On September 4, 1896," he writes, "my jailers received . . . orders to keep me, until further notice, confined to my hut throughout the twenty-four hours with the double *boucle* at night."

The double *boucle* was an ankle yoke similar to the "stock" used by the Puritan settlers to confine their delinquents in public view. But it was made of iron, and confined only Dreyfus' ankles as he lay on his cot at night. An iron bar was stretched across the foot of the bed. To it two iron bands were fastened and, when Dreyfus retired to sleep, his ankles were locked into the bands.

In addition, construction of a double wall was begun. Writes Dreyfus:

The hut was surrounded by a wall over eight feet high, and not quite five feet distant from it. The wall was much higher than the little grated window of the hut, which was hardly three and one-half feet above the ground. Outside the first wall, which was one of defense, a second one was built quite as high and it, like the first, hid everything from my sight.

Dreyfus had no idea why this was happening. All letters and packages to him from the outside world suddenly stopped. They were being withheld. Nor were his letters permitted to leave the islands in his handwriting. They were copied first in the prison office, and only the copy was sent.

For Mathieu had made a move. The silence that had fallen over his brother's case was its worst enemy, he knew. It could have only death in it. He resorted to a hoax to break it.

Through a friend he succeeded in getting published in the *South Wales Argus* in Newport, England, a fabricated report that Dreyfus had escaped from Devil's Island. A vessel, the *Non Pareil*, was invented and given a fictitious captain with the symbolic name of Hunter. The Welsh paper printed the news that the *Non Pareil* put in at Newport Harbor fresh from French Guiana and the hot word from

Captain Hunter was that the famous French traitor had got away from his jailers and was free.

The London *Daily Chronicle* reprinted the item and, as Mathieu had expected, the entire Paris press took it up. Even though Captain Hunter did not exist, *La Libre Parole* published an interview with him from its "special correspondent." The Minister of Colonies spent an immensely agitated hour awaiting an official report from Devil's Island. Dreyfus writes:

> Dating from September 6, I was put in the double boucle at night. . . . When my feet were inserted in the two bands, it was no longer possible for me to move about. I was fastened in an unchangeable position to my bed. The torture was hardly bearable during those tropical nights. Soon also the bands, which were very tight, lacerated my ankles.

This kept on for two months until the double walls around his hut were completed. Where there had been one man watching him day and night, there were now two. "My guards," records Dreyfus, "received orders to report every one of my gestures and even the changes of expression on my face."

One night he woke to the sound of shouts and shots and feet running. A rumor had come to the commander that a foreign warship had been seen in the vicinity of the islands. Everybody's finger was on the trigger. Orders had been given to shoot Dreyfus at the first move.

But he did not move. He lay apathetically—a man whose flesh only was alive in that stone tomb walled off from the world by a wall within a wall on a rock at the end of an enormous sea.

10

"MONSIEUR: I shall wait for a more detailed explanation of the question in hand than you gave me the other day. Please let me have it in writing so that I can judge whether or not to continue my relations with the house R. C——T."

It was a special-delivery post card of the kind sold by the French post office and called a *petit bleu* because of its blue color. It was addressed to Major Count Ferdinand Walsin-Esterhazy. It had been written by a woman friend of the German military attaché and, for some unknown reason, given to him to mail. Perhaps she had written it in his office at the embassy.

Von Schwarzkoppen had never succeeded in mailing it. Indeed, it may have been removed from the letter box itself. The French Intelligence Service naturally had no wish to make it easier for German counterspies to discover that it had more than one agent with access to the embassy. Thus the *petit bleu*, like the *bordereau*, was torn up into thirty-six separate pieces to make it seem to have come "in the regular way" from Schwarzkoppen's wastebasket. If the Germans should ever catch Mme. Bastian (which, incidentally, they never did) they would feel secure. The *petit bleu* was delivered to the Second Bureau as one of her little treasures.

This was in March 1896, fifteen months after the Dreyfus case had been officially and formally closed with a sentence by the court-martial. Changes had taken place in that time in both the Second Bureau and the high command. In a squabble over the granting of railway franchises, the President of the Republic had resigned. This called for a new Government. In the maneuvering among the political parties to form coalitions that could take power one name was omitted as if by common consent—that of General Mercier. The Dreyfus case had made him a controversial figure. General Jean Billot succeeded to the War Ministry.

Colonel Sandherr had been put out of action, too. He had suffered a paralytic stroke. Major Hubert Henry had confidently expected to succeed him as head of the Second Bureau, but he was passed over. Instead, Georges Picquart, now a lieutenant colonel, was given the post. A new efficiency came into the Second Bureau with him. Picquart was a cultivated man. He also had an alert mind.

When the *petit bleu* addressed to Esterhazy arrived at the Second Bureau it was brought to the desk of Captain Jules-Maximilien Lauth. The captain's social disdain for Henry had not lessened with time. He pasted together the thirty-six pieces and brought the *petit bleu* directly to the attention of Lieutenant Colonel Picquart. "What, another spy?" he asked.

The intelligence officers recognized the handwriting as not Schwarzkoppen's but his lady friend's, and there was nothing in the message itself to indicate any crime. But who was Esterhazy and what was he doing getting *petits bleus* via the German Embassy? Picquart ordered a look taken in that direction.

The reports on Esterhazy were provocative. Commander of an infantry battalion at Rouen. A brave officer, but a gambler. Squandered his wife's dowry. Involved in seedy business ventures. Chronically in debt. Picquart ordered an eye kept on him.

In June a French agent in Berlin, Richard Cuers, had told the military attaché there that a battalion commander in the French Army had been selling military information to the German General Staff. The news was late. Still it was news, and Picquart promptly reported it to General de Boisdeffre, the Chief of the General Staff. Picquart had a suspicion who this battalion commander might be.

Cuers was ordered to go to Switzerland, where he might be interviewed with less risk. Picquart originally intended to do the interviewing himself, but he was busy and Major Henry volunteered. The friendship between Henry and Esterhazy was not known to Picquart and he fully trusted the man whom he thought of as "this rough son of the people." So it was Henry who went to Switzerland to meet Cuers.

Later Cuers complained to the French military attaché in Berlin that he had been browbeaten and shouted at by Major Henry, and had been unable to make any headway against an attitude of persistently hostile doubt. Henry himself reported to Picquart that the interview had been disappointing. The agent had been unable to add anything of importance to his original report.

In the meantime Esterhazy had not abandoned his ambitions for an assignment to the General Staff. Perhaps Major Henry had neglected to warn him of what was going on. Or perhaps it was just simple brazenness on Esterhazy's part. At any rate, he chose this moment to make a written application for General Staff duty. The application came to Lieutenant Colonel Picquart's desk.

When he handed over his post Colonel Sandherr had shown Picquart the place in the safe where the "secret file" on Dreyfus was kept. It's best to let sleeping dogs lie, he had remarked. But General de Boisdeffre was a man of a different stamp. He had advised Picquart to get acquainted with the file. Dreyfus had been a brilliant officer. Boisdeffre remembered from the conversation they had had in Dreyfus' student days. The general thought it would be useful to Picquart in his intelligence work to solve the mystery of what motive a man so gifted could have had for committing treason.

Although Picquart had been present at the trial as an observer, he had never had an opportunity to inspect the evidence. That was a "state secret," and even the judges, it may be remembered, had looked at it alone behind closed doors. Now he looked at the file. He did not discover what reason Dreyfus could have had for throwing himself away, but he did see the *bordereau*.

Picquart had been surprised at the meagerness of the evidence against Dreyfus. Some qualms about it lingered on in him—enough to alert him when he received Esterhazy's application. There seemed something familiar about the handwriting. He went directly to the safe, got out the *bordereau* and compared its writing to that of Esterhazy's. Immediately, he summoned Bertillon to his office. To the credit of that number-obsessed man it can be reported that he did not quibble. He studied the *bordereau* again and then examined Esterhazy's application. "This is the man who wrote the *bordereau*," he said.

General de Boisdeffre was the next to learn. "Well," he said heavily, "we were wrong, weren't we?" But General Gonse, his deputy, was more familiar with the details of the case than he. Boisdeffre suggested that Picquart take up his next moves with Gonse.

Gonse was away on leave. Picquart waited. The news was not kept secret from the trusted officers of the Second Bureau. There was widespread resentment. Colonel Sandherr's legacy was sacrosanct. Who was this young upstart who presumed to think any action of the colonel's needed looking into? Picquart was not deterred. He let that dabbler in graphology, Major du Paty, compare a few lines of Esterhazy's handwriting with the *bordereau*. The marquis dropped his monocle, lifted the documents to his nose and squinted with his astigmatic eyes. "Of course it is the same writing!" he exclaimed. Major Henry was unable to suppress his excitement and anger. He was not alone. What was this Picquart trying to do to the memory of Colonel Sandherr?

When General Gonse returned from his leave, Picquart went to his office. Their conversation was testified to subsequently in court.

"You should have kept the two cases separated," the general told Picquart. "The Dreyfus case is closed."

Picquart reminded the general that the Dreyfus family did not think so. They were persisting in their efforts to reopen the case. There would be dire consequences for the Army should the case be reopened and it become known that the initiative had come from quarters other than the General Staff.

General Gonse lost his patience. "What do you care for this Jew anyhow?" he asked.

"He is innocent," Picquart replied quietly.

"And how do you propose to get a new trial started with General Mercier and General de Boisdeffre personally declaring that it is an adjudicated case?"

"General," Picquart said, "the man is innocent."

The lieutenant colonel could not understand why that should not be reason enough to reopen the case. But the general understood. "For me," he said, "truth is what the Minister of War and the Chief of the General Staff tell me is true." Then he added, "If you keep silent, no one need find out anything."

Picquart forgot the difference in rank. He forgot the power of a general of the Army. "General," he cried, "what you say is abominable. I do not know yet what I am going to do. But I will not carry this secret to my grave."

The general did not freeze. He did not bark. He signed an order commanding Picquart to investigate the Intelligence Service on the eastern border. But he did not issue it. He kept it in abeyance. In the meantime he continued to see no reason why Esterhazy should not be brought to justice if there was any evidence against him. But the *bordereau* was not evidence against Esterhazy. It was evidence against Dreyfus, and the Dreyfus case was closed.

But without the *bordereau,* the *petit bleu* proved nothing against Esterhazy. So Picquart waited—for Esterhazy's foot to slip, for something to happen that would change Gonse's mind. For it was very difficult to go over Gonse's head. It meant going over General de Boisdeffre's. Boisdeffre had told Picquart originally to take it up with Gonse, and Picquart had no reason to believe Boisdeffre would not back up his deputy. Going over Boisdeffre's head meant going out of the Army, into politics—a step for which he felt the utmost repugnance. The Army was Picquart's mother, father, wife and children.

The summer went by in waiting. Esterhazy's foot did not slip. But Mathieu's hoax on the press had not been futile. It had revived his brother's name among the people. It had caused talk to start again. On September 14, *L'Eclair,* a newspaper that was frequently a mouthpiece for the General Staff, published an article which had for its declared purpose to "stop once and for all rumors, conjectures and misstatements" about the Dreyfus case:

The Government cannot depart from the reserve that is dictated by diplomatic prudence. [But] we are convinced that the reasons for silence no longer exist, and that we can now publish, without fear that we are being indiscreet, the proof which could not at the time be offered to the public—the irrefutable proof of treason, the proof which produced the unanimous verdict of the officers of the court. . . . In September, the military attaché of the German embassy addressed a letter to his colleague of the Italian embassy. This letter was not placed in evidence. Instead, it was handed secretly to the judges of the court prior to their deliberations. Not even counsel for the defense had knowledge of this fact. The letter referred to espionage in Paris and contained this sentence: *"Decidedly, this beast of a Dreyfus has been demanding."* Thus the *bordereau* —which Dreyfus wrote but did not sign—was only corroboratory evidence in the case.

The article was reprinted by all newspapers. It confirmed the majority in their belief in Dreyfus' guilt. Others began to be puzzled. Intelligence officers never mentioned the most minor agent by name in any communication, even in conversation, unless it was unavoidable. What could be going on in the heads of military attachés that they would spell out in longhand the identity of so precious a source of information as an officer of the General Staff? It seemed incredible. It did not seem possible that this letter had been invented out of whole cloth, but something must have been forged somewhere, and forged very crudely.

Hardly anyone noticed the most significant admission in the article: the Army in presenting its case against Dreyfus had set itself above the law. But Demange noticed it. So did Mathieu. So did a handful of others.

Picquart was not among them. Article 101 was a mere legal technicality to him at that time. If the state felt that public disclosure of evidence would embarrass it with a foreign government, then, of course, the evidence must not be disclosed. But this did not mean that the guilty must go unpunished. The state was entitled to secrets, the guilty to punishment. The chances are that the crucial admission in the article seemed neither crucial nor an admission to him. But the article did give him an opportunity to take up the matter again with General Gonse.

For Lucie Dreyfus immediately filed a petition to the Chamber of Deputies asking it to ascertain whether it was true that "a French officer had been convicted on the basis of a document put before his judges without his knowledge and which he was given no opportunity to dispute." At the same time she appealed to the Pope for his aid in securing justice for her husband. The Pope made no reply. Neither did the Chamber of Deputies. But the press had run the facts and Picquart reminded Gonse of his earlier warning. The case, he argued, was far from over. The General Staff would be better off taking the initiative than leaving it to their enemies.

But Picquart had no more success than Lucie. A deputy named Castelin announced he would ask information about the Dreyfus case. The mouthpiece for the Premier, *La République Française*, hastened to write: "This traitor [Dreyfus] belongs among the safely dead who need not be disposed of a second time." However, Major Henry did not seem to think so. He was moved to an urgent piece of homework.

He had received "in the ordinary way" from Mme. Bastian a dinner invitation extended to Schwarzkoppen by his Italian colleague. It was a conventional invitation that would ordinarily have been thrown away once studied, but Henry put it to extraordinary use. He called into action a confederate of his, a man of many aliases, the latest being Lemercier-Picard. This man obtained a blank piece of paper identical except for the color of the lines with that on which the invitation to dinner had been sent. This was torn up and crumpled as the invitation had been. On it Lemercier-Picard copied, in a handwriting forged skillfully to imitate Panizzardi's, a letter dictated by Henry. Henry had combined ideas of his own with words extracted from the original invitation and had pasted them all up together to compose the following:

Dear friend, I read that a deputy will question the Minister on Dreyfus. If asked by Rome for new explanations, I will, of course, say that I have never had any dealings with that Jew. If asked, say the same. No one should ever find out who was associated with him.

The letter was pasted up under authentic Italian Embassy stationery and to it was appended Panizzardi's authentic signature. Henry then put it away for use when needed.

In the meantime, he was working to undermine his chief, Lieutenant Colonel Picquart. It has never been revealed what the source was for *L'Eclair*'s article. Many officers on the General Staff were ignorant enough to have inspired it. It is not uncommon for a professional officer to feel that the Army is and should be above the law. But Henry was not only ignorant. He was a liar and a forger for his own ends, and while he was cunning he was far from clever. So he was not above suspicion as the source of that fateful article and its devastating admission. However, he planted the rumor that it was Picquart himself who had done it. It was his first step in an unrelenting effort to destroy his chief, for Picquart had become dangerous to him ever since catching on to Esterhazy.

The next step came after General Gonse decided to use the orders he had been holding in reserve for Picquart. On November 16, Picquart left Paris on a tour of inspection of the eastern frontier. If Picquart suspected the reason, the general's friendly letters to him should have set his mind at rest. However, no sooner was his mission accomplished than he received orders to repair, without returning to Paris, to the Italian frontier and inspect the Intelligence Service there. From the Italian frontier he was sent urgently to Algiers, from Algiers to Tunisia—each time with letters of praise and appreciation for work well done from General Gonse.

In Picquart's absence, Major Henry became acting chief and ran the Second Bureau with his huge fist. Picquart's mail, addressed to the bureau, came to Henry's desk for forwarding. Henry began steaming it open. A file on Picquart was started. Into it went whatever compromising material could be found, and if nothing could be found it was invented. Du Paty dabbled in this game, too. One day there arrived a note for Picquart: "Each day the demi-god asks for you." It was signed, romantically, "Speranza"—the pen name of Jane Francisca Elgee, who, in addition to being Oscar Wilde's mother, had her own fame as the author of graceful verse. Of course, it was not Oscar Wilde's mother writing to Picquart, but Mlle. Comminges—as Du Paty knew very well. He frequented the salon of the Comminges family and knew, too, that "demi-god" was the customary demi-mocking way of referring to an Army captain who also frequented it. It was a simple, friendly, somewhat coquettish note to make a man aware that his absence was being noted, but under the ministrations of Du Paty and Major Henry it became quite sinister:

"Your brisk departure put us in confusion," it now read. "The work is compromised. Speak up, and the demi-god will act." Signed: "Speranza."

This letter was duly dictated by Major du Paty, addressed to Lieutenant Colonel Picquart by Major Henry, mailed by Henry, intercepted by Henry and then placed by Henry in the chief's file.

Picquart noticed the irregularity with which his mail was following him on his travels. He had an uncomfortable feeling that it was being tampered with. In January 1897 he received a letter that made him realize he had been practically exiled. It was from a friend who wrote that, whenever he inquired, the Second Bureau replied that Picquart was expected back momentarily. How long is a moment? the friend wanted to know. Picquart wrote an indignant letter to Major Henry. He wanted to resign from the General Staff.

Henry wrote an equally indignant reply—remarkable from a subordinate to his superior. He accused Picquart of a mishmash of incompetencies and wrongdoings: of having opened letters to Major Esterhazy without authorization; of attempting to persuade Captain Lauth and Félix Gribelin that the *petit bleu* which had been written to Esterhazy by Schwarzkoppen's lady friend had been written by the German military attaché himself; of having opened a plainly marked "Secret File" as a result of which indiscretions were committed from motives that had no connection with the good of the service.

Picquart must have fumed and foamed when he received this insolent letter with its outrageous inaccuracies and misinterpretations. But he was under orders from General Gonse and had to remain in Africa.

Then an intimation of mortality struck Picquart. It is difficult for a young man, unless he is in an Army at war, to believe that the day will come when he actually will be dead. But it happened to Picquart. He fell from his horse. He jumped up uninjured, but it had been a close call and he remembered that he had told General Gonse that he would not carry the secret to his grave.

He sat down and wrote a letter, dated April 2, 1897. It began: "The undersigned, Picquart, Marie-Georges, Lt. Col., formerly Chief of the Intelligence Service of the Ministry of War, certifies on his honor to the truth of the following facts. Their suppression, which was attempted, shall be impossible."

The letter went on to tell the story of how Picquart had discovered the real author of the *bordereau*. It concluded:

1. Walsin-Esterhazy is a German agent.
2. Acts charged to Dreyfus were committed by Esterhazy.
3. The Dreyfus case was treated with unheard-of lightness, with a preconceived conviction of Dreyfus' guilt, and in disregard of the law.

Picquart wrote the letter in private and addressed it to the President of the Republic, but he did not mail it. However, two months later he was able finally to obtain leave, and he returned to Paris. There he called on an old friend, a lawyer named Louis Leblois who was a refugee from the annexed area of Alsace-Lorraine. Under the seal of the lawyer-client relationship, Picquart told Leblois his story. He then deposited in Leblois' keeping the letter to be sent to the President in the event of Picquart's death.

Leblois was profoundly disturbed by Picquart's revelations. He did not think Picquart should let it go at that. In the end Picquart gave Leblois permission to impart the secret to reliable friends of the lawyer who were in a position to put it to good use. However, Leblois was not to do this unless he could keep from divulging Picquart's name until Picquart himself consented.

The lawyer felt this could be managed. He made an appointment with the senator from Alsace, the last such to survive, Auguste Scheurer-Kestner. Scheurer, a prominent industrialist with an irreproachable family background, was Vice-President of the Senate and held a position high in public esteem. The news did not catch him entirely unprepared. Being an Alsatian, he had known and respected the Dreyfus family. Mathieu, who had given up all business to devote himself to clearing Alfred's name, had persuaded Scheurer that anti-Semitism rather than evidence had convicted Dreyfus.

But he felt he could not act merely on the basis of an unsupported statement from an unnamed man. And Leblois could not get permission to name Picquart or to present the letter to the President of the Republic.

Part Two

HEROES AND HOOLIGANS

11

In 1789, when the French Revolution began, Frenchmen marched across the old provincial boundaries to meet other Frenchmen and to take this oath:

We . . . fraternally assembled for the public welfare, swear before high Heaven, on our hearts and on our weapons, devoted to the defense of the state, that we will remain forever united. Abjuring every distinction of our several provinces, offering our arms and our wealth to the common country, supporting the laws which come from the National Assembly, we swear to give all possible help to each other to fulfill these sacred duties, and to fly to the help of our brothers of Paris or of any town in France which may be in danger in the cause of liberty.

On the first anniversary of the Revolution, July 14, 1790, Paris itself echoed the oath for the entire country. Before the Altar of the Nation, on the Champ de Mars, some 50,000 delegates from all the provinces took the oath of national brotherhood. Two hundred priests celebrated Mass to the music of 1,200 musicians.

The oath symbolized the integration of the provinces and regions of France, divided by traditions, customs, laws and languages, into one nation, and its first Constitution was published within a year. In a preamble, an "eternal rule" was laid down in this document to cover all future changes in the Constitution. The "eternal rule" was the Declaration of the Man and of the Citizen, and it ran: "The Law is the expression of the general will; it must be the same for all, in protecting men as in punishing them."

This marked an end to arbitrary prerogative, cloaked before this as the divine right of the King, in the government of France. Before the same Altar of the Nation, on the same Champ de Mars, and in the presence of an ecstatic multitude, the Declaration of the Man and of the Citizen was proclaimed.

It erected a bastion against religious persecution and racial prejudice which nothing could shake for more than a century.

Yet now the way in which Dreyfus had been convicted clearly restored a rule of arbitrary prerogative, cloaked this time as reasons of state. And the open admission in a newspaper that this had been done stirred so little apprehension that the Government had not even been called upon to confirm or deny it.

Many of the forces that impelled France to try to reverse its destiny, or to escape from it, had been working deep in French minds since the military catastrophe at Sedan in 1870. A formidable new power, Prussian Germany, had inflicted defeat on Napoleon III in a lightning war. The Emperor capitulated after the battle at Sedan, fell prisoner, and his Second Empire collapsed. But France still refused to surrender. The people of Paris marched to the City Hall to proclaim the Third Republic and their resolution to go on fighting. Léon Gambetta, son of an immigrant from Genoa who had become a grocer in southern France, a man of boundless energy with a mighty head of unruly black hair and a beard, took off in a balloon and flew out of the besieging ring of the enemy to Tours. There, acting as a one-man government, he organized three armies, appointed able generals, raised a loan from the House of Morgan in New York and threw a new France against the Germans. But the main Army of 170,000 soldiers at Metz was commanded by Marshal Bazaine, who regarded republicans as greater enemies than Germans, and he surrendered without firing a shot.

Paris still believed in the invincibility of a free republic, but the country dreaded the invasion of foreign armies. A bloody civil war flared up between the Paris Commune, which refused to give up, and the country, which yearned for peace and order. In the end a provisional government signed an armistice on Bismarck's terms. This quick war was more than a lost battle. It was the symbol of a fateful shift in the balance of power in Europe which threatened to reduce France, the greatest power in Europe for centuries, to insignificance.

Only with a powerful Army could France look forward to a reprieve from this threat. Torn between the dread of ultimate destruction and the longing for revenge, the public voted for parties of peace and order, royalists and Catholics. But they listened in fascination to the magic oratory of Gambetta, who relighted a vision of greatness for the nation. On the platform Gambetta spoke with a force which seemed to move not only his listeners but the very landscape. *Revanche* was the emotion he managed to awaken without using the word. He urged the sons of peasants and craftsmen to invest their future in the Republic, to become officers in the Army, officials in the civil service and, above all, teachers to carry the spirit of republicanism back to every village and hamlet in the land. This was the way, he said, to make France strong again.

To the Army, all this smacked of recruiting an Army of insurrection. To the royalists and Catholics it boded a return to the egalitarianism of the Great Revolution and another step toward anarchy.

In 1881, the elections returned the parties of the Republic to the majority. The cult of the Great Revolution became strong again in public life. Once more an optimistic faith in science emerged. It promised to counter superstition and prejudice and to ensure well-being for all; Frenchmen began again to talk of that faith in reason which had informed their forefathers. The Chamber passed laws to democratize the Army. Yet at the same time in the schools a veritable army of monks and nuns, still using the old textbooks, was propounding the duty of every Christian to obey the King and to help restore the temporal power of the Pope. The republican parties struggled to free education from the influence of the Church. Primary education was made free, general and non-denominational. Catholic universities were deprived of the right to confer degrees; unauthorized religious orders were dissolved.

However, the Right had little reason for alarm. The representatives of the upper middle classes, headed by the President of the Republic, Jules Grévy, were determined to prove that the Republic, now safe from clericalism, could be made as conservative as any monarchy. Thus they became allies of the royalists and Catholics against the Radicals, who were insisting that the Republic must complete the interrupted work of the Great Revolution against its old enemies. Gambetta was the acknowledged leader of the nation, but except for a few months as Premier, Grévy succeeded in keeping him out of the Government. In Grévy's view, Gambetta was an extremist and a warmonger. Grévy, himself a rich industrialist, had made clear to the distressed

Scheurer-Kestner, the last senator from Alsace, that the upper middle class wished for peace and prosperity after the defeat of 1870.

"Do not believe," he said, "those fools who say that we should never renounce Alsace. It is their fault that our misfortunes have been made worse by a hopeless struggle." The so-called Moderate Republicans stood firmly by this position. Whether the French or the Germans would administer the lost provinces was to them secondary to the issue of fruitful economic relations with Germany. "These opportunists do not want war," Bismarck remarked with contempt. "They are nothing but Jewified businessmen." The nightmare which had haunted him ever since Alsace-Lorraine had become part of the German Reich began to recede.

The newly established parliamentary system did not accurately reflect the spirit of the French people. A mood of business-minded conservatism had invaded the parties of the Republic. Yet in the popular mind concern for the future role of France in the world was still paramount. If there were troubles in finance and banking or in the country's colonial involvements, the people reacted to them in terms of their meaning to the national life and security which were threatened by the German colossus. It seemed doubtful whether the Republic and Parliament could stand the strain. The Boulanger case was to bring matters to a head.

Gambetta did not long survive his short premiership. He died early in 1883, only forty-four years old. Trying out a new type of army revolver, he fired it accidentally and blistered the palm of his hand. The burn became infected. The doctors were so preoccupied with treating the hand that they neglected to notice his appendix until it had perforated. The whole nation took part in the funeral. But the stubborn and resentful grocer who was Gambetta's father refused to give up his son's body. He insisted that it be interred in the family crypt at Nice. Later he relented enough to give permission for his son's heart to be removed and placed in the Panthéon.

When Gambetta died, a very different man took his place as leader of the republicans. He was not a son of the poor, but the scion of country squires from the Vendée. It was this province that had taken up arms against the Great Revolution when it had moved against the Church. But Georges Clemenceau, like his father Benjamin, was an atheist. Benjamin Clemenceau was a physician who was arrested by Louis Bonaparte in the course of a general purge of his potential enemies when Georges was only sixteen. Benjamin was taken to jail in chains, but he was spared deportation on the intervention of his fellow townsmen. The Clemenceau family was an old and respected one, and Benjamin had spent his life giving his services as a doctor free to all who asked for them.

Georges, too, started adult life as a doctor. But politics attracted him early and the sight of his revered father in chains had filled him with a passion that determined his life. It was a cold passion. It made him a member of the Radicals—a party proud of the heritage of the Great Revolution. He was contemptuous of human weakness and was one of those who did not love men but loved mankind. He disdained any quality that made for popular appeal. If ever he felt emotion, he declined to show it in public. He strove to gain power by logic and by force. A breaker of governments, he made no effort to head one. Short, powerfully built, meticulously dressed, he cut a strange figure with his round, bare Mongolian skull, his sleek-skinned face, slanted coal-black eyes and drooping mustache. He was a poor speaker by deliberation. He regarded oratory as a national vice. His speeches carried weight by their logic. They bristled with short sentences that rattled like a machine gun. In those turbulent days when every castigation was answered by a challenge to a duel, he was feared as much for his marksmanship with the pistol and his skill with the sword as for the sarcastic words with which he attacked his opponents.

Clemenceau accepted the Great Revolution as a whole, including the dread Terror which had earned it such a bad name among the comfortable and well situated of the world. He stood for the Revolution's fulfillment. But he rejected socialism and the factory laws put forth by the extreme left. At a time when elsewhere in Western Europe governments were yielding to clamor for the eight-hour day and other social legislation, he appeared at an election meeting in a working-class district. France had an eleven-hour day and child labor went on almost unrestricted. His hat pushed back on his round head, cigar in mouth, he told his audience of workers that he refused to share a concept that would make "a monastery" of society.

Clemenceau had been personally responsible for the cometlike career of Georges Ernest Jean Marie Boulanger, that handsome, fair-haired and bearded republican general with a martial mustache under his protruding nose, a strong chin and dreamy blue eyes.

In his youth he had attended the same secondary school as Clemenceau at Nantes, and the Tiger (as Clemenceau was to be known later) remembered him from those days.

Boulanger's father had failed in the insurance business and left to his son nothing but debts. But he succeeded in turning to an asset his humble origin and his mother's good looks. She was a girl from Aberdeen, Scotland. And the Republic had a flair for the sons of the people.

In the Army, Boulanger had been decorated and promoted in the Crimea, in Africa, in Indo-China and in the war against Prussia. Nor had his awards and promotions been merely political. He had suffered wounds in combat. But his great fame came in 1881.

Boulanger was a colonel then and had been chosen to represent France at the celebration of the centenary of Cornwallis' surrender at Yorktown. Gambetta had frowned at the selection. The great tribune had lost the sight of one eye in an accident suffered when a child. The young colonel had two eyes, he remarked, but never looked anyone in the face, while he managed to do so with only one eye. Finally Gambetta consented and Boulanger set sail for America aboard the *S.S. Canada.*

A salute of twenty-one guns was fired when he landed, and he was escorted ashore complete with scarlet trousers, gilt braid, epaulets and blond beard. On October 15, Secretary of State James G. Blaine led the party of dignitaries aboard the *City of Catskill* for the steam down to Yorktown. Boulanger noticed that the German flag was being flown alongside the American and French. He refused to go aboard until it was hauled down. A heavy fog kept the *City of Catskill* offshore at Yorktown. When the fog lifted, Boulanger noticed that in honor of Steuben and other German heroes of the American Revolution and as a concession to the millions of German-Americans, the American warships present were also flying the German flag alongside the French and their own. Boulanger refused to leave the *City of Catskill.*

Blaine tried all his eloquence while German officers in full dress stood about furiously. But the young colonel remained obdurate. Finally a compromise was reached. At sunset all flags were hauled down and the next morning only the American flag was raised. Whatever effect it had elsewhere, it made Boulanger the hero of all France.

Boulanger's every action was taken with one eye on public acclaim. At the time he became military commander, Tunisia was a new French protectorate and had a very large, influential Italian population. One night in an ovation at the conclusion of her performance, an Italian actress was presented with two bouquets—one from an Italian clerk, the other from a French officer. On the open stage in full view of the audience, the actress thrust away the French officer's bouquet and embraced the Italian's.

A brawl followed. It ended in court, and the judge angered the French garrison by his clemency toward the clerk. Boulanger promptly issued an order authorizing military personnel in Tunisia to defend themselves against insults with the sword.

The French High Commissioner, then busily engaged in the delicate business of wooing the resident Italians to support the new protectorate, lodged a protest against the order with the Government in Paris. Boulanger was ordered to defer to the High Commissioner. He immediately resigned from the post of Military Commander and, without awaiting orders, left with his family for Paris. They settled in the Hôtel du Louvre, where they soon received an important visitor —Clemenceau.

The Moderates and the Radicals had got together at last to form a government headed by an all-republican Cabinet. Clemenceau wanted the Ministry of War to go to his Radicals. He scanned the political horizon for a suitable republican general. After a brief interview, he settled on Boulanger—then only forty-eight, immensely popular and a republican. *La France Militaire* commented: "For fifteen years we have waited for a man of his cut who would reconquer for our beloved France her rightful place among the great powers."

In addition to Clemenceau, Boulanger acquired yet another powerful supporter—Henri de Rochefort. Of aristocratic descent, Rochefort had been the idol of revolutionary circles in Paris for thirty years. He was a pamphleteer of mordant wit and his ridicule had done more than the entire opposition combined to discredit Napoleon III and his Second Empire. For a time he had to flee the country. His weekly *Lanterne* was smuggled in from Belgium. When he returned to France he expressed his contempt for the bourgeoisie and his ardor for *revanche* on Germany in his daily *L'Intransigeant*, fighting the Moderates and supporting the Radicals even though he stood far to the left of them.

Boulanger set to work. He staffed his office with young men. His avowed mission was to strengthen the confidence of the people in their Army. He paved the way for the reduction of military service from five years to three, and the introduction of conscription without exemption even for candidates for the priesthood. He improved and modernized instruction in the Army, gave the soldiers a dashing new-style uniform, ordered tables and plates in the barracks so that soldiers no longer had to eat on their cots, provided furloughs for peasants' sons at harvest time, made Sunday a day of rest, gave soldiers permission to grow beards. There was an unremitting flood of reforms, great and small, and the public followed his activities with mounting enthusiasm. Soon he became almost the only topic of conversation in Paris.

When the officers of a cavalry regiment expressed their contempt for the Republic in the aristocratic salons they visited, Boulanger ordered the regiment garrisoned elsewhere. A right-wing deputy rose in the Chamber to take him to task. His order was reviving the Law of Suspects of the Terror. Amid cheers from the Radicals, Boulanger retorted: "Is France a Republic, yes or no?"

"All right," replied the deputy. "Let the Army be the judge."

Cried Boulanger in a fiery voice: "As long as I am in command, the Army will not judge. It will but obey."

Even the Center jumped to its feet at this assertion of civilian control over the Army to join the Radicals in applauding a truly republican general.

A more serious incident gave him the opportunity to endear himself to the workers. The miners struck at Decazeville. One of the executives of the coal company was thrown out of a window of his office. The Government dispatched troops, and protests were hurled from the Left.

"Yes," Boulanger stated, "the soldiers are there—in readiness. They take no sides. Do not complain of their presence. At this very moment, perhaps, one of them is sharing his soup with a miner."

On July 14, France's national holiday, the President, cabinet ministers, deputies and diplomats crowded the grandstands to watch Paris' military parade. But they were only a background for the youthful General Boulanger, mounted on his famous black charger Tunis, surrounded by Spahis in their colorful uniforms, and with 300 generals in his retinue. At the mere sight of him the immense throng burst into cheers and that very night a songwriter named Paulus wrote *"En Revenant de la Revue"* ("Back from the Parade"), a gush of melody which was to become the theme song of the movement that went down in history as Boulangism.

The Moderates were now alarmed at Boulanger's popularity. France had had enough of men on horseback. They pressed the Premier to ask for Boulanger's resignation. Instead, the Premier him·self resigned. But his successor refused to provoke the ire of the Radicals and the public. Boulanger remained as War Minister in the new Cabinet.

In April 1887 a French customs official was invited by German guards to step across the border to take part in a conference on the regulation of traffic. The official, a man named Schnaebele, was arrested immediately on reaching the other side. Two German detectives had been waiting there to pounce on him. Schnaebele succeeded in dragging the two detectives back to the French side, so that by the time they got the handcuffs on him and rendered him powerless he was actually on French soil.

The Cabinet held an emergency meeting. The President of the Republic, Jules Grévy at that time, presided. Without a word, Boulanger put before him for signature an order calling for general mobilization. Grévy and the Moderates were taken aback. It seemed an act of utter irresponsibility. Unexpectedly, the royalists and Catholics of the Right sided with the Moderates. They sent word privately that they would support the Premier in the Chamber in his efforts to preserve peace. This assured Grévy of a majority. Instead of an ultimatum, a protest was made to Berlin. The Germans then released Inspector Schnaebele.

The public, unware of what had gone on behind the scenes, believed General Boulanger had forced the hand of Germany's Iron Chancellor. Overnight he became "Le Général Revanche" in the popular view.

The Moderates resolved that Boulanger was too dangerous to be left to his devices. They decided to get rid of him by improvising a government crisis. The reorganized Cabinet simply would not include him as Minister of War.

The Cabinet resigned according to plan. But the plan leaked out. Rochefort in L'Intransigeant urged his readers to write in the general's name on the ballot at a Paris by-election. The general was not a candidate; as a soldier on active duty, he could not be one. But 40,000 voters wrote in his name in a single district and the whole nation began to seethe with demands and resolutions that he be kept in the Cabinet. Four hundred different songs extolling Boulanger competed for the public's larynxes. Hucksters and peddlers offered busts, pipes, soaps, and pins labeled with the golden name.

Like the proverbial woman, no Cabinet could live either with him or without him. The crisis dragged on. Boulanger set up headquarters in the Hôtel du Louvre. His visitors grew daily in numbers and importance. *La France Militaire* proposed a military dictatorship with Boulanger at the head as the only way out of the crisis. But the politicians found another way. In May 1887 a new Cabinet was formed. Premier Maurice Rouvier ordered General Boulanger to a tour of duty with the provincial garrison at Clermont-Ferrand.

A great outcry followed. Rochefort called on the hero to disobey the order. But Boulanger decided the time had not yet come. On July 8 he set out for Clermont-Ferrand to take up his new post. The crowd at the Gare de Lyon was so great that it tied Paris traffic into a knot. They sang Boulangist songs. Three thousand of them stood on the tracks and refused to allow the train to move. Finally, under cover of darkness, the police smuggled him aboard a locomotive on another track and got him out of Paris.

But he was not gone for long. In the fall of that year the son-in-law of the President, a deputy with the improbable name of Daniel Wilson, was discovered to be selling Army decorations for cash. President Grévy was able to prove that he was not involved in his son-in-law's shady dealings. But Clemenceau and the Radicals were determined to use any pretext for riding him out of power. Grévy's clandestine acceptance of royalist support in the Schnaebele case had alarmed the Tiger. He judged correctly that a combination of the Center and the Right would imperil the Republic itself.

So Daniel Wilson's wrongdoings were magnified to force a government crisis. Clemenceau and his Radicals planned their moves in a fashionable café. Grévy, it was clear, was finished. But whom to select as his successor? The chances were that the Moderates and the Right would settle on Jules Ferry, an esteemed statesman opposed by the Radicals because of his stand on colonialism. The Radicals had to have a candidate to prevent the election of a President dependent on the royalists.

Into their deliberations strolled General Boulanger with the nonchalance of an intimate. He had read in Clermont-Ferrand of the crisis and had come to throw his popularity behind any government supported by the Radicals. Clemenceau greeted the offer coolly. He took Boulanger at his word and did not go beyond it.

When Grévy's resignation was forced, the members of the Chamber of Deputies and the Senate assembled at Versailles to select a new President on the day and in the manner decreed in the Constitution. At the same time a committee set up headquarters in the City Hall, traditional launching site of revolutions. Déroulède's League of Patriots and large numbers of Paris' workers jammed the streets, ready for action should the Right and the Center combine to elect Jules Ferry. Clemenceau put forward as his candidate not Boulanger but François-Marie Sadi-Carnot, grandson of Lazare Carnot, who, a century before, had organized the army of the Great Revolution.

Carnot was elected and Boulanger resumed at a breakneck pace his changeover from Left to Right. His offer to Clemenceau had been his last gesture in deference to his republican past.

During his trip to America, Boulanger had met a former schoolmate of his at St.-Cyr, the French officers' academy. This man, Arthur Marie-Dillon, had become an important executive of the Mackay Transatlantic Cable Company. Now he was back in Paris, his future staked on Boulanger's. Dillon approached the royalists.

There was the Comte de Chambord, Bourbon pretender to the throne. In the first panic of the defeat of 1870, a royalist majority had returned to the Chamber. They invited him to become king. "As king by the grace of God," he had declared, "I cannot accept the Constitution. I shall not be king by the grace of the Revolution as was my ancestor [Louis XVI] until he was beheaded for his folly." He refused to accept the tricolor. Pointing to the white flag of the Bourbons, he said that the flag that had stood over his cradle would stand over his tomb. The royalists had had to give up on him, hoping that when he died his heir would prove more realistic.

Now Dillon sounded out the intimates of the Comte de Chambord. He found his way to the Duchesse d'Uzès, heiress of the champagne firm of Veuve-Clicquot. She was ready to sacrifice all her great wealth to Boulanger if her "king" approved. Eventually Boulanger met all the royalist leaders. They proposed that he seize power in a popular movement which they would help foment. A council to create a royalist constitution would then be created. The general was to submit the new constitution to a plebiscite of the people.

But Boulanger had other advisers. Friends of Jérôme Bonaparte, nephew of the late Emperor Napoleon III, argued that Bourbons would never be accepted by the French people. The name of Bonaparte, however, still rang gloriously in the native ear. The general listened cautiously. On January 1, 1888, dressed in mufti, he slipped secretly across the Swiss border to Prangins and met the head of the House of Bonaparte. He was shown the sword of Napoleon I and promised he would be allowed to carry it into battle to reconquer Alsace-Lorraine.

Boulanger's secret supporters were enthusiastic but formed quite a potpourri. There was Déroulède and his League of Patriots who still stood for an authoritarian Republic; Rochefort, out to destroy the Republic of appeasers and businessmen; Bonapartists with Jérôme as their emperor; royalists with a Bourbon as their king.

The Duchesse d'Uzès made more than half a million dollars available to Dillon. The Transatlantic Cable man was not impressed. "I found eight million dollars to drop into the ocean," he said. "I'll surely find five to give the general a chance."

La Cocarde was started as a Boulangist daily. Millions of pamphlets emerged. Dissolution of Parliament and revision of the Constitution were demanded. A well-financed, full-fledged grass-roots groundswell started on its powerful way.

The Government moved to block it. It was announced that Boulanger had made three unauthorized visits to Paris, one of them while in civilian dress and further disguised by dark glasses and a limp. He was bounced abruptly to the retired list.

Retired generals are celebrated bores. But now Boulanger could devote all his time to politics. He had but one week in which to campaign for a seat in the Chamber in a by-election in the north. It was a challenge. He accepted it defiantly and won a spectacular victory. Miners and peasants deserted the Radicals and cast 173,000 votes for the general the politicians had ousted from the Army.

It began to seem as if no one would be bored by the man. The most exclusive salons now vied for the general—even Mme. de Caillavet's, the meeting place of literature and the arts. One of the ladies noticed that the general had beautiful hands, and said so. "Ah," replied Boulanger, dumfounded, "you should see my feet!" The remark was not kept secret and the ladies wondered whether all great men in history had been as disillusioning as Boulanger. Yet some of the great were attracted to him—Anatole France, the novelist Maurice Barrès. But, as it turned out, most significant for history was the one he was attracted to: Marguerite de Bonnemains, a beautiful young woman but recently divorced after a disastrous marriage. They met at a salon—a man of destiny, a woman of fate.

On June 4, 1888, the general announced a speech in which he would state his program. When he drove to the Chamber his followers lined the streets and cheered him. In the Chamber he outlined a program drafted for him by the harpies that were now his entourage. The Chamber of Deputies was to be abolished and an authoritarian Republic set up in its place. That was the program. The rest of the speech was an attack on parliamentarianism, which, he said, could produce nothing but fruitless debates.

Clemenceau answered him bitingly. "These debates honor us all," he said. "They prove our ardor in defending the ideas we believe to be right. . . . Yes, glory to the lands where men freely discuss their differences. Shame to those where no voice is raised."

But the barb that bit deepest was a witticism from the Premier, Charles Floquet: "What have you accomplished, *M. le Général*, to entitle you to talk like Napoleon the Great? At your age, Napoleon was already dead."

Boulanger challenged Floquet to a duel. The Premier was sixty-five years old at the time and had spent his life in the sedentary practice of the law. Still, the great soldier took no chances. Neither did Arthur Dillon. Are you a good swordsman? he asked Boulanger. The general was not certain. He hadn't touched a foil, he said, in thirty-two years, not since his cadet days at St.-Cyr. Dillon summoned a famous fencing master, Xavier Feuillant, to help Boulanger brush up.

The duel was not fought until July 13, six weeks after the remark which had occasioned it. It took place on Dillon's estate at Neuilly. At the edge of the field, an elegant coach waited; in it, a lady heavily veiled—Marguerite de Bonnemains. All Boulanger's practicing only enabled him to last through one round against Premier Floquet. The old man scored a second-round knockout, piercing Boulanger's neck with his sword to a depth of ten centimeters. The hero of France was carried languishing to the elegant coach and the arms of the lady within it. She was seen to lift her veil to press her lips against his face and heard to murmur: "I knew as soon as the day was chosen—Friday the thirteenth."

It was Marguerite's first public appearance in her new role in life. But the fact of her existence could not damage a French reputation, nor—surprisingly enough—did the glamour boy's unglamorous performance on the field of honor. By January, Boulanger's headquarters was ready for a showdown on the matter of his taking power and overthrowing the Constitution.

Under French law at that time, a man could be a candidate for the Chamber in as many election districts as he chose. No matter how many districts returned him to the Chamber, he could represent only one. But it was a way, and in fact the only way, for a man to demonstrate a national following at the polls. A by-election in Paris for a seat in the Chamber was scheduled for January 27, 1889, and the Boulangists chose it as a test of strength on the crest of which Boulanger would ride into the Chamber and sweep it aside.

Clemenceau accepted the challenge. He founded the Society of the Rights of Man "to defend to the last the Republic against dictatorship and reaction." He induced the political parties to agree on a single candidate against Boulanger in order not to divide their strength. As a concession to the revanchist and leftist temper of Paris, the candidate chosen was a member of the Radical party.

So, cleanly, the battle lines were drawn. But it was a time when politicians kept their ears to the ground for the rumble of the winning bandwagon. It was estimated that no less than half the Radical deputies were ready to abandon Clemenceau and join Boulanger at the first sign of victory. But the right wing was equally opportunistic. The Church was reluctant to commit itself openly to the general until it was sure he would win. Boulanger strove mightily for the Church's support. Prominent Jews were active in his camp, even on his staff. "One of the first things we will have to do," he promised, "is rid France of the Jews." Then he declared, in a Catholic newspaper, that he would never be a party to "religious persecution."

The campaign was fought furiously. Dillon poured a fortune into it, mobilizing an army of poets, artists, journalists, photographers to flood not only Paris but the whole country with Boulangist propaganda. The signal was to be victory in the by-election and the country was to be prepared to hear it rapturously.

On election night, as the ballots were being counted, the streets of Paris were jammed. The President of the Republic sat in the Elysée Palace and awaited the roar that would greet the appearance of Boulanger as he walked in to take over. The Republican guard posted about the building to defend his office ostentatiously read Boulangist literature, wore Boulangist buttons. The crowds in the streets, poor as well as rich, female as well as male, chanted Boulangist songs. Cries of "Boulanger, Boulanger!" and "To the Elysée!" were continuous. Boulanger himself chose to receive the returns at the strategically located Restaurant Durant on the Rue Royale. It was only a short walk from there to the Elysée.

But while the President sat in the Elysée, Marguerite may have sat in Boulanger's apartment. She had contracted tuberculosis and the winter night's air was dangerous for her. Marguerite was no old fool's folly. The general, at the perilous summit of a man's life in his earliest fifties, was estranged from his wife. She had not been able to endure his vanity, she said. After that he had had a series of trivial, even vulgar affairs. Marguerite, a delicate soul, young and cultured, was the first to fall in love with him rather than with what he had to offer.

A woman at whose house the couple met said of her: "A queen on her throne could not be more majestic in her beauty. She will make of him what she wants him to be. If she loves him more than she loves herself, she will make him great. If not, he will be lost."

What thoughts went through Boulanger's mind as he sat in the Restaurant Durant that night can only be guessed. But he knew of Marguerite's consumption and that only a few more years of life were left to her. He knew, too, that if he staged a *coup d'état,* he could not spend these years with her. He would have to spend them in the crowd at work.

The news came. Boulanger had won the election. A fever of expectation swept the streets. The mobs clamored exultantly for action. Walk, begged Boulanger's aides, walk. It is only a few steps. Now or never, pleaded Rochefort. It cannot be tomorrow. Dramatically he took out his watch and held it in his hand. He counted out the quarter hours as they passed. The Day would end at midnight. It would never come again, he assured Boulanger.

At midnight the streets began slowly to empty. The Restaurant Durant emptied. The lights in the Elysée were turned out. Boulanger had gone to his apartment and to Marguerite, and did not emerge.

Léon Blum, in his memoirs of the Dreyfus Affair, has left this analysis of Boulangism:

Do not always judge the impact of political movements by their success or failure. When an attempted revolution succeeds, it becomes part and parcel of history; if it fails it leaves in men's memory but a faint trail of derision. Yet failure and success are but a hair's breadth apart.

Boulangism that failed appears today as buffoonery, incoherent and ridiculous. For all that, it held France in thrall for two years running, and touched on the very roots of her being. The Boulangist leaders were sure of victory and, verily, they held it in the palms of their hands. Only a miracle could have lost it for them, or, rather, a new miraculous concatenation of circumstances.

If history, in happening, followed the logic of an adventure story, Boulanger would have occupied the Elysée on January 27, 1889, after the Seine by-election. In the General Elections [which would have followed] a Boulangist majority would have been returned. On the face of it, the chances of Louis Napoleon's coup d'état which succeeded were far slenderer than those of the Boulangist adventure which lost itself in a vague and piteous outcome.

M. Blum wrote after Boulangism had failed. But it was a long time happening. The leader of a movement is only its symbol. When he walks out on it the passions that brought the movement into being do not walk out on themselves.

Meanwhile, in the aftermath of Boulanger's defection, a new Government had come into power, composed of men who agreed on only one thing—republicanism—and were determined to make a firm stand. Plans were made to arrest and prosecute Boulanger and his chief advisers, Déroulède and Rochefort, for an attempt to overthrow the Government by force and violence—a crime that came under the jurisdiction of the Senate.

But a police official slipped the news to Marguerite de Bonnemains. Fearing he would be separated from his beloved, Boulanger fled with her to Belgium. He did not even risk waiting for confirmation of the news. The police watched over their flight. Frontier guards were ordered to permit the couple to pass without incident.

On April 1 the general's followers were shocked by the news in the press that their leader had fled rather than fight with them against a legal prosecution. Nevertheless, in the general elections in September, held while he was still in Belgium, a Paris constituency returned him to the Chamber. Forty-four other Boulangists were elected deputies.

But Boulanger refused to leave Brussels. He would not risk trial. After all, a trial, even if it resulted in acquittal, would have meant embracing what he had turned his back on the night of January 27. Marguerite was mortally sick. He did not leave her bedside.

The young woman died two years later, in 1891, at Brussels. Boulanger mourned her for two months. Then he went to her grave and killed himself on it. In his last will he asked that one tombstone be placed over the two graves inscribed with these words: "How did I survive for two months without thee?"

And now, even though Boulanger was dead, Boulangism was not. Wrote M. Blum: "The Dreyfus affair cannot be understood at all unless one recalls that the storm broke less than eight years after a revolution that misfired."

The misfire did not mean that the explosives had fizzled out; they were just waiting for a new match. The royalists waited, the anti-Semites, the hooligans and adventurers, the zealots, the opportunists and the fear-ridden mass of the people, in terror of the power of Germany, watching that power rise and spread. In the awful shadow of Prussian might, what were the Rights of Man? A Protestant plot? A Jewish plot? A philosopher's dream?

12

THE POLITICAL CONFUSION from which General Boulanger rose to become a popular hero was not of his own making. A strong emotional undercurrent had been sapping the base of the French political structure, which all but collapsed when the handsome general appeared on his famous charger.

Patriotism had been giving way to nationalism.

Patriotism was the heritage of the Great Revolution. It included the cult of the Army, that Army of the Revolution which had defeated the coalition of kings and princes in 1792, broken down the Old Order and opened the way for other peoples to free themselves and join the French in a brotherhood of nations. Patriotism, even as distorted in Napoleon's camps, carried abroad a vision of freedom and of human rights, and never entirely lost that generous emotion that permeated the nation during the opening years of the Revolution.

"I love myself, but I love my family better, and I love my country more than my family, and humanity better than my country. One must be ready to sacrifice one's self for them: one's self for the family, the family for the country, the country for humanity." So wrote François Xavier-Joliclerc, volunteer in the republican army from Franche-Comté, in a letter to his mother, at the time of the French Revolution.

Léon Gambetta tried hard to evoke this patriotism of the Revolution after Sedan, which was to prove a catastrophe for France and all she stood for. Necessarily he had to set as his immediate task the building of a strong Army at all cost, and lost sight of the importance of the spirit of the Army. When it came to appointing a general to head the War Office, Gambetta chose a first-rate military man and by-passed other candidates in whom the flame of revolutionary patriotism was still alive. Eventually he was branded an opportunist and defeated in his own working-class electoral district in Paris by those politically closer to his heart.

Gambetta's favorite veterans' organization, the League of Patriots, went even farther in shifting away from the traditional patriotism of the Left. Paul Déroulède, poet of the barracks, a sincere man with a single-track mind dedicated to *revanche* against Germany, had been encouraged by Gambetta to launch this rally of veterans all over the country. Gambetta had expected that it would keep the great issues of the nation alive while the Chamber was being fragmented by political factions. But Déroulède, who started out as an admirer of Gambetta, ended up with his League of Patriots on the side of the anti-Semitic hooligans who were to use the Dreyfus Affair as an excuse to overthrow the Republic.

The new nationalism conceived of all questions only in their relation to national interest. It was ready to sacrifice the basic ideas of the Great Revolution—human rights, liberty and equal justice—for national strength. Thus the genuine place of the new nationalists, as in so many other countries, was on the Right. Eventually the word "nationalist" became synonymous with the Right, the Catholics and Conservatives who were still fighting the Revolution with the arguments of the *ancien régime*.

The case of Captain Dreyfus helped the new nationalism to acquire, as a by-product, a new anti-Semitism. This was a different anti-Semitism from that which had been latent in the country during the first half

of the nineteenth century and which had broken out time and time
again against Jews prominent in the rise of modern commerce, railroad
enterprise and finance. The older anti-Semitism had abated as fast as
it appeared, whenever the advance of industry absorbed its driving
force.

In the Great Revolution, Hébert had denounced Jews and moneybags in one breath. Again on the eve of the February revolution of
1848, a Socialist pamphlet, entitled *Jews, the Kings of Our Age*, hit
out at business and money-making. "Jew, usurer and merchant are
one," the author wrote. The Protestant nations were branded "birds
of prey." Anti-Semitism became particularly ferocious in the Second
Empire when Napoleon III granted railroad licenses to his Jewish
banker friends. The railroads developed into strongholds of plutoc-
racy. Outbursts against their Jewish owners were fanned by the anti-
industrial feelings of the rural population, which was being uprooted
in the rapid spread of capitalism. Later, in 1870, the Communards
wrote and spoke of "Jewish molochism." A leading Marxist, Jules
Guèsde, occasionally declared that the social question was first of all
a Jewish question. A newspaper of his faction demanded the ex-
propriation of all Jewish fortunes. This was considered simply a re-
covering of wealth which the Jews had amassed by fraud and exploita-
tion in the course of a century. Identification of the Jews with the evils
of capitalism was made easier by the fact that in a country with a population of 39,000,000 there were only about 70,000 Jews. Most of
these lived in Paris and in the larger provincial towns. Most Frenchmen had never seen a Jew. In their eyes there was something monstrous
about these descendants of the crucifiers of the Son of God. They
might be anywhere, unseen. In this they seemed like the forces of
finance, pervasive and invisible.

Edouard Drumont, in a voluminous and learned work titled *Jewish
France*, introduced a significant shift. The only child of a civil-service
clerk, he had lost both parents at an early age and was raised by relatives on his mother's side who were poor artisans. He did not marry
until he was thirty-eight, and his wife died two years later. A bitter,
violent man with a biblical face, he had bushy black hair and wore a
beard which left only narrow patches of his face visible. His obsessed
black eyes glittered from behind glasses, and many called him "the
rabbi of anti-Semitism."

Drumont was possessed by a nostalgia for the France of old, where life had been rooted in a Christian order of family, profession and community and where privilege went with responsibility, work was guaranteed and ennobled, since the lowest labors were recognized as vital to the community and therefore honored as the highest. This France of old—which of course never existed in actuality—had been a casualty, in Drumont's view, of the Great Revolution. The liberty which it created had broken down the legal and moral restraints on the Jews. Its equality made them individuals, the same as everybody else. Frenchmen came to realize their presence only after they had entrenched themselves in the wealth of France, in society, literature, science and government. Nothing but a complete reversal of the Great Revolution, Drumont wrote, would suffice to undo this.

As late as 1886 the book rotted unsold. In 1889 he founded an Anti-Semitic League. It collapsed a year later. Finally, in 1892, Drumont's efforts came to fruition. The Jesuits decided to finance a newspaper, *La Libre Parole*, dedicated to anti-Semitism. Edouard Drumont was made its publisher and editor. The newspaper throve on the "moral enormity" of the Panama scandal and its influence spread throughout the country. It ruined reputations and made scoundrels respectable. Drumont's word determined the fate of ministers, cabinets, Presidents of the Republic.

This was one of the results of the Panama affair. It had others. Ferdinand de Lesseps, the hero of the Suez Canal, had been given the task of building a Panama Canal. He proposed a new Bosporus—a passageway between the Atlantic and the Pacific, without locks. The Suez Canal had been the glory of the Second Empire. The Panama Canal would be the glory of the Republic. The influence in Latin America the canal would bring France would be the answer to the rise of Germany on her border. It would bring the nation the power for which she yearned. The French bourgeoisie rallied to invest in the canal almost as passionately as they had rallied to pay off the enormous indemnity Bismarck had imposed (five billion francs) and get the German troops out of the country a year before the deadline.

But De Lesseps ran into engineering difficulties. More money was needed. Public subscriptions began to lag. Jacques de Reinach, named a baron by the King of Italy for his work on an Italian loan, was approached to raise the money. His work was complicated by the fact that it was thought undesirable to let the public in on exactly how much difficulty the engineers were encountering, and finally Baron

Reinach petitioned the Minister of the Interior for a government license to hold a national lottery.

The Minister refused, so the company the baron had formed approached Dr. Cornelius Herz. Herz, a Frenchman by birth, had emigrated to the United States, become a U.S. citizen and taken degrees both in medicine and engineering. When he returned to France, he had supported the Radical Republican party, published a republican newspaper himself and helped Georges Clemenceau's paper. In 1886 he had become Grand Officer of the Legion of Honor. He was offered 10,000,000 francs—600,000 in advance, the balance if and when a license for the lottery was granted.

Now, with the aid of further bribes, a press campaign was started to put pressure on the Government. More than 150,000 separate holders of Panama obligations petitioned for the license, and under their urging the Chamber requested a report from the Government on the progress of the canal.

The report was discouraging. Nevertheless, Baron Reinach's company paid the Minister of Agriculture one million francs to present a bill to the Chamber authorizing the lottery. Finally, in 1888, the lottery was held and proved disappointing. De Lesseps resigned and the enterprise went into bankruptcy. Some half a million small investors lost their money. Almost one and one-half billion francs had been sunk in the project—over half of it for bribes, inducements and commissions.

A national roar went up. The hero of Suez and his son were prosecuted for fraud and sentenced to prison. However, the sentence was annulled under the statute of limitations and the matter might have ended there, with the two victims, except that Dr. Herz had not yet been paid the balance of his ten million francs for getting the lottery.

He threatened Baron Reinach and his company with exposure of their unsavory dealings. The baron decided to be clever rather than wise. He went to see Edouard Drumont, whose newspaper, *La Libre Parole*, had been languishing, and made the following proposition. He would give Drumont the inside story of the Panama Canal scandal provided Drumont protected his, the baron's name. Dr. Herz got wind of this and he decided to be ferocious rather than wise. He went with his own inside story to *La Cocarde*, an equally extremist right-wing paper.

The result was general slaughter. Baron Reinach committed suicide. Dr. Herz fled to England. Five former ministers, twelve deputies and senators, a chief of police and numerous bankers went through criminal investigations. Only one of them confessed—Bailhaut. He alone was convicted but all suffered politically, and the infamous *La Libre Parole* was on its way.

In the wake of the uproar over the Panama Canal scandal Clemenceau suffered. With everybody accusing everybody else, an opposition deputy took the floor of the Chamber and offered documentary evidence that Clemenceau was a paid agent of the British Government. It was proved that the documentary evidence was a crude forgery and the republican deputies threw the man who had offered it out of the Chamber bodily. Still, the incident cost Clemenceau his position in public life. It was an age of suspicion and mere charges were enough. Clemenceau was defeated for re-election and, he then believed, was out of politics irretrievably.

Drumont's thesis was simple: The villains of the affair were Jews. Had not Dr. Herz worked for the Protestant British, who had once before, with Jewish help, stolen from France her national accomplishment, the Suez Canal? And had not the Panama affair aroused the Tsar's suspicions about the stability of the French regime? Was this not a conspiracy of Protestant Germany, England and America with the Jews to frustrate, weaken and isolate Catholic France?

Treason has been the central issue of the long civil war which has dominated the last hundred years of French history. Treason was the legacy of defeat. When Gambetta was about to reverse the capitulation of Sedan, Marshal Bazaine had handed over to the enemy an intact Army in a key fortress. He was court-martialed and sentenced to death. But the royalists, still in power, had commuted the sentence to twenty years. The marshal was moved with his family to the island of St. Marguerite. One night, tired of the magnificent view of the Gulf of Juan, they all disappeared and found a new, luxurious home in Spain. But the idea of treason remained, and struck deep roots.

Fear and suspicion of the internal and external enemy were channeled relentlessly by *La Libre Parole* in a single direction. It hammered on its one article of faith, that the Jews were the enemy within, working to ruin France, hand in glove with the enemy outside.

13

SENATOR SCHEURER-KESTNER could not rest easy with the secret which had been entrusted to him by Lieutenant Colonel Picquart's lawyer. It was only practical to do nothing about it until the mysterious officer whom Attorney Leblois represented was willing to come forward with proof. But there are moments when even very old men find it impossible to be practical.

It seemed to Scheurer, as the days went by, that he was becoming an accomplice in this dreadful miscarriage of justice. He whispered a tip to the office of the President of the Senate. There was evidence of Dreyfus' innocence.

It was as if he had whispered at a sleeping snake. He was hissed at and spat on. The news reached the press: Scheurer believed Dreyfus innocent. He was accused of being the dummy of a syndicate of Jews. This "syndicate" purchased documents, hired forgers, bought witnesses, it was charged. Its aim was not only to rescue Dreyfus but to destroy the French Army and thus deliver France to Germany. It was not only in the gutter and yellow press that this kind of thing appeared. A Catholic paper wrote of Scheurer that Drumont was right in calling Protestants semi-Jews. Other papers advised the senator to take his seat in the Prussian parliament. Muck was thrown at his private life and that of his relatives.

Scheurer sat and took it. He could make no move without Picquart. He had given his word to respect Leblois' confidence as to the identity of the officer who had the proof. He could not even associate himself with the Dreyfus family. Picquart had enjoined Leblois and anyone he informed of the secret against that.

Mathieu Dreyfus meanwhile had persuaded a young literary critic, Bernard Lazare, to write a factual story of the Dreyfus case. Lazare was of Jewish extraction but had become an Evangelical Christian. He had gained a reputation for an almost superhuman impartiality with a pamphlet, *Anti-Semitism: Its History and Its Causes*. Published in 1894, it was a reply to Drumont's massive and apoplectic *Jewish France*, and even the "rabbi of anti-Semitism" had found words of praise for it.

As a peg on which to hang his Dreyfus pamphlet, Lazare used the article that had appeared in *L'Eclair*. He interviewed Major Forzinetti, the director of Cherche-Midi prison, and Demange, Dreyfus' lawyer. His pamphlet dealt with the letter *L'Eclair* had printed as coming from the German military attaché and which referred directly to "this beast of a Dreyfus." Lazare stated categorically that whether the letter was true or false, it had never formed part of the secret evidence handed to the court. There had been but one document referring to a person by the initial letter "D." But the contents of the document proved that the "D" had no connection with Dreyfus, Lazare wrote. The rest of the pamphlet was devoted to demonstrating why Dreyfus could not have written the *bordereau*.

To avoid prosecution, Mathieu had Lazare's pamphlet printed in Brussels. Copies were mailed in sealed envelopes to all deputies, to numerous important personalities and to all newspapers. That was in November 1896. Again the fact that the Army had violated Article 101 was ignored—even by Lazare. All that was noticed about the pamphlet was that it was sponsored by the Dreyfus family and thus automatically could be discounted.

Suddenly a bold headline appeared in *Le Matin*: THE PROOF! Under it appeared in facsimile the *bordereau*. France's largest daily had got hold of it from one of the handwriting experts, who had violated his instructions and kept it as a souvenir.

One effect of the publication was to strike panic in Esterhazy. Schwarzkoppen, he knew, had been puzzled by the Dreyfus case. It will be recalled that the attaché had never seen the *bordereau* before; now he could not only recognize Esterhazy's handwriting but recognize the items listed in the *bordereau* as material Esterhazy had delivered to him under separate cover.

Schwarzkoppen was an officer and a gentleman. He could not let Dreyfus expiate a crime committed by another man. Of course, neither could he name one of his own agents. It seemed to Esterhazy that Schwarzkoppen would find a way out of the dilemma by assuring the President of France confidentially that he had positive reason for believing Dreyfus innocent.

Esterhazy had been having a precarious time anyway. His Army record was good, but Esterhazy was not the man to let well enough alone. His superior discovered that the count had falsified an order of the day in order to honor himself with a citation for energy and character.

The discovery convinced Esterhazy that his health was poor and he withdrew from the Army temporarily, moving to his country home. He was at low ebb, short of money and of prospects. But something always turned up for him, and in this case it was the toes of a relative of his, a bourgeois, who in dying left his estate to his widow. Esterhazy rushed to console the grieving widow and offer his help in investing her inheritance securely and advantageously. He hinted at his close ties with the Rothschilds.

The bewitched widow gave him 35,000 francs to invest for her. He sent her interest from her "investments" punctually every month until the money was gone. For, of course, there had been no investments. Esterhazy had been living on the capital.

Helping him do this had been the widow's twenty-year-old son, Christian Esterhazy. The count grew fond of the youth, who in his turn adored the count's bubbling way of life. The count employed Christian on delicate errands to various scented and silken boudoirs in Paris and began looking around for a rich girl for him to marry. He imparted to Christian his wisdom: only scoundrels could get ahead in a court where Money was king; governments sold out unhesitatingly; politicians and newspaper editors were in the pay of bankers and gangsters; generals were in the clutches of Jews and had to do their bidding. His one kind word was for traitors. Poor devils, he called them, who sold documents about dubious plans that would never be followed in battles that would never take place because France would never be able to wage war while her governments dealt in treason wholesale.

When the precious pile of widow's francs dwindled toward the vanishing point, Esterhazy renewed his efforts to get into the Ministry of War. He buttonholed everyone he knew, and when no one could offer a tangible hope he threatened to make disclosures about generals from De Boisdeffre down. In a letter to the deputy, Jules Roche, he almost gave himself away. He wrote that only a position in the Ministry of War could save his life. Roche did not have to be inspired to deduce that Esterhazy wanted the position in order to get military secrets he could sell. After all, the only legitimate money he could earn at the ministry was his Army pay, and that he could earn at any time by resuming his commission as a major. But Roche refrained from making the deduction.

Among those Esterhazy threatened vaguely with disclosures was his old friend, now Lieutenant Colonel Henry. The thought of helping a traitor gain access to secret documents must have been repugnant to Henry. Particularly repugnant to a man like him was the thought of sticking his neck out. He recommended Esterhazy to General Gonse.

The only outcome of this was that General Gonse informed Henry that Picquart and Bertillon were no longer alone in identifying Esterhazy as the author of the *bordereau*. Senator Scheurer had mentioned it confidentially to General Jean Billot, the Minister of War. Billot had demanded proof, but this, of course, Scheurer was prevented from offering.

General Gonse would not tolerate Esterhazy on the General Staff. But he felt that the case against Esterhazy was all a plot of the Jews to blame a Christian for what a Jew had done and that Senator Scheurer was a dupe of it. He told Henry to make sure that the plot did not work, that Dreyfus remained in jail for writing the *bordereau* and that Esterhazy remained out of it.

Henry was relieved. He knew Esterhazy. He had been afraid the shameless blackguard, if his situation became desperate, would flee the country and sell to newspapers abroad what he knew about the Dreyfus case. This actually was to happen subsequently, but in the meantime Henry was out to prevent it. He sought guidance as to ways and means from that mastermind of the Third Bureau, Major du Paty de Clam.

The precious pair requested General Gonse to send an order to General Leclerc in Tunis, dispatching Lieutenant Colonel Picquart to the Tripoli border. Skirmishes had been taking place on the border. They did not, of course, know of the letter Picquart had written to be delivered in the event of his death. They felt that a bullet in the right place would successfully stop any reopening of the Dreyfus case. General Gonse sent the order.

When General Leclerc received it, he was astonished. He could see no reason why an intelligence officer should be dispatched to a combat zone to set up a spy network. He asked Picquart to tell him in confidence what the General Staff had against him. Picquart told him, and General Leclerc wrote orders dispatching him toward the border but commanding him to advance no farther than Gabes, where the border skirmishing did not reach.

While waiting for their happy bullet, Henry and Du Paty decided to maintain contact with Esterhazy. Perhaps they honestly believed in the "Jewish syndicate" and its plot. No vaporings were too thin to cloud minds already besmogged from within. At any rate they sent

Gribelin to the apartment of Esterhazy's mistress, Marguerite Pays, with a message. The message informed the count that he was in danger but that powerful friends were protecting him, and concluded by asking him to go to Montsouris Park the following afternoon to meet an "important person," not otherwise identified.

In the meantime there had been the facsimile reproduction of the *bordereau* in *Le Matin*. In his panic over it, Esterhazy had rushed to his friends on *La Libre Parole* and *La Patrie* with fresh material about the "Jewish syndicate." This duly published material, according to Gabriel Monod, the historian, bespeaks in its frantic imaginings not a hired slanderer or deranged patriot, but a criminal at bay and lashing out madly.

Now, on the way to his mysterious tryst at Montsouris Park, Esterhazy stopped off at the German Embassy to see Schwarzkoppen. Take the bull by the horns was his idea, and what he, in his misery, ended up by doing was to stage a remarkable scene. Unfortunately the dialogue has not been preserved; only the gist of what went on is known.

The count told Schwarzkoppen that their connection had been discovered and would soon be made public by a leading senator. He suggested that Schwarzkoppen go to see Mme. Dreyfus and assure her that her husband had actually committed treason. Schwarzkoppen refused, and Esterhazy then said that he had reached the end. He would kill himself right here and now in Schwarzkoppen's office. The prospect failed to alarm the military attaché, and Esterhazy became enraged. He threatened to make public Schwarzkoppen's relations with a lady whom he named. Schwarzkoppen coldly rang for an attendant and ordered Esterhazy shown forcefully into the street.

Esterhazy jumped into a cab and drove to Montsouris Park. He waited a few moments. Then a carriage stopped before him and a strange figure alighted—a man wearing dark glasses and well muffled up in a long black coat. It was the Marquis du Paty. He assured Esterhazy on behalf of the General Staff that there was nothing to fear, that matters were well in hand.

On the way back from this melodramatic meeting Esterhazy stopped once more at the German Embassy. He was a changed man. He glowed rosily with euphoria. He boasted to Schwarzkoppen that he owned the General Staff. Every man on it was behind him.

The clandestine meetings continued, now in a park, now in a street. On one occasion, Du Paty brought Esterhazy the draft of a letter which he was to copy and mail to General Billot, requesting a brief audience with the War Minister to inform him of an impending scandal in which his (Esterhazy's) name would be involved. Du Paty coached Esterhazy in what to say, but the count didn't get a chance to say it. When he arrived for his appointment with Billot he was met by an aide who advised him to put it all down in a letter.

This letter, too, was written out for Esterhazy by Du Paty. It was a long letter. In it Esterhazy explained that Dreyfus probably had got samples of his handwriting from Jewish money-lenders with whom Esterhazy, alas, had had dealings. Dreyfus, he said, had then imitated his writing on the *bordereau* and now Esterhazy had been warned that he would soon be charged with having written the *bordereau* himself. Could nothing be done to protect the honor of an officer?

General Billot did not answer the letter. The general, it later developed, was well aware that strange and extra-legal doings were the regular order of business in his Second Bureau and preferred to know as little about them as possible.

At this moment the press carried a report that Senator Scheurer-Kestner, whose lips were still sealed in public, had made a private call on the President of the Republic, Félix Faure. Du Paty told Esterhazy to write President Faure a letter similar to the one he had sent the War Minister. Esterhazy added a typical touch of his own. If the President, too, refused to protect the honor of a French officer, he would be compelled to turn to the Emperor of Germany, suzerain of the Esterhazy family. The Kaiser would not fail to defend the honor even of an enemy officer.

The President responded to the letter as had General Billot—with silence. In the meantime Schwarzkoppen had sent a report to Berlin on Esterhazy's two performances at the embassy. His superiors decided he had better get out while the getting was good, before the brewing scandal boiled over. They promoted him to command of a regiment in Germany. But before leaving Paris, Schwarzkoppen did the most that a spy can do for his own self-respect. In bidding the President a formal farewell, the German assured the French chief of state privately and on his honor as an officer that he had had no dealings with Dreyfus. Again the President responded only with silence.

Now a new figure entered the act being put on by the muscular peasant and the perfumed little marquis. A woman, so heavily veiled that she almost had to grope her way, met Esterhazy clandestinely at night. It turned out that under all those veils there lurked only Du Paty, with a document—a letter which Schwarzkoppen had written to Panizzardi, or vice versa, but now so altered that it referred to Dreyfus. Esterhazy took one look at it and entitled it ecstatically "The Liberator."

Emboldened by his possession of "proof" of Dreyfus' guilt, the count wrote a second letter to the President. He complained about getting no answer to his first letter and added:

> The service for over a century and a half of five generals whose name I bear must not be rewarded by infamy and by letting a scoundrel go free. I am forced to use all means at my disposal. A high-minded lady, who also warned me before that the friends of Dreyfus with Col. Picquart's assistance would launch their attack on me, now has given me a document that Col. Picquart stole from a foreign embassy. It will grievously compromise certain diplomatic personalities. If help and justice continue to be denied me or if my name be mentioned, I shall have to resort to publishing this document which is already abroad in safety.

Again there was not even an acknowledgment from the Elysée that the letter had been received.

Henry had sent the document to Esterhazy to use if and when necessary. Once published, of course, it must become known that Esterhazy had got it from the files of the Second Bureau. With typically shameless and crude cunning, Henry attempted to cover his tracks. He sent a query to General Leclerc, Picquart's commanding officer, asking whether a secret document had not been stolen from Picquart while he was serving as head of the Second Bureau. Information had reached the War Ministry, Henry cabled, that such a document, involving a foreign military attaché, had been photographed by a woman.

Picquart replied that no such theft had occurred. But he now knew Henry. He wondered uneasily whether Henry was cooking up something against him with the *petit bleu* Schwarzkoppen's lady friend had written to Esterhazy.

While he was still wondering, Picquart received an amazing letter from Major Esterhazy. The plot of the comedians was thickening. Esterhazy accused Picquart bluntly of conniving to foist the guilt for Dreyfus' treason on Esterhazy himself. The proof of the accusation was that Picquart had surreptitiously given secret documents to Dreyfus' friends. Esterhazy said he knew this because one of the secret documents had come into his possession.

Thus did Henry build up his story. He had "information" that a secret document had been photographed illegally by a woman while Picquart commanded the Second Bureau. Esterhazy had "knowledge" that a secret document had been slipped by Picquart to the Dreyfus camp and could back it up with evidence of the document itself.

Then two baffling telegrams were received by Picquart:

THERE IS PROOF THAT THE PETIT BLEU WAS MANUFACTURED BY GEORGES. (Signed) BLANCHE.

HOLD THE DEMI-GOD. EVERYTHING IS DISCOVERED. SITUATION GRAVE. (Signed) SPERANZA.

The first telegram was plain enough to Picquart. The *petit bleu*, of course, along with the handwriting on the *bordereau*, was the evidence thus far to prove that Esterhazy had been the spy. The "Georges" supposedly proved to have manufactured it was himself.

The second telegram must have bewildered him. He knew the "demi-god" as an Army captain who shared the hospitality of the salon at the home of the De Comminges. He knew "Speranza" as the pen name of Oscar Wilde's romantic mother and the pet name of Blanche de Comminges. But he was not aware that months before, when he had first left the Second Bureau, Henry and Du Paty had altered an innocent letter to him from "Speranza" to make it read like a message from a conspirator and then had "intercepted" their own forged letter and placed it in the file they were building up against him.

But, though bewildered by the form the plot was taking, Picquart was not puzzled by the motivation behind it. He was sure that if Lieutenant Colonel Henry had not sent these two telegrams himself, he must at least have copies in his possession. He immediately wrote the Minister of War, enclosing a copy of the letter Esterhazy had sent to him and requesting an investigation into the grave charges contained therein.

In the meantime Henry was busy drawing up reinforcements with a forger's pen and ink. Colonel Sandherr died and Henry took advantage of his former chief's permanent departure to let out the news that he had discovered yet another secret file in Sandherr's office safe. This file, he declared, contained documents—shoals of them—certifying

Dreyfus' guilt. There were no less than seven letters in Dreyfus' own hand to the German Emperor. There was even one answer Dreyfus had received from the Kaiser. It was a few words to the German Ambassador scribbled by the Kaiser on the margin of one of Dreyfus' letters. The general effect of this marginal notation was that "the scoundrel" was getting more and more demanding but was to be kept satisfied.

But seven letters forged in Dreyfus' handwriting plus a bit of marginalia from the Kaiser were not enough for Henry. The farmer's son really poured the manure on. In this same "secret file" of Sandherr's he discovered what he identified as proof that what had been offered at the Dreyfus trial as the original of the famous *bordereau* was in fact only a copy on thin paper traced by Esterhazy at the command of Colonel Sandherr. On the real original, as opposed to its copy, appeared yet another marginal notation from the Kaiser, Henry "discovered." Colonel Sandherr had been informed that the German Ambassador was threatening war if his emperor's involvement in a squalid spy case were made public, and had demanded the return of the *bordereau*. That was why the colonel had ordered Esterhazy to copy it, reproducing only the contents and eliminating the imperial marginalia. The original, Henry declared, had been written on a standard-weight paper rather than the light-weight graph paper Esterhazy had used in copying it.

So Henry thought to undo in advance any handwriting experts Picquart might produce to prove that Esterhazy had written the *bordereau*. He felt perfectly safe. The Germans would deny the whole incident, but what Frenchman would believe them, and anyway how is it possible to prove a negative? How could the Germans prove they had not demanded back from Colonel Sandherr the *bordereau*, and had not received it? If they proved that they did not have it, how could they prove they had not destroyed it? Who could subpoena the Kaiser to testify, and, even if it could be done, how could he prove he had not seen a document and not written a note on its margin? As for Colonel Sandherr, he could deny nothing. He was dead. And as for Major Walsin-Esterhazy, he was jubilant.

The news of Henry's "find" appeared in Rochefort's *L'Intransigeant*. Esterhazy graciously granted interviews to the royalist, Boulangist and anti-Semitic newspapers. The feeling of being safe at last flowed like wine to his head. He returned to the Ministry of War that

forged document, "The Liberator," which had been handed to him by
the lady swathed in veils. The ministry now promptly acknowledged
the receipt of his letter and its enclosure.

The country felt that the Army's prestige was fully restored. The
alliance with Russia, which was France's answer to Germany's alliance
with Austria and Italy, was being implemented by a program of fortifications on the eastern frontier. Tsar Nicholas II had come to visit
France. The President of France, Félix Faure, a rich hide merchant
from Le Havre, was about to repay the visit. Was this the time to rain
contumely on the General Staff?

Premier Jules Méline officially took his place beside General Billot.
He made a public reply to a statement by Senator Scheurer. There was
no such thing as a Dreyfus Affair. The case was closed. A traitor had
been convicted.

The Chamber supported its War Minister and Premier without
question. The right wing did not even have to be counted. But the
Radicals were with them, too. Their cult of the Army as the foundation
of national dynamism and *revanche* was too dearly cherished. The left
wing remained indifferent. The Socialist press repeatedly assured its
readers that a squabble between generals and Dreyfus' rich capitalist
friends did not concern workers. At Kronstadt, the Tsar raised his
glass to Faure and proposed a toast to "two nations, friends and allies."
The Russian autocrat embraced the pompous hide merchant while the
Tsarina, pale, stood aloof. Germany sent an invitation to France to
send some warships to the opening Kiel Canal. The bully boys were
showing one another their fists.

However, in the light of all that had been happening, Mathieu
Dreyfus' tactics had changed. Where previously he had avoided a clash
with the authorities by printing and distributing Bernard Lazare's pamphlet from Brussels, now he deliberately courted arrest. The second
edition of *A Judicial Error* appeared in Paris and was sold openly on
the streets. But no arrests were made. Any number of charges could
have been framed: libel, inciting to riot, conspiracy, falsification; none
was. Apparently it was thought desirable to avoid stirring things up.
Outrage was allowed to speak and even to be heard—in the thin cries
of street vendors muffled by the surge and din of Paris traffic.

The second edition of Lazare's *A Judicial Error* had been enlarged.
The cover was now a reproduction of the *bordereau* as *Le Matin* had

printed it. Experts had been hired by Mathieu to give their opinion whether the *bordereau* was in Dreyfus' handwriting. Their testimony that it was not and their expert reasons for the decision had been added to Lazare's own examination of the Army's case.

The still, small voice of truth fell at last on an ear that heard it. In a moment of idle curiosity, a stock broker named Castro bought the pamphlet. Why he had not recognized the handwriting when it had appeared in *Le Matin* is not known. Perhaps he had not bought the newspaper that day. At any rate he had had business dealings with Count Walsin-Esterhazy. Like most of those who had, his only return for it had been an acrimonious correspondence. Now he knew who had written the *bordereau*.

Castro went to Mathieu Dreyfus with the letters Esterhazy had written him. Mathieu embraced him and on November 15, 1897, three years and one month to the day after Alfred's arrest, formally charged Esterhazy with having written the *bordereau*.

Under the criminal code of France, as in the United States, anyone with knowledge of a crime can bring a charge. The accused must be arrested, the charge investigated.

14

UNDER FRENCH LAW, following the arrest of an accused person, there is a proceeding that bears substantial resemblance to the inquiries conducted by American grand juries. The major difference is that no jury sits, only a *juge d'instruction,* a recommending judge. Like a grand jury, he has the power to dismiss the charge but no power to convict on it, only to recommend the defendant for trial. For the rest it is much the same. The American grand jury investigates the charge made. So does the French recommending judge.

Esterhazy was not arrested when Mathieu Dreyfus made his charge to the Minister of War. No one thought it necessary to explain the reason for this tender regard for the feelings of the accused. However, an investigation could not be avoided. It was entrusted to General de Pellieux, and a civilian aide was assigned to guide him in the law—Judge Paul Jules Joseph Bertulus.

Pellieux was no chair-warmer. He was a general of the line—an Alsatian, blunt and commanding, as quick to lose his temper as to recover it. He summoned Mathieu to present his proofs. Mathieu had none except a facsimile reproduction of the *bordereau*. He suggested that handwriting experts be called.

General Pellieux was under orders to exclude the Dreyfus case as closed and therefore, under law, inadmissible. When he announced this, the investigation was over. But the French General Staff was at the mercy of the whims of an adventurer. Esterhazy had the effrontery to claim that he could not allow his reputation to remain under a cloud. He insisted on a complete vindication. Where the General Staff would have been content to dismiss Mathieu's charge as not proven, now it had to disprove it. The "investigation" continued.

While all this was taking place, a small circle had begun to form around Senator Scheurer-Kestner. The senator was being abused daily in the press, his honorable silence mocked or cited as proof of his duplicity. His political friends had turned hostile. But a new newspaper had made its appearance in October—*L'Aurore*, edited by Georges Clemenceau.

Clemenceau may have been driven out of politics in the general laying-about by the electorate after the Panama Canal scandal, but his pen remained as stilleto-like as ever. Revering the Army as all Radical party members did, he had absolute confidence in a military court and it had never occurred to him to doubt Dreyfus' guilt. But he also respected Scheurer, and went to see him. He was unable to accept Scheurer's unsupported word that Dreyfus was innocent. But there was one important outcome to the meeting. For the first time Clemenceau was struck by the fact that the judicial process against Dreyfus had been in fact illegal. He joined Scheurer in demanding a new trial on that basis. A right-wing newspaper, Paul de Casagnac's *L'Autorité*, took the same position: convict Dreyfus, yes, but convict him legally.

L'Aurore, L'Autorité—they were fringe papers of small circulation. Others of the same kind began to fall into line—*Le Siècle*, edited by Yves Guyot and Joseph Reinach, the *La Fronde* of Mme. Séverine, a spirited woman who had reversed the usual course by going from the extreme right to the left. Then a figure almost as redoubtable as Clemenceau got into the battle.

Emile Zola, France's leading novelist, even then a writer of world renown, had been shocked by the filthy spew of anti-Semitism that accompanied Dreyfus' conviction. He had consulted with Alphonse Daudet, famous for his tales of southern France, and the poet François Coppée. Daudet, whose son Léon was doing just that, believed that writers should not mix personally in the hurly-burly of human affairs. Coppée believed that they should, and then, in the end, emerged on the side which demanded death for Zola.

But that lay in the future. At this time the columns of *Le Figaro* were open to so distinguished an author, and Zola began writing in them. But even so, the circulation of newspapers impressed with the need for a reconsideration of the Dreyfus case remained small. *Le Figaro* was a paper for the well-to-do and the high-brow. *Le Matin* sold more copies on one boulevard of Paris than *Figaro* and the others combined sold in the whole nation.

While the rigidly restricted investigation being conducted by General Pellieux went droning on, the legal blinders making it like the study of a book whose pages could not be opened, everybody daily awaited some revelation from Scheurer. But he could not speak, and neither the Government nor the Army as yet wanted to. They were reluctant to identify their cause openly with Esterhazy.

But they did not mind doing it secretly. The popular press was crammed with revelations of how guilty Dreyfus actually had been. It was stated that he had been convicted on fourteen separate counts. There was a photograph, it was said, snapped in Brussels showing him in the company of the German attaché. Word about the "secret file" Henry had invented after Colonel Sandherr's death leaked out. The file, it was "reliably" disclosed, showed that Dreyfus had sold not merely the trifling inconsequentialities listed in the *bordereau* but information of immense importance. Proof of it could not be publicly produced even now without, in the first place, risking war and, in the second place, divulging the still secret information itself. Thus, those Dreyfusards who were urging the War Minister to produce the proof were urging him to commit a crime against all.

However, *Le Figaro* did a job of reporting. It brought up from the *bordereau* that telling bit: "I am off to the maneuvers." Where Lazare had been able to prove that Dreyfus had known the previous May that he, as a probationer, would not be present at the maneuvers in September, *Le Figaro* was now able to prove that Esterhazy had actually attended them. Esterhazy denied it, but *Le Figaro* published an interview with his fellow officers, who added the piquant information that they had never considered him "a Frenchman." *Le Figaro* also published side by side reproductions of the *bordereau* and of Esterhazy's handwriting so that its readers might judge for themselves. The mass-circulation papers retorted with two voices at the same time: one group said the handwritings were not at all identical; the remainder said they had been "reliably" informed that Dreyfus had imitated Ester-hazy's handwriting.

Finally Scheurer felt impelled to make a public declaration, but his speech in the Senate was an anticlimax. The honorable old gentleman from Alsace spoke with sealed lips. When he sat down without offer-ing any solid evidence for his belief that Dreyfus had been convicted unjustly, only one senator dared stand up for him—Ludovic Trarieux, a former Minister of Justice. And Trarieux did not speak for Dreyfus. He merely pointed out in a few words what in the past everyone had known, that Scheurer was a man of unassailable integrity. In the com-ing year, 1898, a general election was to be held and the other legis-lators knew well how the country was reacting to anyone who sought to impeach the Army. They kept away from Scheurer.

But the climate was worsening. It was no longer enough merely not to impeach the General Staff. One had to beat one's breast in favor of it. The Minister of Labor paused in the Chamber for a moment's chat with Scheurer. So great was the muttering that he hastened to take the floor to announce that he had only asked his colleague for the address of a pastry shop. President Faure had had the bad luck to receive Scheurer as a visitor on some legislative matter. He asked Scheurer to deny that they had spoken about the Dreyfus case. General Billot issued a statement that the latest events had not shaken the Government's view that the case was closed. The statement seemed too temperate to the press. A storm of abuse was unleashed. The War Minister was ac-cused of allowing his personal debts to be paid by Scheurer and Joseph Reinach. He was "exposed" as having stolen 100,000 francs from the Army's secret fund, and was declared to be selling out the Army of which he was guardian to the "Jewish syndicate." *La Libre Parole* published a sensational article accusing the President and the Cabinet of being Dreyfus' accomplices in espionage.

The Catholic youth held a protest meeting and adopted resolutions: no one should deprive France's soldiers of the confidence they had in their leaders; Jews should be excluded from the Army and from the civil service. Posters went up all over Paris with a message from the Royal Pretender, Philippe d'Orléans. Conscious of his duty, his rights and the virtue of monarchical institutions, the unemployed heir to a nonexistent throne assured the nation of his capacity to defend the honor of French soldiers. Royalist-minded students blocked traffic for a riotous demonstration in front of *Le Figaro*.

Day by day the press rehashed "proofs" of a world-wide conspiracy whose aim was to destroy the Army and thus France. One of the greatest orators of the day, the Catholic Albert de Mun, took the floor of the Chamber of Deputies to interpolate into the proceedings a few remarks:

We must reveal the facts about the mysterious and occult power, strong enough to throw suspicion on the commanders of the Army, on the men who have to lead the Army and direct the war when the hour strikes. Let us discover whether that power is great enough to subvert the entire country. . . . You wonder perhaps whether my interpolation is not inspired by party considerations. No, we know no government and opposition. There are here today only . . . Frenchmen anxious to preserve that common domain of our unflagging hopes—the honor of the Army.

The Chamber rushed through a resolution paying homage to the Army and excoriating those who instigated odious campaigns to disturb public confidence.

It seemed almost as if Esterhazy, who had wanted only a little corner on the General Staff from which he might empty wastebaskets and peer into files, was going to end up as Minister of War, firing the generals who had refused to hire him. The press, including not only the anti-Semitic sheets but *Le Matin* and *Le Petit Journal*, discovered that the "Jewish syndicate" it had invented had its headquarters in Berlin, that it had spent 6,000,000 francs already in forging documents and corrupting prominent Frenchmen, and that for two years now the French Government had been in possession of the names of those acting as the syndicate's chiefs.

In the midst of this, Rochefort in his office at *L'Intransigeant* entertained an important visitor—Major Pauffin de Saint-Morel, chief of General de Boisdeffre's personal staff. Rochefort, who had been dubbed by Clemenceau "a subversive in retirement," emerged with a colossal bang. He did not reveal his informant's name (that was disclosed by a rival newspaper) but he revealed the "information":

The "syndicate" had been collecting samples of the handwriting of French officers for two years. The purpose: to find one that resembled Dreyfus'. Finally they had settled on Esterhazy's. But their long effort was all in vain. The evidence vindicating Esterhazy was impregnable and was so comprehensive that it revealed the major as the victim of a criminal conspiracy and exposed Dreyfus in all his treachery. Won't the "syndicate" be surprised when it learns of this clinching piece of evidence?

So *L'Intransigeant's* report of Major Pauffin de Saint-Morel's disclosures went. The press contrasted this revelation of facts too long withheld with the "timid" and "hesitant" conduct of the War Minister. General Billot called General de Boisdeffre on the carpet. Boisdeffre protested he had had nothing to do with it. Billot ordered his enterprising Chief of Staff put under house arrest for thirty days.

Esterhazy was spending most of his time in newspaper offices, handing out juicy bits of information about the "syndicate" from what seemed to be a bottomless basket. He painted his own portrait in glowing colors. He was, it seemed, a superbly courageous man of indomitable will power, fanatically jealous of his honor. His every word was enshrined in print for posterity and debated avidly. When he said he was going to kill Mathieu Dreyfus like a dog, *La Libre Parole* felt that the idea was sound but that whipping was more appropriate.

It did not bother Esterhazy in the least to contradict himself. Nor did it seem to bother anyone else. He came dangerously close to making truly damaging admissions. An experienced liar, he knew the value of half-truths. He said that his relatives in Austria were intimate friends of the German military attachés and that he himself had visited the German Embassy, but in full military attire. He even let out the name of Picquart, asserting that Senator Scheurer's accusations rested on forgeries given him by the lieutenant colonel. He described the visit of the heavily veiled "lady" and the delivery of the document that identified Dreyfus as a spy. He had taken it to London for safekeeping at first, he said, then later he had turned it over to the War Minister.

Paris was at Esterhazy's feet. Wrote *L'Echo de Paris*: "To treat Jesus as Judas is not only atrocious, it is also self-defeating."

The stories printed about the *bordereau* were magnificent. The police, it was said, had stolen it from the German Embassy and, when discovered, had dived into the Seine to get away. Esterhazy himself, it was said, had seized the *bordereau* during a fire at the embassy. He had been assisted by police disguised as firemen.

Oscar Wilde, out of jail then and an exile in Paris, seemed to relish the spectacle of a rogue raised to the status of absolute ruler of the public mind in the Country of Enlightenment. He sought the acquaintance of Esterhazy and fed him odd bits of information from the mixed society he frequented.

Esterhazy was having so much fun that he even visited *Le Figaro* daily. The paper was making new discoveries about him all the time. For example, it found out that his story about having gone to London to place in safekeeping that document he called his "Liberator" had nothing more behind it than a Paris mailing service that called itself "Alibi" and did its chief trade among errant husbands who wanted their letters mailed from cities where they had not been and did not intend to go. Esterhazy in fact had had some letters he had written mailed from London by "Alibi" while he himself was in Paris, but that was the only fact involved in his romantic story about his secret flight to London to hide all that stood between him and dishonor. The major turned not a hair over any of these disclosures. He read them in the editorial offices of *Le Figaro* surrounded by the journalists, and laughed, and everybody laughed with him. For he was in a state of relief so great he was in danger of getting unhinged. He lived as in a dream on top of an opium cloud, and wallowed in it and shivered in it—a man who, if not quite psychopathic, was at least giving a good imitation.

The major had accumulated a long backlog of villainies, both major and minor, through life and it was inevitable, now that he was riding the crest of the wave, that some soul he had embittered would reach out from the past to try to pull him down. Such a one was the widow of a Colonel de Boulancy, who had her own private reasons for hating every sight and sound of Esterhazy's name. Esterhazy was not one of those lovers who keep enough control over themselves never to write love letters, and Mme. de Boulancy had a quiverful of them, containing passages of a sort that went right to the point of this moment in his career. ". . . These people [the French] aren't worth the cartridges it would take to kill them . . . and if one night I should be told that I, serving as a Captain of Uhlans, should die massacring the French I should be entirely happy. . . ."

That was one. Another read: "I would not harm a puppy, but I would kill 100,000 Frenchmen with pleasure. . . . What sorry figures they would cut in the red sun of battle if Paris were taken by storm and left at the mercy of 100,000 drunken and plundering soldiers. This is the feast I dream of."

These orgies of hate and spite in which Esterhazy had vented what he really felt about his life as a liar, a thief, a blackmailer and a traitor, and all the humiliations and terrors it had brought him, were taken by Mme. de Boulancy to her attorney. She instructed the lawyer to use them in the way that would damage Esterhazy the most. He turned them over to Senator Scheurer to hand to General Pellieux, whose hearings into Mathieu Dreyfus' charges were still dragging on.

Esterhazy got wind of it from the General Staff. His nerves unraveled. He was sure the letters would send him to the guillotine. He demanded help. The letters must be suppressed, he insisted. If they weren't, he would ruin the General Staff. When I go to the guillotine, he warned, I will not go alone. But the letters could not be suppressed. Henry told Esterhazy to take it easy and just say that the letters were forgeries. But Esterhazy was in no condition to take anything easy. He ran to his suitcase and packed for a flight from France. This had always been his ace in the hole—to get out of the country, and then, when safe from prosecution, sell the whole story. But before he could play his ace, Henry coolly trumped it. The frontier guards were alerted and ordered to take Esterhazy into custody should he attempt to cross a border. Esterhazy remained in Paris and waited with a blizzard in his blood for France to turn on him with the same venom he had felt for it.

But Henry had estimated the temper of the times better than Esterhazy. The letters were duly published in *Le Figaro,* but the darling of France could do no wrong. "Atrocious forgeries," the mass-circulation newspapers proclaimed. "The Major is so infuriated he is ready to whip his enemies to death," one stated. "His lawyer has called on General Pellieux, who will soon confirm the letters are forgeries." And *Le Petit Journal* announced it would not publish the letters; it did not care to insult the intelligence of its 3,000,000 readers.

In *L'Aurore,* Clemenceau shrewdly put a blunt question: Who was the man on the General Staff protecting what Clemenceau called "the Uhlan captain"? *Le Figaro* took up the question. It promised to answer it by publishing the name.

But the name of Lieutenant Colonel Hubert Henry was not published. Suddenly *Le Figaro,* far from answering the question, even stopped asking it. The General Staff had cracked an obscure but painful whip somewhere. By December 1897, Zola no longer found a place in *Le Figaro*'s columns. The newspaper had turned anti-Dreyfus.

Henry seemed to play the French press as if it were his pipe organ, now muffling one, now pumping hot air to another. There were the seven letters that Henry had forged, making them appear to have been written by Dreyfus to the Kaiser. Rochefort in *L'Intransigeant* printed everything about them except that Henry was their author. Dreyfus, it seems, had asked for the boon of serving in the German Army. The Kaiser had replied that the greatest service Dreyfus could perform for Germany was to remain where he was. The originals of the letters, Rochefort wrote, had had to be returned to Ambassador Münster under threat of war. But they had been photographed before being returned.

General Pellieux's investigation began to pick up speed. Poor Mme. de Boulancy. The high-brow *Revue des Deux Mondes* observed that there were frontiers which one in all propriety could not cross. Pellieux took her to task for having smeared the Army.

But Esterhazy had had a fright and did not want another. He was now so public a figure that Du Paty no longer dared risk meeting him, even in veils. Messages between Esterhazy and the General Staff were carried back and forth from the home of Esterhazy's mistress, Marguerite Pays, by the count's nephew, Christian, who was enjoying the adventure of a young lifetime. Du Paty was sifting through the roster of handwriting experts to come up with some who would clear Esterhazy once and for all of having written the *bordereau*. The argument he used was born of desperation: if Esterhazy had written it, he would naturally have disguised his handwriting. But since the *bordereau* was in Esterhazy's ordinary hand to the dot over each *i*, was it not obvious that a forger had written it? Finally Du Paty found three experts who were persuaded by his argument. But Esterhazy wanted them to identify his Uhlan letters as forgeries, too. It took some doing, but finally even that was managed—at least partially. The experts were willing to say that the letters to Mme. de Boulancy gave indications of being forgeries. But they had no reservations about the *bordereau* being one.

Henry apparently had decided that it was unnecessary at this time to use his big gun on the *bordereau*—the one that would identify it as not the original at all but only a copy made by Esterhazy at the late Colonel Sandherr's request when Ambassador Münster had demanded the return of the original because of the Emperor's note on the margin.

Why fire a cannon when a popgun would do as well? Henry let the three handwriting experts go ahead and swear their addled heads off.

Under ordinary procedure in France, when a charge is made and the investigation produces insufficient evidence to support it, that ends it. No further proceedings are held. That was the course the *juge d'instruction* recommended. But the General Staff was well aware that the legalistic hairsplitting by which it had separated the Dreyfus case from the investigation into Esterhazy had aroused more suspicion than anything else it had done. So, against the recommendations of the judge, the Military Commander ordered a trial for Esterhazy. The official announcement emphasized that Esterhazy was not being tried. His innocence had already been established. The trial, it was declared, was being held only in justice to Esterhazy. It would be the accusation rather than the accused who would be tried, the purpose, declared officially in advance, being to make Esterhazy's innocence as widely known as the suspicion of him had been.

Mme. Séverine reminded the readers of *La Fronde* how fallible handwriting experts can be. She cited a case in which they had identified a document as not having been written by a defendant although some footnotes on it, they swore to a man, had been. It turned out that the footnotes in question had been written by the presiding judge of the court.

But the tiny band of writers who had rallied to Dreyfus were fighting a lost cause. The trial was not a search for truth but an official endorsement of the virtues the overwhelming majority had already seen in Esterhazy. Since the press had already expended whole forests of pulp in extolling those virtues, chief journalistic attention centered on the presence as a witness of Lieutenant Colonel Marie-Georges Picquart.

General Pellieux had summoned Picquart from Africa in the course of his investigation into the charge against Esterhazy. While en route, the young officer's home had been searched for evidence against him. He himself had been placed under orders to talk to no one. Witnesses had sworn to the customary half-truths and outright lies. He had opened the file Colonel Sandherr had placed in his safe and had marked "secret," but he had done it at General de Boisdeffre's suggestion. They swore he had done it "in the absence" of the then Major Henry and had shown some of the secret documents contained therein to an unauthorized person—his attorney, Leblois. They characterized the *petit bleu*—which identified Esterhazy as having contact with the German Embassy—as a forgery, but did not yet name Picquart as the forger.

Now, while waiting for the trial to begin, Picquart, isolated by the enmity of his fellow officers, stood alone at a window of the courtroom—a proud figure, handsome and poised. Only Senator Scheurer greeted him, and Mathieu and Lucie Dreyfus, and Demange, who had been retained to represent Mathieu, and a young lawyer named Fernand Labori who had made a reputation for his eloquent defense of an anarchist and had been retained to represent Lucie. They chatted briefly. Picquart said he expected to be deported to a prison island for his testimony, but was going to give it anyway.

Clemenceau stepped up from the press table to draw Picquart aside and whisper a reminder of the lieutenant colonel's promise not to carry the secret of Dreyfus' innocence to the grave. He suggested to Picquart that he solemnly break his sword and resign from the Army. That, he pointed out, would regain for him his freedom as a citizen whose conscience was not in the keeping of the Army.

But Picquart saw no necessity for that. The Army, he felt, was the faithful guardian of his conscience. He distinguished sharply between the uniform and the man who wore it. A criminal could not truly wear the uniform. He could only soil it. It was his duty, Picquart felt, to protect his beloved Army from being debased, even by his superior officers.

The press printed in advance that Esterhazy would be taken into custody for one day to conform to regulations, that preliminary proceedings would be open to the public but that the testimony of Picquart and the other military personnel would be taken behind closed doors to guard "military secrets," and that at the end of the trial Picquart would be arrested. So it all came to pass. Arguments were heard and the judges decided to exclude the attorneys for Mathieu and Mme. Dreyfus from active participation in the trial. Then the public, which had been lining up for seats since five o'clock in the morning, buzzed and tensed expectantly. Esterhazy had been called to the stand.

It was the same building in which Dreyfus had been tried—the old Military Court in the Rue Cherche-Midi, hard by the military prison. A gloomy light came into the bleak room through the tiny windows cut into the thick stone walls. The judges of the court were all officers. They sat at a table covered with green baize. The only decoration in the room was a large painting of Christ which had been hung in 1873 when Marshal Bazaine was tried for his treason at Metz.

Esterhazy made a calm and reserved witness. He was very chivalrous about the veiled lady who had delivered "The Liberator." He did not know who she was and regarded it as a matter of honor to refrain from inquiring into the source of the document she had given him. A judge wondered why the police had been unable to discover any clue to it all, not even to the carriage in which she had traveled. Esterhazy burst out fervently: "All I have said is as true as that I am innocent." It is perhaps the one honest statement he made.

Then it was Mathieu Dreyfus' turn. Esterhazy's attorney criticized him sharply for circulating a reproduction of the *bordereau.* "You may defend your brother before the court but nowhere else," the lawyer told him. "I shall defend my brother everywhere," replied Mathieu, and the throng in the courtroom hissed its hate so loudly that it had to be called to order.

Senator Scheurer testified quietly and without equivocation that he was convinced Dreyfus could not have written the *bordereau.* Then came a man who opened a door, briefly, on the surging hell in which Esterhazy, for all his public air of confidence, had been living. The witness was the landlord of the building in which Esterhazy's mistress resided. The lease on Marguerite Pays's apartment was in Esterhazy's name. Mlle. Pays seemed to have become a remarkably levelheaded woman, one of those who, however furious the breaking storm, nevertheless manages to think of all the little precautions that must be taken. The storm that had broken over her little bower was the charge Mathieu Dreyfus had made that Esterhazy was a traitor. On the same day the charge was made she had gone to see the landlord, and told him that Esterhazy was going to commit suicide. She wondered what her position under the lease would be.

The door on that hell was quickly shut. The presiding judge observed that the witness seemed to feel little good will toward Esterhazy. The landlord replied dryly that he had seen the major only twice in his life, and had no reason for good or ill will, but did have a reason—his conscience—for telling the truth.

The bulk of the testimony was taken behind closed doors. At the end, the public prosecutor formally dropped the charge against Esterhazy. Nevertheless, Esterhazy's attorney summed up in a speech which lasted five hours. The court deliberated for three minutes.

Then the courtroom doors were thrown open and the public was allowed to come in. The presiding judge read the verdict of the court. It was unanimous for acquittal.

A pandemonium of joy broke out. It was as if France had won a great victory on the battlefield. Officers, newspapermen, women and men, old and young, rushed up to Esterhazy to press him to their bosoms with tears in their eyes. More than a thousand people, unable to crowd into the courtroom, jammed the exit. When Esterhazy at last began to make his way through them, a voice shouted, "Hats off to the martyr! Death to the Jews!"

Hats were removed and the crowd cheered. That night triumphant processions marched through the streets of Paris chanting, Long live Esterhazy! Long live the Army! The next morning a gendarme entered Picquart's apartment and arrested him. He was taken to the fortress of Mont Valérien.

And on Devil's Island, five thousand miles away, Dreyfus' guard was increased to thirteen men and a warden. A tower was built to watch over the sea. A large gun was mounted on its top. Dreyfus had no idea why. All mail privileges had been denied him. For three months no letter had reached him and the guards had obeyed their orders against speaking to him.

15

THE ACQUITTAL of Esterhazy and the arrest of Picquart made black headlines around the world. France is no more, Europe mourned from Lisbon to Salonica and Moscow. It was now, when France in her extremity had fled from her senses, that people in every part of the globe realized how much this one country had come to mean to them. Clemenceau, the Tiger, wept as he read the foreign papers. He wrote:

France discovered certain human rights of justice and liberty, which were to secure for modern societies a development towards a happiness unknown before. This was mirrored in the beautiful words: Every man has two countries, his own and France. For a country is made up not only of its soil, its rocks, its waters, forests and fields . . . but also of the ideas that knit the souls together, inform the actions of the people, determine their influence on the civilized world. Happy or unhappy, free or oppressed, victorious or vanquished, France in modern times has made the most magnificent effort to achieve justice for the whole of mankind. . . . When it will be perceived that right and justice in our country are words deprived of significance, that brute force has become the only arbiter, when once more we shall have become persecutors of races and religions . . . when the watchwords of tolerance and liberty will have yielded their place to the clamors of hatred . . . then, we may still have the same fields, the same rivers, the same mountains. We may still sit on French soil. But we shall have ceased to be the France our fathers desired to create and left to us to make into a reality.

But Clemenceau's inspired invocation of the spirit of France was lost even on his own party, the Radicals. They were traditional worshipers of the Army, dedicated to the idea of *revanche,* and the Army in their eyes could do no wrong. Even the mildly independent line taken by their leader Godefroy Cavaignac, a man of eminent republican ancestry, made them uneasy. Cavaignac wanted all existing proofs of Dreyfus' guilt brought into the open, no matter what the consequences. He was firmly convinced that Dreyfus was a traitor and wished to see even the shadow of a doubt on this point dispelled. But his party appeared to think this reflected on Esterhazy. If there were a shadow of a doubt about Dreyfus' guilt, the shadow must fall on Esterhazy—and that was political suicide.

The governing Moderates were keen to disown every link between their own republicanism and the Great Revolution. Their sole concern was that the Catholic, nationalist and anti-Semitic press might not find them fervent enough in their assurances that no such thing as a Dreyfus Affair existed, or that Dreyfus had not only received a just sentence but also one that conformed to the requirements of due process of law. The deputies in the Chamber vied with one another when it came to applauding a speaker who dwelt on the sacred duty of the Chamber to protect the Army.

For the Socialists the fuss about Dreyfus continued to be a family quarrel of the bourgeoisie. If what had happened to Dreyfus had happened instead to a worker, who would care? they asked. Scheurer, or Trarieux, or Joseph Reinach? They had all voted for the so-called "wicked laws," ostensibly passed against anarchists but applicable against all forms of political revolt. The Dreyfus Affair was between two rival factions of the same class. It did not concern the workers.

The spirit of the Great Revolution, its message of equality and justice for all, was on the wane even among its former protagonists. Enthusiasm had faded with Gambetta. In the words of a contemporary of his, "There began to be discernible a distaste for life, an incapacity for effort, a renunciation of ideals. It was a period of fatigue and decline, of mysticism and sensuality in literature and the arts. The heroic ages were past, and the country had lost faith in its destiny."

Renunciation came from two eminent thinkers of the time: Hippolyte Taine and Ernest Renan. They were by no means descendants of the *ancien régime*. Both stemmed from the *petite bourgeoisie*. Yet both despaired of the equalitarianism inherited from the Revolution. In Taine's view, it destroyed the family, the Church and social distinctions for the sake of vague abstractions. Renan condemned popular elections. Society, he taught, is strong only if it recognizes natural superiorities. The victory of the Prussians over France was that of an *ancien régime*, aristocratic and hierarchic, over equalitarian democracy. Both Taine and Renan maintained that it was futile to admire the principles of the Revolution or approve of some of its results while rejecting its crimes and excesses. For it was the principles themselves that had produced the crimes and excesses.

That the agnostic Taine and the skeptic Renan should become converted to the pre-revolutionary traditions and accept the Church, the throne and the aristocracy as the sum total of their lives had a tremendous impact on the intellectual life of their day.

Maurice Barrès, novelist and Boulangist deputy, developed the astonishing creed of the new nationalism. He initiated the cult of the graveyards. The French, he wrote, have accepted as their guide the pillar of light in the sky, forgetting that the real light is under their feet and in the tombs of their ancestors. Their only salvation is to prostrate themselves before their dead and their soil, and, in the spirit of penitents, to take these unto themselves. Even atheists ought to be Catholics, added Jules Soury, another theoretician of this school, not for the sake of the Catholic faith, but in order to live like their ancestors who had been believers and to meditate on the same maxims of life.

In the eyes of the nationalists, the Protestants stood outside of the nation. To be faithful to France in the mere world of the intellect was not enough. The Protestants, unlike the Catholics, could never be part of that physico-mental continuum which mystically encompassed the nation.

To the Church militant the time seemed to have arrived. The nation, as if by a miracle, was ready to come back under the wings of the Church. The Pope had advised the French Church to recognize the lay Republic as having been permitted by God. This was construed as constituting a misreading of French history. The throne might never be restored, but it was believed that France could be turned into a Catholic state. A hundred years of history were being reversed. The nation was returning as an errant sheep to the fold.

The new, reactionary nationalism fed on the frustrated greatness of a people torn between the fear of a new invasion and the passion to prevail over such an invasion—a passion expressed in *revanche*. The Army was their shield in all trials.

And yet, in the case of one Jewish captain found to have been a traitor by seven of his fellow officers, a stubborn clique insisted on incriminating the military court and the General Staff rather than the convicted Jew. The papers which the public read, the men whose opinions it respected, asserted that the clique consisted of Protestants and a few intellectuals, misguidedly invoking the principles of the Revolution. The public also read and heard that in the Protestant countries and in countries where the influence of Jews and Free Masons prevailed, public opinion unanimously demanded that France destroy her Army rather than keep a Jew deported—all in the name of the principles of the Revolution. The fear grew that the nation might become the victim of her own principles. Would it not be better to sacrifice the principles and settle for survival? A consistent, purposeful and determined coalition of institutions, church and royalist, right and center, vested with the prestige of a long tradition and endowed with all the means for shaping public opinion, put the choice on this basis: the Revolution's Rights of Man must die, or France must.

To the majority of the people, the Revolution still meant the end of the feudal system of privileges, the advent of national unity and the triumph of the sovereignty of the people. And the majority of the people kept voting for the republican parties, solidly and increasingly. But on the unique issue of the Army, where the security of the nation, so they believed, was at stake, they were ready to follow the Church militant, the authoritarians, the anti-Semites and the royalists, and even sacrifice the Republic itself rather than face the fact that the Army which they regarded as their only salvation was untrustworthy.

The *Civilità Cattolica*, official organ of the Jesuit Order in Rome, gave the signal for the great offensive:

The emancipation of the Jews was the corollary of the so-called principles of 1789, the yoke of which weighs on the neck of all Frenchmen. These French Jews grew in number by the immigration of German Jews, and now they total 130,000.

They got control of Masonry (Dreyfus is a Jew and a Mason as well), and Masonry is notoriously the master of the French State. This is the way they keep the Republic in their hands; it is more Hebrew than French. . . . Of 260 billions that constitute the wealth of France, the Jews possess 80. They direct home as well as foreign policy. The abandonment of Egypt [a reference to the concession to the British of De Lesseps' Suez Canal] was the work of these Jews who, at the behest of the government of London, corrupted the press, the government and parliament.

The condemnation of Dreyfus was a terrible blow for Israel. It branded the forehead of all Jews in the world, most of all in their French colonies. This mark they swore to wipe off. But how? With their usual subtlety, they invented a case of miscarriage of justice. The plot was hatched in Basle at the Zionist Congress, held under the pretext of discussing the deliverance of Jerusalem. The Protestants joined in common cause with the Jews and established a Syndicate. The money came mostly from Germany. *Pecuniae obediunt omnia* is the principle of the Jews. They bought consciences and those newspapers which were for sale in every country of Europe. . . .

The Jew was created by God to serve as a spy wherever treason is in preparation. Moreover, ethnic solidarity ties the Jews to each other and prevents them from becoming loyal citizens in spite of naturalization. The Dreyfus affair reveals this fact clearly. Thus anti-Semitism will become, as it should, economic, political, and national. The Jews allege an error of justice. The true error was, however, that of the *Constituante* which accorded them French nationality. That law has to be revoked. . . . Not only in France, but in Germany, Austria, and Italy as well, the Jews are to be excluded from the nation.

Then the old harmony will be re-established and the peoples will again find their lost happiness.

Cardinal Rampolla, Secretary of State of the Vatican, told a diplomat: "The attempt at a revision of the Dreyfus sentence is a Jewish-Protestant machination. The duty of every good Catholic is to stand by Premier Méline in his anti-Semitic endeavors."

Albert de Mun, the Catholic leader, sounded the clarion call in a speech at the French Academy. He proclaimed the bankruptcy of the French Revolution and hailed the return of the Middle Ages. "By an irresistible evolution the ancient ideas reappear to fulfill new tasks. Our flag unfurls proudly; it shows the cross and the glorious device: *In hoc signo vinces.* Our aim is clear: this is a new revolution that puts the rights of God against those of men."

La Croix and other newspapers of the Assumptionist Order followed suit, heralding the crusade against the enemies of the Army and of Christ. And parish priests of five thousand churches throughout France echoed the battle cry.

The aristocracy descended into the political arena. People who had kept aloof in their castles or secluded in their salons responded to the call. Their young joined the mobs on the streets. Adults went to mass meetings, mixing freely with anarchists, Drumont's anti-Semites and Déroulède's patriots, in a combined effort to destroy the bourgeois republic.

Esterhazy's acquittal created a morally upside-down world. In the words of the young journalist Paul Brulat, "the fraudulent glorified fraud, and the impostors erected a monument to imposture." The public sang hosannas to a criminal whose crime was being expiated by another man.

Such moral enormity could be sustained only in an atmosphere of terror and intolerance. It was the popular press that silenced dissent. It went after people, demolished their position in life, material or moral, and exposed them to contempt. In their fear of the invented "syndicate" the people had created a real power of destruction. A teacher in Paris told Clemenceau: Do not expect high-school teachers to come out for you. If I gave you my name, I would soon find myself retired, to rot somewhere in the depths of Brittany.

The terror did not come from the Government. The Government itself was terrorized. So were the deputies in the Chamber. The nationalists and clericals by themselves could not have silenced dissent by sheer threat. It was the people. The bulk of the nation had identified itself with the Army. Yet even with the Army secure from Dreyfus, the feeling of insecurity continued. The offensive continued—but where was the enemy? And where was the opposition? When Paul Brulat was asked by a foreigner, "Where are the honest men in this country?" he replied, "They are frightened." No tyranny weighs heavier on society, Brulat added, than the tyranny of public opinion. It crucified Jesus, burned John Hus and Savonarola at the stake, it

persecuted Galileo, delivered apostles and martyrs to the hangman.
Voltaire knew it when he wrote:

> *Oui, le public, ce fantôme inconstant*
> *Monstre à cent voix, cerbère dévorant,*
> *Qui flatte et mord, qui dresse par sottise*
> *Des statues et par dégoût les brise . . .*

Courageous men defying tyrants were never wanting in history,
Clemenceau said, but it required true heroism to defy the tyranny of
public opinion. Who risks being rejected by his own community and
being expatriated in his own country?

No such men could be found in the Government. "Egotism and
fear," wrote Anatole France, "were in the chair at cabinet meetings.
A vague suspicion of an injustice began to spread. But it seemed to be
sustained and defended by both public and secret forces so strong that
even the firmest of men hesitated. Those whose duty it was to speak
out kept silent. The best, who were not afraid for their own person,
were fearful of exposing their party to terrifying dangers."

Contemporaries estimated the number of dissenters at about one
per cent of the population, which was the proportion of Protestants in
the country. This did not mean, however, that dissenters and Protestants were the same individuals. The hostile nationalist propaganda
against Protestantism in France may, in fact, have kept French Protestants from going along with the multitude, as it kept the Jews from
doing so. But not all Protestants were Dreyfusards either. André Gide,
who came from an eminently Protestant family, once told the story of
how he had yielded to Léon Blum when the latter, as a young Dreyfusard, requested his signature to a protest. "I could not refuse to
sign," he said, "and later developments proved that I did right. But
how I was blamed by the family!"

The Jews constituted only a fraction of one per cent of France's
population and they kept away from the Dreyfusards. They wished to
remain unnoticed, afraid of giving any sign of race solidarity with a
traitor. They blamed the revisionists for a campaign that stirred up
even fiercer anti-Jewish feelings than Dreyfus' conviction had.

But dissenters were found in all walks of life. The papers of the
revisionists sold altogether about a hundred thousand copies daily.
However, they hardly reached the small towns. Arriving with the

other papers by the Paris train, they were left lying in a bunch, untouched and undelivered. It was not advisable to read them, anyway. A reader would have been shunned like a leper by the man in the street.

Yet there were a few men of indomitable courage and sense of responsibility who continued to brave the storm of indignity, threat and calumny. With Esterhazy acquitted, they expected to be isolated from their compatriots. As men who refused to share the prejudices of the community, they would be exiles even if permitted to remain in France.

Some, like Bernard Lazare, believed in Dreyfus' innocence. So did Senator Scheurer. The old man had been able to find no peace once the first doubt of Dreyfus' guilt had assailed him. It kept gnawing at him until it was resolved, and what resolved it was a definite conclusion that Dreyfus was innocent. Others, like Clemenceau, believed in Dreyfus' guilt but were alarmed by the dangers to every citizen if an unlawful conviction by a military court should be allowed to stand. Not until Esterhazy stood revealed as the obvious writer of the *bordereau* did Clemenceau reinforce his position with the knowledge that Dreyfus was innocent. Clemenceau wrote some eight hundred articles in the course of the Dreyfus Affair. Day by day he hammered out his arguments in *L'Aurore* with clarity, force and inexorable logic. There was no such thing for him as condemning a man unlawfully but justly; lawlessness was itself a form of injustice. The law alone was the safeguard of justice. He was merciless toward the opponents of revision who maintained that they protected the prestige of the Army by involving reasons of state:

Reasons of state—have they force against the law? If so, stop talking of law. Arbitrary power would take the place of law. Today it hits Dreyfus, tomorrow it will hit others, and the reasons of state, without reason, will, in the name of public interest, swoop down on the ranks of the opposition with a sneer, and the crowd will look on in stupefied terror. Reasons of state, once introduced into the régime, cannot again be discarded. They provide the answer to everything. They do not admit of shades, nor will they suffer distinctions. If they are of use against Dreyfus, they will be found effective against anyone. . . . The first gesture of the Great Revolution, in the dawn of the new times, was to destroy the great fortress of the reasons of state: the Bastille.

Jean Jaurès, whose humanism had drawn him into the Socialist ranks, had been convinced by Scheurer-Kestner of Dreyfus' innocence.

He alone in the Chamber raised his voice for Dreyfus after Esterhazy's acquittal. His position was doubly difficult. The majority of his own party held slogans such as "right" or "justice" to be nothing but words in the bourgeois vocabulary, traps set for simpletons to enlist them into one of the bourgeois factions.

Clemenceau warned Jaurès' opponents in the Socialist party: "The rights of the least among men cannot be violated without endangering the interests of all oppressed. The cause of the Rights of Man is indivisible. One can be only either for or against it." But he also found words of explanation for the Socialists' reluctance: "Themselves the victims of so much injustice," he wrote, "why should they hasten to take up arms against yet another act of arbitrary power, this time one that visited the camp of their masters, felling one of them? They are dreamers. Nothing less than the total eradication of all injustice will do: a dangerous illusion that might well lead into a total catastrophe."

Jaurès tried to explain why Socialists should take sides in this bourgeois affair. "Whether Dreyfus or the Uhlan [Esterhazy] is guilty, or innocent, I don't care," he wrote. "But what I am concerned about is the tyranny of the sword. The military courts should not be permitted to seize without legal safeguards any citizen under whatsoever pretext, be it Jewry, the flag, the nation, or what you will. This is the question at stake, the real and only one." True to his humanism, he tried to evoke sympathy for Dreyfus, who by his fate had ceased to be a member of the ruling class and had become a symbol of human suffering.

In the vanguard of the early Dreyfusards was Emile Duclaux, director of the Pasteur Institute. A great scholar, he was resigned to human folly, yet his nights were sleepless until he raised his voice in protest. He held out little faith in the victory of justice. Yet he followed Voltaire's words to fight for it as resolutely as if he believed that it might yet prevail in human affairs.

Another among the early Dreyfusards was Anatole France, whose irony only veiled his love and pity for man in his weakness. He was a bitter critic of the Third Republic, but he would never part company with the cause of reason and would never support fanaticism. Yet another was Ludovic Trarieux, the senator and former Minister of Justice, who lent the full weight of his authority to the cause.

This handful of intellectuals, with the aged Senator Scheurer-Kestner in the lead, gave voice to dissent. They were an example to honest and courageous men, who began slowly, one by one, to line up with them.

Esterhazy's triumph had come as a shattering blow even to the most optimistic among them. They began now to share Duclaux's somber outlook. It seemed as if it would take years before a different constellation of political factors would bring about a situation in which the rehabilitation of Dreyfus could be taken up again. The battle, if not the war, appeared lost.

Then came January 13, 1898. On January 13, 1898, the leaden atmosphere of despondency was dispelled as if by the elemental force of a hurricane. Zola's *J'Accuse!* appeared. It was a challenge to France and to every Frenchman to hold by cherished ideals and stand up and be counted. Zola's article appeared in Clemenceau's paper, *L'Aurore*. It was in fact an open letter addressed to the President of the Republic, Felix Faure.

"It was freedom of thought and the freedom to express it," said Clemenceau later, "that saved France from mortal peril."

Zola was then at the peak of his world fame. His novels were best sellers in almost all civilized languages. He was the most controversial author of his time both at home and abroad. Zola claimed he applied the scientific method in literature and the arts to discover the realities of the human condition. Thirsting only for truth, he delved into the brute facts to isolate the forces that determine human fate; he collected in minute detail observations of places, people and their ways of life, and these he unified into his vision of the world.

The mass popularity of his books undoubtedly was due in part to his unprecedented disregard of the taboo of conventional decency, both in scenery and language. Many readers, absorbing his books in rapid succession, were on the lookout for pornography; many others sensed the purity of his intention and were elevated by its masterful achievement.

Emile Zola's father had come from Italy. He was a successful engineer in southern France, where he settled and where his son was born. Emile Zola was in Italy at the time of Dreyfus' conviction. When he returned he read incredulously of the anti-Semitic excesses that had followed the conviction. His firm belief that scientific thinking was bound to put an end to superstitions and religious prejudices received a shock when prejudice in its basest form broke loose in the most civilized land of Europe. At the house of his friend, the novelist Alphonse Daudet, he heard from the mouth of Daudet's son, Léon (sub-sequently a royalist leader), an account of Dreyfus' public degrada-ton and how his protestations of innocence had been drowned out by the clamor of the mob. He was revolted at the indignity to which a human being had been put, even if he was, as Zola had no reason to doubt at that time, a criminal.

But only when Scheurer-Kestner, in his solitary protest, stood up for what he was convinced to be the truth did Zola sense the drama that was beginning to take shape in the public life of France. He was attracted at first as a writer, and became increasingly involved. When he eventually recognized the innocence of Dreyfus he was over-whelmed by the deepest sympathy for the victims.

He had often said that writing novels no longer satisfied him. To crown his achievements, he desired to be part of a great and significant act of faith. Zola had written of his admiration for Scheurer-Kestner, of his indignation over the press; he had warned the young people not to turn their backs on truth and justice. But not until Esterhazy, the scoundrel, was glorified, and Picquart, the champion of truth, was treated as a villain did Zola realize that only the stark witness to faith —a martyr—could break the spell that had descended on the nation. He felt the discouragement among the fighters for the truth and knew that his time had come. He did not consult anyone, but wrote for a night, a day and another night until he had finished his appeal to the President of the Republic. Zola intended to publish his letter as a pamphlet. But before doing so he walked over to the office of L'Aurore and showed it to Vaughan, the publisher, and to Clemenceau. Both men felt its formidable power. Clemenceau gave it the title J'Accuse!, the headline under which it was to appear and take its place in the annals of history.

L'Aurore had continued to be a paper of insignificant circulation. But on the day on which Zola's protest appeared in its columns it sold 300,000 copies. Between attacks on and polemics against Zola's step, the whole nation eventually took cognizance of it. J'Accuse! became a byword, forever associated with Zola by the whole world.

Its immense appeal lay in the magic insight that pierced the smoke-screen of fraud, confusion and contradictions, unraveled the events as though he had been behind the scenes to witness who and what had made them happen, and then revealed them with precision and clarity. More than that: he gave the public a consistent interpretation to set against the only one they had had until then of the affair. Against the current version of an international Jewish syndicate that operated with paid spies and traitors to undermine and paralyze Catholic France and deliver her into the hands of the enemy, he showed how the General Staff, having committed a fateful blunder, had attempted to cover it up and had sunk into a morass of fraud and forgery.

At a time when even the staunch handful were hopeless in their hearts and the broken and submissive had turned to hunting with the pack, Emile Zola, singlehanded, threw into the scales all he had attained in a lifetime's creative achievement, to prove, personally, that the highest generals of the French Army had acted as weak-kneed scoundrels.

J'Accuse! began by apostrophizing the President and came to the point at once:

A court-martial has but recently, by order, dared to acquit one Esterhazy—a supreme slap at all truth, all justice! And it is done; France has this brand upon her visage; history will relate that it was during your administration that such a social crime could be committed.

Since they have dared, I too shall dare. I shall tell the truth because I pledged myself to tell it if justice, regularly empowered, did not do so fully, unmitigatedly. My duty is to speak; I have no wish to be an accomplice. My nights would be haunted by the specter of the innocent being expiating, under the most frightful torture, a crime he never committed.

And it is to you, Mr. President, that I shall call out this truth, with all the force of my revolt as an honest man. To your honor, I am convinced that you are ignorant of the crime. And to whom, then, shall I denounce the malignant rabble of true culprits if not to you, the highest magistrate in the country?

The truth, first, on the trial and condemnation of Dreyfus. One pernicious individual arranged, planned, concocted everything—Lieutenant Colonel du Paty de Clam, then only Major. He is the whole Dreyfus affair. . . . He appears as the foggy, complicated ruling spirit, haunted by romantic intrigues, devouring serial novels, titillating himself with stolen papers, anonymous letters, strange trysts, mysterious women who come by night to sell crushing testimony, secrets of State. He it was who conceived the idea of studying the man in a room entirely lined with mirrors. . . . I declare simply that Major du Paty de Clam, designated as prosecuting officer, is the one who is first and most guilty of the fearful miscarriage of justice.

Then Zola described how the *bordereau* arrived at the office of the Second Bureau:

A search was made then; handwritings were examined at home; it was all a family affair; a traitor was to be found right under their noses, and to be expelled. . . . And Major du Paty de Clam enters as the first suspicion falls on Dreyfus. Henceforth it is he who conceives, creates Dreyfus; the affair becomes his affair; he extends himself to confound the traitor; to precipitate him into complete confession. There is also the Minister of War, General Mercier, at work, whose intellect seems but mediocre; there is also the Chief-of-staff, General Gonse, whose conscience adjusts itself readily to many things. But at the bottom, there is at first no one so busily involved as Major du Paty de Clam, who leads them all, who hypnotizes them, for he is also interested in spiritualism, occultism; he talks with spirits. The experiments to which he had the unfortunate Dreyfus submitted, the traps he laid, seem incredible; the mad investigation, the monstrous hoax, a whole harrowing romance.

. . . And thus the charges were drawn up as in some tale of the fifteenth century, in an atmosphere of mystery, brutal tricks, expedients, all based on a single, inane accusation, that of having written the idiotic *bordereau,* for the famous secrets delivered were found to be almost valueless. And, I insist, the core of the problem is here: it is from here on that the real crime issues, the shocking denial of justice which renders all France sick. . . . At the outset their part had involved nothing more than negligence and silliness. . . .

But there is Dreyfus before a court-martial. The most rigorous secrecy is preserved. A traitor might have opened the frontier to the enemy and led the German Emperor clear to the Cathedral of Notre Dame and no more extreme measures of silence and mystery would have been taken. The nation is horror-stricken, the most terrible details are whispered of monstrous treasons that make all history cry out; obviously the whole nation bows to the court. No punishment is severe enough for the criminal; the country will applaud the public degradation, she will want the guilty man to stay eternally on his rock of infamy, devoured by remorse.

Is there any truth in those whispered unmentionable things, capable of setting all Europe aflame, that they must needs be buried in the deep secrecy of star-chamber proceedings? No. Behind those doors there were only romantic and insane fancy, and the imaginings of a Major du Paty de Clam.

Ah! the inanity of that accusation! That a man could have been condemned on such a charge is a prodigy of iniquity. I challenge honest people to read it and not be overcome by indignation, and not cry out their revulsion at the superhuman expiation of the man on Devil's Island.

. . . We were told of fourteen charges in the accusation; in the end we find only one, that of the *bordereau*; and we learn, even, that the experts were not unanimous on this; that one of them, Mr. Gobert, was roughly handled for not having come to the desired conclusion. . . . It is a family trial, one is completely among friends, and it must be remembered, finally, that the General Staff made the trial, judged it, and merely reaffirmed its judgment.

. . . It is said that in the council chamber, the judges were naturally in favor of acquittal. And, therefore, as justification for the condemnation, we may understand the desperate obstinacy with which they maintained the existence of a secret paper emanating from a foreign office, something overwhelming, impossible ever to reveal, which legitimizes everything done, before which, in short, we must bow as we do to the almighty and unknowable God! . . . Here then, Mr. President, are the facts that explain how judicial error has been committed; and the moral proof, the prosperous situation of Dreyfus, the absence of motives, his continued cry of innocence, combine to show him a victim of the extraordinary imaginings of Major du Paty de Clam, and of the clerical milieu in which he found himself, of the whole persecution, in short, of the [atmosphere of] "dirty Jew" that dishonors our time.

Then Zola deals with the *petit bleu* and Major Esterhazy:

. . . Colonel Sandherr had died, and Lieutenant Colonel Picquart had succeeded him as chief of the Secret Service. It was in the course of duties that the latter found one day a little dispatch addressed to Major Esterhazy by the agents of a foreign power. His duty was to open an investigation. It is clear that he never acted against the wishes of his superiors. . . . But the impetus was extraordinary, for the condemnation of Esterhazy involved fatefully the revision of the Dreyfus verdict and it was this above all things that the General Staff wished to avoid at any cost.

. . . Observe that General Billot, new Minister of War, was yet in no way compromised in the previous affair; his hands were clean; he could have established the truth. He dared not; in horror no doubt of public opinion, certainly also in fear of abandoning the whole General Staff. And so there was no more than a moment of struggle between his conscience and what he felt to be the Army's interests. When that moment had passed, it was already too late. . . . Do you understand that! Here it is a year since Generals Billot,

Boisdeffre and Gonse learned that Dreyfus is innocent and they keep the fearful thing to themselves! And those men sleep, and they have wives and children they love!

Zola then came to Esterhazy:

Witnesses show Esterhazy maddened at first, prone to suicide or flight. Then suddenly, he gambles on a daring front, he amazes all Paris by the violence of his gestures and attitudes. Help had come to him. . . . From now on the duel is fought between Colonel Picquart and Colonel du Paty de Clam, the one with frank, open face, the other masked. We shall find them both soon before the bar of civil justice. But at the bottom, remember, it is always the General Staff defending itself, refusing to avow a crime whose consequences pile up from hour to hour.

. . . Ah, we witness the infamous spectacle of men weighted down with debts and crimes being proclaimed to all the world as innocent and virtuous, while the very soul of honor, a man without a stain, is dragged in the mire! When a country, when a civilization has come to this, it must fall apart in decay. . . .

How could any expect a court-martial to undo what a previous court-martial has done? . . . Now we know . . . that to require the guilt of Esterhazy would be to proclaim the innocence of Dreyfus. Nothing could enable them to get out of that charmed circle.

They have rendered an unjust verdict, one that will forever weigh upon our court-martials, and which from now on will cast the blot of suspicion upon all the decisions of military courts. The first court-martial might have been stupid; the second was necessarily criminal. . . . They speak to us of the honor of the Army; they want us to respect, to love it. Yes, by all means, yes— that Army which would rise at the first menace to defend French soil, which is, in fact, the whole people, and for which we have nothing but tenderness and reverence. But . . . it is a question of the sword, the master that we shall probably have forced upon us tomorrow. And as for kissing the hilt of the sword, piously—great God, no!

Dreyfus cannot be vindicated unless the whole General Staff is indicted. . . . What a cleaning up the republican government must institute in that house of Jesuits, as General Billot himself called it. . . . And what abominable measures have been resorted to in this affair of folly and stupidity, smacking of low police practice, of unbridled nightmare, of the Spanish inquisition— all for the sweet pleasure of a few uniformed and accoutered personages who grind their heel into the nation, who hurl back into the throat the cry for truth and justice, under the lying guise of "reasons of state."

Zola praised Scheurer and Picquart, though they waited for God to act while the Devil was busy. However, it was the President's duty to act, rather than theirs.

I do not despair in the least of ultimate triumph. I repeat with more intense conviction: the truth is on the march and nothing will stop it! . . . When the truth is buried underground, it grows, it chokes, it gathers such an explosive force that on the day it bursts out, it blows everything up with it. We shall soon see whether or not we have laid the land mines for a most far-reaching disaster of the near future. . . .

To close his long letter, Zola made these accusations:

I accuse Colonel du Paty de Clam of having been the diabolical agent of the judicial error, unconsciously, I prefer to believe, and of having continued to defend his deadly work during the past three years through the most absurd and revolting machinations.

I accuse General Mercier of having made himself an accomplice in one of the greatest crimes in history, probably through weak-mindedness.

I accuse General Billot of having had in his hands the decisive proof of the innocence of Dreyfus and of having concealed it and of having rendered himself guilty of the crime of *lèse* humanity and *lèse* justice, out of political motives and to save the face of the General Staff.

I accuse General Pellieux and Major Ravary of having held a scoundrelly inquest, I mean an inquest of the most monstrous partiality, the complete report of which composes for us an imperishable monument of naïve effrontery.

I accuse the three handwriting experts, MM. Belhomme, Varinard and Couard, of having made lying and fraudulent reports, unless a medical examination will certify them to be deficient of sight and judgment.

I accuse the War Office of having led a vile campaign in the press, particularly in the *Echo de Paris* and in *L'Eclair*, in order to misdirect public opinion and cover up its sins.

I accuse, lastly, the first court-martial of having violated all human rights in condemning a prisoner on testimony kept secret from him, and I accuse the second court-martial of having covered up this illegality by order, committing in turn the judicial crime of acquitting a guilty man with full knowledge of his guilt.

Zola stated that he was aware that he was committing a felony by making these accusations.

The action I take here is simply a revolutionary step designed to hasten the explosion of truth and justice.

I have one passion only, for light, in the name of humanity which has borne so much and has a right to happiness. My burning protest is only the cry of my soul. Let them dare to carry me to the court of appeals, and let there be an inquest in the full light of day!

I am waiting.

16

THIRTY THOUSAND LETTERS and telegrams from all parts of the world greeted Zola's appeal. They testified to the immense relief felt everywhere at this turn of events and to the irritation which had mounted over the dim-out of reason in France. The eloquence of Zola and his moral stand had put the world on notice not to give up too hastily the country of the Great Revolution. Zola's act of faith heralded the coming of great battles for the conscience of the nation.

Europe, outside of France, believed almost unanimously in the innocence of Dreyfus. That France remained impervious to the truth was attributed to her moral decline. The English, Scandinavian, Netherlands and German publics had undergone a revulsion of feeling at the moral decomposition of France. The French population in Belgium and Switzerland had despaired at the extinction of French glory. Newspapers even of such backward countries as Russia and Rumania reproached France for its relapse into barbarism. Russian papers went so far as to ask whether France still had the right to be called the nation of the Enlightenment.

Overnight, America became interested in the strange backstage commotion of this drama of justice. Mark Twain, in the New York *Herald*, declared: "I am penetrated with the most profound respect for Zola and [filled] with boundless admiration. Such cowards, hypocrites, and flatterers as the members of military and ecclesiastic courts the world could produce by the million every year. But it takes five centuries to produce a Joan of Arc or a Zola." Björnstjerne Björnson lamented that France did not care for the sympathy of other nations.

She turned a deaf ear to the great writers of the world, despised their sentimentality and scorned their judgment of herself.

But in her domestic ordeal France resented the interference even of such friendly nations as Russia. Following Zola's protest, the internal tensions broke into violence. In Nantes, Bordeaux, Toulouse, Montpellier, Le Havre, and Orléans huge crowds plundered Jewish stores, beat up Jews, publicly burned Zola's article and hung Zola in effigy. In Paris the mob paraded along the boulevards carrying standards: "Death to Zola! Death to the Jews!" Huge protest meetings were held, ending in bloody clashes. For a month or more, the towns all over the country were in an uproar. The police were often powerless to prevent bloodshed, and the military had to be called out. In Algiers, pogroms claimed numerous victims, French and Arab making common cause in raiding Jewish shops.

In Paris, the police were called to keep students from storming Zola's house. The students had to content themselves with stoning it and shouting, "Death to Zola! Long live the Army!" At universities in Belgium, Italy and Switzerland resolutions were passed hailing Zola's stand for justice. In France only the few who had privately dissented all along dared to raise their voices. Many French intellectuals inscribed their names on a list to do homage to Zola.

The country was possessed of violent excitement. No time, thought or passion seemed left for the business of everyday life. Life consisted of turning to the papers, arming oneself with arguments, fighting with the word and the fist. People ceased to read books or to go to the theater. No thriller, no play could compete with the drama of which France was the stage, her citizens the actors, and the civilized world the audience.

This fever was destined to keep a hold of varying intensity on the country for years. The constant awareness of conflicting and contradictory events vested life with the magic of a higher plane of existence. The man in the street re-evaluated the past, revised principles and spoke his mind. Life was lived as if every day were a red-letter one, towering over that gray maze of time which in the ordinary run is wasted on petty, individual cares.

The Cabinet was at a loss what to do about Zola. It could not very well let his accusations stand unchallenged. He had charged that two Ministers of War, Mercier and Billot, had been accomplices in one of the worst crimes in history; that General Pellieux in conducting the investigation against Esterhazy had behaved like a scoundrel. No lofty declaration that the honor of the insulted personages was above any calumny from a writer who was merely trying to keep up his dwindling sales would satisfy the public, even less the nationalist papers. All were demanding a harsh punishment for Zola. On the other hand, if the Government prosecuted Zola for a libel on the Minister of War, or on General Pellieux, the law gave the defendant the right to attempt to prove the truth of his statements. For all practical purposes it meant that the Dreyfus case, together with its corollary, the Esterhazy case, would be reopened.

The Cabinet finally found a way to save its face while depriving Zola of any direct opportunity to air the well-buried secrets of the Dreyfus case. It decided to charge as criminal libel only that passage of *J'Accuse!* in which the author stated that a court-martial "acting on orders" dared acquit Esterhazy. This would give Zola the right to produce evidence against Esterhazy but not in favor of Dreyfus.

This halfway house pleased most people but it did not please Esterhazy. He dispensed opinions on Zola in daily interviews in the nationalist press and to English newspaper correspondents in Paris. He deplored the passing of the less legalistic times of yore when such an insult as Zola's was punished on the spot without giving the felon a further opportunity to insult the Army and the nation. The author of *J'Accuse!* should not be prosecuted, he insisted, for to do so was beneath the dignity of generals. He felt the turmoil whipped up by Zola's appeal would subside in a few days, and that it merited no better treatment than to be ignored.

Esterhazy had good reason to fear a new airing of his case. It would be in a civil rather than a military court. Mme. de Boulancy was furious at the "expert" opinion that Esterhazy's letters to her had been forged. She flatly denied the existence of an unknown criminal who might have written the notorious "Uhlan" letter in which the major dreamed opulently of commanding drunken hordes that would butcher the French in the streets of Paris. In addition, the major's new friend, Oscar Wilde, warned him that Panizzardi, the Italian military attaché, was talking. The gossip made its way through various salons that the German War Office was in possession of quite a collection of Esterhazy's letters.

In sum, it seemed to Esterhazy that the Government's decision was to throw him to the wolves. He planted the news in *La Libre Parole* and in *L'Intransigeant* that General Billot, the Minister of War, was financially in the meshes of the Jewish syndicate.

Since Esterhazy's trial, General Pellieux had come to like this strange figure. The general admired his flamboyant imagination and saw in the wretch the knight-errant come down from the times of reckless bravery and lost in the *petit-bourgeois* world that cared for nought but moneybags and security. Thus it was to Pellieux that Esterhazy now communicated his old familiar threats. Pellieux transmitted them to General Boisdeffre: Esterhazy was going to talk, if betrayed, and would drag generals down with him. Boisdeffre hastened to reassure Esterhazy of the continued protection of the General Staff. He was all the more anxious to do so since he had begun to suspect that the Minister of War might be unwilling to allow himself to become more deeply involved in the practices of the General Staff. The game was getting too gamy for Billot, and if the provocation were strong enough he might walk out on it. However, at Boisdeffre's urging, Billot agreed that the General Staff should stand behind Esterhazy in the trial.

Zola no sooner received the indictment than he saw through the legal maneuver. He protested in *L'Aurore* in an open letter to the Minister of War. He repeated his previous accusations in full, and asked how the Minister, the officers of the General Staff and the judges of the first court-martial could let him get away with such public statements. He added: "The law would be mendacious if it imposed on me [the need] to prove the accuracy of my statements, and at the same time deprived me of the means of doing so." But Méline, the Prime Minister, declared that the honor of generals did not need support from the courts. Generals were above suspicion.

Famous writers, artists and composers in Italy sent a declaration of sympathy to Zola, who in their eyes embodied the real France, the France of the Rights of Man. But in France a menacing poster appeared on the billboards on the eve of Zola's trial. "The honest and patriotic population of Paris will be its own police," it proclaimed. "It will take up its own defense, if the Jews continue to endanger the country." And the president of the Republican Association warned in the press that "the interests of the Republic as well as of the Israelites themselves demand that the instigators of the Dreyfus affair call a halt to their activities."

On February 7, 1898, the trial of Zola opened.

17

LIBEL COMMITTED in the press was a matter for a jury. The trial was held in the so-called jury room of the Palais de Justice.

A well-fed, chubby judge named Delegorgue was in the chair, with two associate judges at his side. He seemed pleased to be presiding over a case of world interest and at the same time aware that a false step might have unfavorable consequences for his career. The verdict, of course, would not be his to give. That belonged to the jury. Yet his conduct of the trial would admit or suppress those facts which form the judgment of the jury. Its members are cautioned to consider no more of the case than what they learn at the trial. Yes, the judge was indeed on tiptoe, and Van Cassel, appointed by the Minister of War to appear in behalf of the court-martial, was notorious for the vigor of his assaults on opponents.

Zola engaged as his lawyer Fernand Labori, a handsome man full of vitality, called by his colleagues "lungs of steel" for his thundering voice. The law made the publisher a co-defendant. He was represented by Albert Clemenceau, brother of Georges. By common consent Georges Clemenceau appeared for *L'Aurore* even though he was not a lawyer. The brothers Clemenceau looked strikingly alike. There were the same round skull, slanted eyes, smooth Mongolian face, alert eyes—Albert a milder copy of Georges, in whose face their common traits were more powerfully molded.

Small shopkeepers and artisans sat on the jury, attentive, bewildered by the parade of so many generals, celebrities and renowned speakers. They remained awestruck to the end. The vast hall was packed with officers, journalists, lawyers, society women, aristocrats and rabble-rousers of the Anti-Semitic League. The building was surrounded by a mob. The garrison of Paris stood to arms at the ready in the barracks in the event the police needed assistance.

This is how Albert Bataille described the audience:

For twenty-five years I have attended trials in criminal courts, but I cannot remember any audience so rough as this was. The President [the presiding judge] refused to give the public exceptional privileges, yet they invaded not only the places reserved for the audience, but took the seats around the judges and jurors, sat on windowsills. Some climbed on the stoves. The lawyers sat along the walls, and on the steps; some young men sat on the floor, their legs crossed like Turks, right in front of the jury. [The women's] beautiful flowery hats brought a gay note to this sea of tumult.

Zola looked like a professor, thin, neat, serious and calm. His creased forehead gave his face the anxious appearance which nearsighted people often have. He sat quietly on the defendants' bench and twisted his cane absent-mindedly. The publisher of *L'Aurore* sat at his side as co-defendant. Back of them sat Fernand Labori, Zola's youthful counsel, and the brothers Clemenceau, cold, alert and sharpminded.

Zola advised his lawyer to defend Dreyfus rather than him. Indeed, Zola's public appeal had had no other purpose than to reopen the Dreyfus case before a civilian court. But Judge Delegorgue was on guard. He made every effort to prevent the witnesses from wandering out of the narrow area embraced by the indictment. Nevertheless, the Dreyfus case could not be barred entirely. Delegorgue kept repeating, "The question is out of order." It became the signature of the fifteen-day trial.

Zola read his plea, assuring the jury that he was not going to defend himself. If the jury condemned him, they would be raising him to the height of the honored and saintly who had suffered in the cause of right and justice. He had no political ambitions. He was a free writer, dedicated to work. But he resented attacks made on him which would have it that he, born of a French mother in France, was not French because his father, whom he had lost at the age of seven, had come from Italy. His forty books written in French bore witness to his being a Frenchman, and whatever honor they brought to his name, they brought to France as well. Not he, and not Dreyfus, were on trial, he said, but France. The question was whether France was still true to her character as the guardian of justice and humanity. The hour was grave. The salvation of the nation hung on the decision of the court.

Zola ended his speech with these words:

Dreyfus is innocent, I swear. I vouch for it with my life and honor. In this solemn hour, before this court, before you, gentlemen of the jury, who represent the nation, before France, I swear that Dreyfus is innocent. By my forty years of work, by the respect earned by the work of my life, I swear that Dreyfus is innocent. By all I have gained, by the name I have made, and my contribution to the growth of French literature, I swear that Dreyfus is innocent. May all of this perish, my work fail, if Dreyfus is not innocent. He is innocent!

The room was breathless. For an instant it seemed as if the Dreyfus case must be heard in public at last. The tension was increased when an elderly lawyer, Salle, took the witness stand. He told the court how he had once questioned a friend of his, an officer who had been a member of the military court which had convicted Dreyfus, about how they had been able to convict Dreyfus on such shaky evidence as the *bordereau*. Out of order, out of order, Delegorgue kept crying. Labori asked Salle: "Do you know of any fact pertinent to the defense of Monsieur Zola?" "The question is out of order!" thundered the presiding judge. Labori looked at him with astonishment and Delegorgue himself asked the witness, "Do you have anything to say in respect to the case of Major Esterhazy?" Salle answered, his lips trembling, that in respect to the case of Major Esterhazy he had nothing to say.

Then Albert Clemenceau, in his indifferent-sounding drawl, turned to the witness: "We understand that this witness heard from a judge of the military court that a secret document had been served on that court. . . . Would you please confirm or deny this in one word, so that the President will not have time to stop you?" Salle, pale and frightened, hesitated. "Speak!" Clemenceau exhorted him. "How is it possible that the word doesn't slip from your lips, even in spite of you, old man?" Delegorgue shouted, "Do not answer!" and ordered the witness to leave the witness box.

Later on in the trial a witness was successful in uttering the key word. When Demange, who had been counsel for Dreyfus, took the stand he told quietly how he had originally intended to appeal for an annulment of the verdict in the Dreyfus trial on the grounds of a violation of the law, but had advised his clients the appeal would be hopeless until calmer days came. Twice Delegorgue refused to allow Labori to question the witness about why he believed that the law had been violated. Then Albert Clemenceau stepped in again. Without putting stress on his words, apparently absorbed in shuffling his papers, he said, as if in an aside, "Wasn't it a judge of the military court who affirmed that secret proofs existed?" "Yes, of course," Demange hastened to reply. The cat was out of the bag and in the trial record.

Bearers of illustrious names were called to testify to the altruistic

nature of Zola's act. Among them were Anatole France, Emile Duclaux and Edouard Grimaux, the highly esteemed old professor of
chemistry who had taught generations of future officers at the Ecole
Polytechnique. After he had added his signature to the list of *protes-
tateurs* approving Zola's appeal, he had been deprived of his chair and
laboratory at the Sorbonne. He cried, "I—not a patriot?" He enumerated his soldier ancestors and said, "Those who are ridden by fear
insult the Army, not us. It was they who told us at the beginning of
the Dreyfus affair: let an innocent man suffer an undeserved punishment rather than arouse the temper of a foreign power. But we have
now the entire nation enrolled in the Army, led by twenty thousand
officers ready to sacrifice their lives on the battlefield. Why should we
fear?"

As the old man left the room, he noticed a lieutenant, a former
student of his. He extended his hand; the lieutenant refused it. Outside, he was booed by the mob.

The audience was fascinated by General Pellieux, whose commanding personality bulged under his honest indignation at seeing the
Army suspected of fraud. While conducting the investigation against
Esterhazy he had been told by General Boisdeffre that there was to
hand incontestable proof of Dreyfus' guilt: a letter which mentioned
him by name. The one thing General Pellieux could not quite understand was why the General Staff did not produce the document and
put an end to the embarrassing and shameful situation.

He spoke from the witness stand with a voice of iron—the offended
honor of the Army personified. Two separate courts composed of soldiers, some of whom had shed their blood in battle for their country,
had passed judgment. One had convicted Dreyfus. The other had
acquitted Esterhazy. Could there be doubt of their honesty? Were
they to be dragged in the mire of suspicion and malice? The general
became more and more indignant. Suddenly it was out. The general
was testifying that the Ministry of War was in possession of conclusive proof of the guilt of Dreyfus. Under questioning he even quoted
from the document, giving his best memory of the wording.

Lieutenant Colonel Henry must have been horror-struck. The quota-
tion came from the famous "Liberator" letter—the one Henry had
forged originally when Deputy Castelin was preparing to put a question in the Chamber on the Dreyfus case. Henry had been using the
fact of its existence to make propaganda to help Esterhazy. It had been

a kind of money in the bank for the conspirators. But in a public trial it would have to be cash on the line. How could it stand examination? Oh yes, the words of General Pellieux must have made Henry groan within himself.

The muscular innocent on the witness stand concluded, "I confirm it on my honor, and refer to General Boisdeffre." He sat back. That ended it all, he was sure.

But it had only begun it. "Very well," said Labori. "Let us see the document." A legal argument started. "No document constitutes proof," insisted Labori, "unless it is submitted for examination and discussion." The lawyers pounced on the fact that the need for a re-trial of the Dreyfus case had now been demonstrated. "If . . . the testimony of General Pellieux [against Dreyfus] is founded on fact," he said, "evidence will have to be produced and subjected to regular legal trial. If the military courts were mistaken, it will be up to the other side to prove it. No matter who the guilty person is, in this way he can be apprehended, and we shall finally be able to resume our regular business—be it peace or war."

General Gonse attempted to rise to the crisis. He asked for per-mission to speak. "The Army is not afraid to reveal the truth," he said, "but there is great need for caution. The proofs, genuine and defini-tive as they are, cannot be disclosed in public."

The reprimand contained in Gonse's words did not escape Pellieux. He forgot that the witness chair was not a saddle from which he com-manded the court. "Get a cab and find General Boisdeffre," he ordered his aide-de-camp.

General Gonse sat down unhappily. "Isn't it strange," Albert Clemenceau asked Pellieux, "that the Minister of War made no men-tion of so convincing a document when Castelin asked his question in the Chamber?"

"General Billot may say what he pleases, I don't care," the general replied. He was furious. His face reddened. He had had no experi-ence of civilians who presumed to doubt that a general's word of honor settled everything. "Besides, there are still other proofs. General Boisdeffre will tell you when he gets here."

Court was adjourned to await Boisdeffre. The noise the crowd made in leaving was frightening. Voices were raised, fists shaken openly at the attorneys. "Miserable wretches!" the mob outside cried, and a vast growling roar went up: "Death to Zola! Death to the Jews!"

These were a people aroused by the right wing to revolution, and hunting for a place where it could happen.

Mme. Séverine left the court. She wrote afterward:

> As we went down the stairs of the Palais de Justice, we found ourselves surrounded by the roaring crowd. And then I saw the hero [Zola], more beautiful than the imagination of mankind ever pictured him; the man who truly deserved the name of hero. He was clumsy, shortsighted, and awkwardly carried his umbrella under his arm. His gestures and manners were those of a scholar. But as he descended the steps one by one, in the midst of the roars of hatred, among the crowd that clamored for his death, he walked under the arch of uplifted clubs and canes like a king descending the palace stairs beneath an arch of naked swords unsheathed in his honor. This was the greatest sight of my life. It was the triumph of a conscience, a truth, and an individual.

The press that night threatened a massacre of the Jews. "The idea of a Saint Bartholomew is getting hold of the soul of the French people," *Le Gaulois* wrote. "If Israel's appeal to Germany were heeded, and Germany should go to war against us, then I am certain, not a single Jew would be alive in France the next morning. . . ." *La Patrie* wrote: "If the tocsin were sounded that the country is in danger, millions of voices would cry: Death to traitors! Trarieux and Reinach would then cringe on their knees before us. But there would be no pardon, no mercy. . . . No one can gainsay that Generals Boisdeffre, Mercier, Gonse, and Pellieux are well informed and competent. No one can believe that they conspired to keep an innocent victim subject to torture. It would occur to nobody that General Billot would have lied six times in the Chamber when he stated that Dreyfus was justly condemned."

On the following day General Boisdeffre duly appeared in court and testified:

> I shall be brief. I confirm the deposition of General Pellieux in all particulars, and I vouch for its exactitude and authenticity. I have nothing more to say. I have no right to say more. You are the Jury; you are the nation. If the nation has no trust in its military leaders—those who are responsible for national defense—then those leaders are ready to leave their arduous task to others. It is up to you to decide. I have nothing further to add. Permit me to retire.

Amid the ovations of the crowd, the Chief of the General Staff left the court. It is quite possible that he had had at that time no doubt of the authenticity of Esterhazy's "Liberator."

After his departure, Labori rose to his feet. The presiding judge had been measuring out the law with a very uneven hand. The generals had been given a free hand in their testimony about Dreyfus. But when a witness for the defense so much as opened his mouth the cry of "Out of Order" shut it. However, Labori was not a witness but a lawyer, and as such could argue. He argued, and thus got into the record the fact that "the proof" had not been produced in court and therefore did not constitute evidence. The implication that he could still doubt the sworn testimony of such generals as Boisdeffre, Gonse and Pellieux caused a wild stir in the crowd.

Then Lieutenant Colonel Marie-Georges Picquart was called to the stand. A disciplinary committee of the Army had tried him for a breach of regulations, the allegation being that he had divulged the contents of a secret file to his attorney, Louis Leblois. Lieutenant Colonel Henry testified to the truth of the allegation. Leblois testified that the only file he had ever seen on Picquart's desk was an unclassified one. The Minister of War reserved decision on the recommendation of the Army committee. It was apparent that he was being given an opportunity to redeem himself in the eyes of the Army at the Zola trial. The decision on which depended his future in the Army remained in reserve, dangling over his head like the sword of Damocles, but he was permitted to travel from the fortress of Mont Valérien to the Palais de Justice and return unguarded.

Isolated by the hatred of the officer corps, who regarded him as a traitor to them and thus, of course, to France, Picquart had the serenity of a man who has committed himself irrevocably to what he knows is right. His tranquillity mystified the crowd. His quiet voice and his patent care to tell the truth and no more than the truth without characterizing the actions of others made him a smashing witness.

"I also should like to speak of the document," Picquart said. "But to do so I should have to be released from the obligation to secrecy by General Gonse. It would be good to submit to verification the authenticity of certain documents, particularly the one which arrived at just the right moment—that is, the one of which General Pellieux spoke. I would not have mentioned it now if General Pellieux had not done so yesterday. That document is a forgery."

When the tranquil voice ceased, there was utter stillness. A sense of shock had fallen upon the courtroom. The presiding judge called upon General Gonse to take the stand. It was a long moment or so before Gonse could rise. His mind must have been working very rapidly, but his feet worked slowly. He declined to take the stand. "The document is authentic," he said, "but I have no right to say anything more."

And General Pellieux? The general had no direct knowledge of the circumstances but he had utter confidence in what his colleagues had testified to on their honor and under oath. He was ready to resume the stand. But first Picquart asked permission to clarify a minor point to the jury. The press, he said, had smeared him viciously. He quoted as an instance the published report that he had been married and was now divorced and that he had children who were being educated in Germany. "The fact is," he declared, "I am a bachelor."

Picquart stepped down from the stand and General Pellieux stepped up. He stared directly at Picquart. His testimony was as follows:

> I said that everything was strange in this affair, but what I find most strange —and I say this to his face—is the attitude of a *monsieur* who still wears the uniform of the French Army and who comes to court to accuse three generals of forgery and of having used forged documents. This is all I wanted to say.

There were about a hundred officers in the courtroom. They jumped spontaneously to their feet and gave General Pellieux a standing ovation. Picquart sat silently.

Then Lieutenant Colonel Hubert Henry took the stand. Of the whole detailed file he had so laboriously and feloniously constructed against Picquart, he could reveal nothing. In view of the Army's position on documents, he limited his testimony to a statement that he had seen Picquart show a secret document to an unauthorized person, Leblois, when the attorney had visited the Second Bureau.

Picquart joined in the questioning. He made the Second Bureau's present chief define exactly where he had been sitting when he saw Picquart hand Leblois the document. Then he showed that from this position Henry could not possibly have seen what the document was and thus could not say whether it had been a secret one or not.

Henry pounded furiously on the witness box. "I maintain everything I have said," he shouted into Picquart's face, "and I maintain that Picquart lies."

Picquart grew very pale. He lifted his arm to strike Henry. Then, with a massive effort, he lowered it, and turned to the jury. His lips trembled with his struggle to control himself. These men who were striving to destroy him, he said, were the prime movers in the Dreyfus Affair. He had started out thinking that they had acted against Dreyfus in the belief that they were right. "I have come to think otherwise," he continued. "When I was at the head of that office and my doubts were aroused, I wanted to clear up matters and I believed there was a better way to defend a case than to wrap oneself in blind faith. . . . For months I was in a horrible situation for an officer. My honor was attacked and I was unable to defend myself. All this did not stop me when I thought I had to search for the truth and for justice. I did it, and I think I have rendered more service to the Army and to the country in this way. As an honest man, I think I have done my duty."

The presiding judge closed the scene characteristically, with an understatement: "You two are certainly in disagreement," he said.

There were moments in the trial when the tension relaxed. The Marquis du Paty de Clam paced the corridor, trying unsuccessfully to suppress his annoyance at the position Zola had put him in. Zola had impaled him on his pen as not only a knave but a fool. To make matters even more ignominious, the name of the Countess de Comminges had been introduced into the trial. There had been testimony about the innocent letters she had written to Picquart, and the use the marquis had made of her signatures "Blanche" and "Speranza," and of the fact that he had imitated her writing on certain letters and sent telegrams in her name. It was a preposterous situation for a bemonocled marquis of celebrated ancestry.

But when the marquis sought to improve it from the witness stand, he only made it worse. Was it true, Labori asked him, that at one time he had wanted to marry the countess and his hand had been rejected? The marquis thought such questions should not be asked. The attorney thought they should be, that they showed motive for the action of the marquis in involving the countess in letters that cast grave suspicion not only on Picquart but on her. Labori asked again: Was it true the marquis had once hoped to marry the countess? Du Paty asked the court to rule out the question. French honor prohibited a gentleman from discussing such matters in public. The name of the young lady had no connection with the trial, he said. Labori pointed out dryly that the young lady in question was fifty years old and that it was Du Paty himself and his ridiculous machinations that had brought her name into the affair.

Poor Du Paty de Clam. Labori brushed him away with a wave of the hand. He disdained to take his testimony on any point other than "Speranza." The marquis had taken the stand as a publicly described knave and a fool. He stepped down from it a publicly jilted lover, too, who had tried to take a sneak's revenge on the lady of the hard heart. Dismissed from the stand, he popped his monocle, bowed to the judge and the jury and marched off the stand as stiffly as a toy soldier. Audible laughter followed his parade toward the exit.

No less ludicrous was Bertillon, France's great detective who had originally identified as Dreyfus' the handwriting on the *bordereau.* When Bernard Lazare in his pamphlet had published the contrary opinions of world-famous experts, Bertillon had expressed profound contempt for them. They were graphologists, he had said. He was a scientist and used scientific methods. There was a rhythm to the writing on the *bordereau,* he had explained, as there is in any writing. This rhythm corresponded to a geometric rhythm, the equation for which could be found on the blotter used in drying the writing. To reproduce Dreyfus' writing, he had claimed, he had only to study the blotter Dreyfus had used.

When Bertillon took the stand, Labori could not question him on Esterhazy's handwriting and how the sight of it had made him change his mind about the *bordereau.* Instead, he questioned him about his scientific method of handwriting analysis. He offered a photostatic copy of Bertillon's own diagram of Dreyfus' writing, saying that, since no one thus far had been able to understand it, an explanation might be helpful. In his appearance at the Dreyfus trial, Bertillon had testified that his diagram exposed "the arsenal of the spy, lugubriously advised." Now he said that the photostat of the diagram was not enough; it lacked the blotter. Labori put the photostat down. Just explain the theory, he said, and how and where it applied. Bertillon launched into such complexities that even he bogged down, and the audience laughed.

Labori turned sternly. "The only proof is the *bordereau,"* he cried into the laughter, "and here is its expert!"

The presiding judge came to the rescue. He told Bertillon he was not obliged to answer any questions about the Dreyfus case.

At all other times, however, the tension remained high, and each new witness screwed it higher. Esterhazy awaited his turn in a frantic rage. It had become public knowledge that he was suffering from tuberculosis and he used it to his own advantage. The generals and the Minister of War, he told the press, had fallen stupidly into Zola's trap. He predicted that before the trial was over, 100,000 corpses would litter the streets of Paris. The Jews, he claimed, knew that he was a sick man and were trying to hound him to death, but he would kill them like rabbits in the end. He would stuff a hundred of them into one cell and horsewhip them to death. He had only one lung left, he said, and was on the brink of the grave. Only his desire for revenge kept him alive. If Zola were acquitted, Paris would rise, with himself as the leader. Should Dreyfus set foot on French soil, 5,000 Jews would die in Paris alone.

The General Staff had a conference before Esterhazy took the stand. They were worried about Labori, the crafty thunderer, and Albert Clemenceau, who worked on witnesses with the cold, premeditated cunning of a spider. They did not think Esterhazy would be a match for them. A strategy was devised. General Pellieux was the only one left who still believed Esterhazy innocent, and thus was the only one Esterhazy trusted. He was delegated to impart the General Staff's strategy. Esterhazy was to refuse to answer any questions put to him by the defense. Esterhazy blustered. He wanted, he said, to hurl the defense's lies in their teeth. But he did not really seem to want it too much. Will you make it an order? he asked General Pellieux. The general made it an order.

Pale, thin and stooping, a mere shadow now of a life of unscrupulous gaiety, his sunken eyes burning with fever, Esterhazy took the stand and declared his willingness to answer all questions coming from the judge and the jury. "But," he added, pointing a contemptuous finger at Zola, "as for these people, I shall answer nothing they ask me."

The audience applauded.

When Labori tried to question him, he refused to answer. Labori then asked the presiding judge to forward questions to the witness. The judge did so. Still Esterhazy refused. Whatever the voice that spoke them, the questions still came from "these people." The judge declined to direct Esterhazy to answer, and Labori sat down.

Albert Clemenceau rose quietly. He addressed Judge Delegorgue.

He had prepared some questions for the witness. In view of the position the witness had taken, he would ask that they be transmitted by the judge. When the witness heard the questions, he could then make up his mind whether to answer them.

Clemenceau began reading the questions. There were sixty of them. Each was one of those loaded "Is it true that you . . . ?" questions. They encompassed every known shabby or criminal act in Esterhazy's disreputable life. Slowly and pitilessly, loaded question followed loaded question. It was a barrage. A great inquisitor and his victim stood face to face. The strain grew. It became immense.

"Does the witness acknowledge having written the following to Madame Boulancy? 'This is the fine Army of France. A shame. I would leave tomorrow if it were not for this job. I wrote to Constantinople. Should they offer the rank that suits me, I will go down there. But not until I have taught these scoundrels something in my own way . . . !' "

THE JUDGE: "Major Esterhazy has already stated that he will not answer the question. Please continue."

CLEMENCEAU: "I want to establish that the major had acknowledged that he had written the letter in question. Will he confirm that he wrote to Madame Boulancy the following: 'Our chiefs, a pack of cowards and idiots, will soon crowd the German prisons'?"

THE JUDGE: "Please continue."

CLEMENCEAU: "Does the Major, officer of the Legion of Honor, acknowledge that he wrote these letters after the war of 1870–71?"

THE JUDGE: "Please continue."

CLEMENCEAU: "Does the witness admit that he has been in contact with the German military attaché in Paris, Colonel von Schwarzkoppen?"

THE JUDGE: "Please do not ask questions which concern foreign policy."

CLEMENCEAU: "There is no question here of foreign policy, Mr. President."

THE JUDGE: "You should not mention foreign officers."

CLEMENCEAU: "So I have no right to speak of an accomplished act carried out by a French officer?"

THE JUDGE: "The honor and security of our country stand above such considerations." [Applause from the audience.]

CLEMENCEAU: "I submit that the honor of the country allows an officer to commit an act, but not to speak of it."

The audience gave an ovation for the Army. A man who hailed the Republic was beaten up and hustled from the court. The tension, the monotony of the slow questions, and the presiding judge's repetitious advice, spaced by Clemenceau's careful pauses, became unbearable. P. V. Stock, a publisher of revisionist books and pamphlets, wrote: "It lasted no more than thirty minutes, but this half-hour appeared unbelievably long. I tremble even now when I recall it. The humiliation, the shame that this miserable creature had to suffer, no matter how cynical and audacious he was, was painful to the limit of endurance."

Still Esterhazy remained silent. When Clemenceau finally released his prey, the audience stood up in a demonstration for Esterhazy. People embraced and kissed him. As he left the court in the company of General Pellieux, lawyers, journalists, officers and women mobbed him. "Glory to him!" they cried. "Long live the victim of the Jews!" Pellieux broke into tears, while Esterhazy, on the brink of fainting from exhaustion, paused before the Duke of Orléans, who said he came to embrace in him "the French uniform." The jubilant mob carried him to his carriage, and an immense crowd in the Place Dauphin hailed him and roared, "Death to the Jews!"

For fifteen days the simple citizens of Paris who were serving on the jury followed this extraordinary review of the highest officers in the Army and the greatest spirits of science and literature. They heard the great orator Jaurès, whose winged words and penetrating logic held the audience captive, but only for as long as his magic voice trembled in the air. There were a few instances when direct pressure was used in an attempt to influence the jury. The press reported that one of them had a Rothschild among his clients. As a result, the juror reported sick rather than expose himself to further attack. Near the end of the trial, each juror received a mysterious letter offering him a large amount of money if he voted for Zola's acquittal. The signatures turned out to have been forged.

The famed handwriting expert, Crépieux-Jamin, by profession a dentist, told the jury how he had been boycotted and ruined after he announced his opinion that the *bordereau* had not been written by

Dreyfus. Another expert testified that Crépieux-Jamin had tried to suborn him when he had been called in to examine Dreyfus' writing, but retracted his statement when confronted with Crépieux-Jamin.

In those two weeks the jurors witnessed many strange scenes of passion and of artifice. The indirect pressure of public opinion weighed heavily on them. The jury was, after all, a cross-section of the nation, and the great majority of the nation knew of the Dreyfus case only from the newspapers of the nationalist and Catholic press. Perhaps they read these papers during the trial. If so, they became aware of the preposterous distortions the press resorted to. Did it make them wonder? But even if it did, the threats of the mob against all who were not with them were open and voluminous and unmistakably in earnest.

For days on end the jurors observed Zola, musing dispassionately as he sat and listened to his trial. When finally the great writer spoke, his sincerity was so touching, his lack of self-interest in the midst of acute hatred and violent passion so genuine, that he appeared almost out of place.

But against him was the General Staff of the Army, the pillar on which security rested. It had come in person to make common cause with the two military courts, the one that had convicted Dreyfus, the other that had acquitted Esterhazy. Not all of those generals, the cream of the Army, the backbone of national defense, the leaders in time of war, could be forgers, liars and crooks. And not all the lower-ranking officers who had served on the two court-martials could be crooks, too. The General Staff drew the issue clearly. It would resign *en bloc* if the jury acquitted Zola.

Pellieux, with his ordering of people about as in the barracks, his browbeating of the judge and his obvious contempt for the jurors— shopkeepers and artisans, called on to pass judgment on him and his like—had been a blessing to the defense. The jury knew his kind and disliked and resented their arrogance. Being Parisians, they must have been tempted to even old scores. But larger issues were at stake.

The public prosecutor rose and read his speech in a flat, colorless tone, hardly raising his voice. Zola stood before the jury charged with having stated that the court-martial had by order acquitted a criminal. Could he prove it? For fifteen days, witnesses and experts had been called to produce the proof. Could they produce it? They could not.

Labori, whose fiery temperament and mighty voice had had their way with Judge Delegorgue, the witnesses and the audience so often, now, in making his plea to the jurors, appealed quietly to reason.

It was a stupid lie, he said, to say that Zola had been bought by a syndicate. No amount of money could buy such a man, bring about such a purchase. And no amount of money could buy this line-up. He ticked it off slowly: Scheurer-Kestner, Trarieux, Jaurès, artists like Anatole France, Octave Mirbeau, Pierre Quillard, Yves Guyot, Senator Ranc, Mme. Séverine. The common tie which held these people together, he said, was the tie of justice and right, or, even more, the ideal which they defended. He turned to the derisive audience. "This was a syndicate of hope and of altruism," he said. "For money!" a voice shouted. Labori retorted quickly, "Had we bribed *you*, you would certainly have cheered us!" Then he turned to the judge. "I beg your pardon, if I was compelled to attend to my own defense."

The public prosecutor, Labori continued, had been correct in calling Zola's act a revolutionary one—yes, Zola had begun a revolution, and it was now up to the jury to accomplish that revolution by acquitting Zola. "If we honor the Army," Labori said, "need this amount to letting a handful of military leaders do as they please? Are those leaders members of a special caste that stands outside or above the law? . . . I say that there is, and always will be, something mightier in France than the Army; something that is to be honored much more than the Army, and that is the law. Wasn't this the principle that Zola stated? Did he, by doing so, insult the Army?"

For three days Labori reviewed the Dreyfus case. He told what had happened in public and behind the scenes. He dwelt on Dreyfus' suffering, on the intrigues against the man who could not live with a lie—Picquart. Labori spared the military leaders, and even showed some ironic understanding of Esterhazy. "The Major, 'Not Guilty,' since he had been acquitted, was nonetheless under the intimidating pressure of an accusation. First he broke down, then he recovered and went on defending himself with all means at his disposal. In effect, he has been in a state of dire peril to himself."

After Labori had spoken, Georges Clemenceau was allowed to substitute for his brother in speaking in defense of the publisher of *L'Aurore*.

For four years Clemenceau had fought with the pen he had been compelled to substitute for speech in the art of which he had been the dreaded master in the Chamber. But he was no longer accustomed to the noise and the yells of a hostile audience and was visibly uncomfortable at being unable to repay his interrupters in kind. As always, his speech was dominated by compelling logic.

He began by reading his first articles on Dreyfus, written at a time when he still believed that Dreyfus was a traitor. However, he pointed out, after so many startling events, he was inclined now to the belief that Dreyfus was innocent. But this was not the place for him to state his views on that question or for the jury to pass judgment on it. The jury was only to decide whether a court had passed a sentence in disregard of the law. Yet, he went on, if the rights of one man are denied, the rights of the whole nation are put in jeopardy. The nation is the safeguard for all citizens enjoying equal rights, and without such safeguards no country is a nation.

When the public prosecutor asked Zola to show him the General Staff's order, or produce the man who gave the order to the court, Zola's answer was that the order had been given anew in the present courtroom by the generals. When they warned the jury that they would resign if he were acquitted, was that not an order to convict? Clemenceau then took up arguments which identified theirs as a Jewish movement. Of course the Dreyfus family had moved heaven and earth to try and save him whom they knew to be innocent. But the Army itself had come to doubt Dreyfus' guilt. It was Lieutenant Colonel Picquart who had first come to suspect Esterhazy, and he had communicated his suspicions to General Gonse. From the correspondence between the two, the whole affair could be laid bare. General Gonse had gone back on his convictions; Picquart *had not*. Clemenceau continued:

The revisionists were accused of insulting the Army. On the contrary, they honor the Army by demanding that it respect the law, for only through the law can greatness be achieved. We have duties toward the Army, just as the Army has duties toward us. Agreement between the civilian and military sectors in society must rest on the common ground of justice and law.

France had been defeated twenty-five years ago.

Our first aim was to rid ourselves of the despotism of individuals or of the few, to establish in this country a rule of the people, a rule of liberty and equality. The question is, did the two aims contradict each other? The principle of civilian society is liberty and justice, while that of the military is obedience, discipline and order. . . . But the Army is no longer a professional

Army. It is the people's Army. It must embody the same principles as does the nation. If the civilian society in its anxiety over national defense fell into the slavery of the military, then the soil perhaps could be defended, but morally the nation would be lost. By forfeiting the principles of justice and liberty, we would give up what, to the entire world, has been the glory and honor of France. . . . There is no civilian honor and military honor; there is only honor for all.

When the day of judgment comes, what will people hold against us? The adjudged case? Look there, gentlemen of the jury [pointing to the picture on the wall]. You see Christ on the cross. There you see the adjudged case. The picture hangs behind the judge, that he should not be embarrassed by its sight. It should hang rather in front of the judges, they should have it before their eyes as they pass sentence, to see the example of a miscarriage of justice, that our civilization holds to be the shame of mankind. . . .

We destroyed the Bastille and every July 14th we dance in the streets to commemorate the destruction of this monument to the reasons of state. Yet, deep inside, a Bastille remains so long as we are able to accept injustice. In making your decision, there is only one danger to beware: that you do not abandon the cause of justice which you represent. You will not do this. You will uphold civilian law above all prejudices. You will leave unstained the treasure of liberty and justice that we have acquired. Free of racial and religious prejudice, you will render inestimable service to France if you suppress the beginnings of a religious war that threatens to dishonor our country. . . . Gentlemen, we represent the law, tolerance, the traditions of the French spirit. We defend the Army.

The audience broke into laughter and shouts at this, and Clemenceau raised his voice to answer them:

Yes, we defend the Army when we demand that an Esterhazy be kicked out of it. . . . Gentlemen, a general spoke here of your children. Tell me, is there a single man of you who would not hate to see his son in a battalion under Esterhazy's command? Would you entrust your son to be led against the enemy by this officer? It is enough to put the question. The answer goes without saying. . . . Your task is, gentlemen, to judge yourselves rather than us. We appear before you and you will appear before history.

Finally, the jury retired to deliberate. Zola and his friends, twelve all told, drew into a closed circle. They knew that if Zola were acquitted, no one of them would reach home alive. They waited tranquilly. One of them, Emile Duclaux, Pasteur's successor, had written at the beginning of the trial: "It is a great thing indeed to assist at a drama of such heroic grandeur. Depending on the course it takes we shall either become great or be crushed." Now a third possibility loomed. If the jury recognized their greatness, the mob would indeed crush them.

One day in front of the Palais de Justice a young man acclaimed Zola; he was roughly manhandled by the crowd. The mob invaded the building, and Zola had to take refuge in a cloakroom. When he left the building, guarded by his friends, the vast throng outside in the foggy winter night was frightening and fantastic. It pressed forward like a many-headed monster. The police chief had to intervene in person to save the little group. Zola's cab made off in a hurry, and the mob ran after it, shouting curses and hurling refuse.

The next day *La Presse* took the chief of police to task for extending protection to Zola. The police for the most part fraternized with the demonstrators and echoed their slogans. On several occasions there was imminent danger of a lynching. Yves Guyot was nearly thrown into the Seine. A woman pursued him to tear off his button of the Legion of Honor, while the mob cried: "Death to the traitors!" In front of *La Libre Parole* revisionist papers were burned; Jewish stores were broken into, factories attacked and machinery wrecked. *La Libre Parole* regarded these attacks as testifying to the people's noble anger and took pleasure in debating whether it would be better to throw the Jews into the Seine or to grill them alive.

In the provincial towns there were riots that turned into pogroms.

In this mood the country waited for the verdict and Paris waited in a tight, ugly mob outside the courthouse. It took the jury only thirty-five minutes. By an eight-to-four vote, Zola and the publisher were pronounced guilty. They were given the maximum penalty—one year in prison for Zola, four months for the publisher, plus fines for each of three thousand francs. So their lives were saved. The mob that would have feasted on blood feasted on triumph instead.

"I shall not try to describe the riotous, fraternal joy of this evening," wrote Barrès in *Le Figaro*. The military clubs hoisted the flag as on a day of victory in battle. Members of the bar in the provinces wired congratulatory messages to the jury. Political parties vied with one another in claiming the lion's share in the triumph.

"The Jews who foolishly unloosed this prepared campaign of

hatred," said Premier Méline to the Chamber, "brought down upon themselves a century of intolerance—the Jews and that intellectual élite which seems to enjoy poisoning the atmosphere and inciting bloody hatred. From today on," he continued, "those who stubbornly insist on continuing the struggle will not be considered as acting in good faith. We shall apply against them the full rigor of the law. If the powers we now possess are not adequate we shall ask you for new ones!"

The Chamber enthusiastically voted to have the Premier's speech publicly displayed as a proclamation. A resolution was proposed: "The Chamber invites the government to repress energetically the odious campaign undertaken by a cosmopolitan Syndicate and subsidized by foreign money to rehabilitate the traitor Dreyfus, who was unanimously convicted by the testimony of twenty-seven French officers, and who has confessed his guilt." Where or when Dreyfus had confessed was not made clear, but the resolution passed 428 to 54.

Lieutenant Colonel Picquart was retired for "grave shortcomings in service." Grimaux was declared unfit to teach chemistry at the Ecole Polytechnique as well as at the Agronomic Institute. The bar suspended the attorney Leblois for six months for "having communicated confidential information from his client to Senator Scheurer."

Clemenceau drew up an accounting in *L'Aurore*: This was a triumph first of all for the Church, blowing the bugles for a religious war against the Jews, Protestants and atheists. The chiefs of the Army subserviently followed the lead of the Church. Under the cloak of anti-Semitism, the Church instigated movements against the spirit of the French Revolution, movements which may take frightening turns in the future. As for the vanquished: Zola was found guilty of having wanted justice for all and respect shown for the laws of the Republic even by soldiers and judges. He was convicted of this crime. The French people, through their jury, sanctioned this. General Boisdeffre placed his sword on the Code of Law. Touch it who dares. The jury was cautious enough not to do so.

It is no exaggeration to say that the whole civilized world followed Zola's trial with anxiety and distaste. France became an enigma to them. Her moral decay augured ill for the Western civilization of which France for so long had been the vanguard.

The crowned heads of Europe were in correspondence with one another in an effort to find out the truth about Dreyfus. Queen Victoria wrote to her grandson, the German Emperor, asking him confidentially whether Dreyfus had been in his service. Wilhelm II answered: No.

The Times of London wrote: "Zola defended truth and civil liberties. He will be honored wherever people are free." *The Daily Graphic* summed up: "The sentence condemns Zola less than it condemns the Third Republic which is dominated by a military caste that openly derides the law." Other English and Continental newspapers called the sentence savage and barbaric; many voiced the opinion that France was about to disappear from the list of civilized nations. Others expressed fear that the verdict would affect not only France but the rest of the world, and mark a return to international barbarism.

A great Italian paper, *Tribuna*, reassured the civilized world: "The friend of humanity will find consolation in the unanimous cry of protest raised by all civilized peoples against the judicial crime committed in France."

This unanimous opinion was voiced not only in Western countries but also in Russia and in the countries of eastern Europe. Their papers were no less critical than those of the West; in fact, they were even more acrimonious because their aspirations for more freedom and democracy were adversely affected by the collapse of the bastion of liberty and justice.

In America, the New York *Daily Tribune* wrote: "M. Zola had fought a brave fight for the vindication of Captain Dreyfus. There is now needed a champion to fight for the vindication of France." All newspapers of importance in America condemned the military clique that held France captive and expressed admiration for Zola and his friends. The Protestant and Jewish public outside France almost unanimously supported Zola and the revisionists, and so did the bulk of Catholic opinion. Members of the high clergy advocated a retrial. But a minority dissented. Thus *The Globe and Church Progress* wrote: "The peculiar interest that Jewish papers, even in this country, have been taking in the Zola trial, and the amount of sympathy they have displayed with the malodorous novelist and the convicted spy whom he championed, lend confirmation to certain charges that have been going the rounds." This minority, however, was so small that it could not even start an argument.

In France, the public could no longer ignore the hostile attitude of world opinion. They resented the active interest of foreigners in an affair that concerned their national defense. In general, hostility abroad strengthened the prevailing opinion and reinforced the propaganda line about Jewish power throughout the world.

The unity of the foreigners in refusing to understand why the French stuck to their guns in defending the prestige and integrity of their Army made it easier for the French public to dismiss any appeal, advice or opinion coming from outside. France thus became an isolated field, in the confines of which propaganda worked with intense effect and with hardly any interference or resistance. The small group of revisionists, and their potential supporters among the Protestants and Jews, merely served the need the propaganda machine had for providing a definable enemy within.

But now that the Dreyfus case had slipped from the shabby clutches of frightened little men, worried about their careers, into the sphere of a nation's morality, there were men abroad who perceived that there was greatness in France's convulsion. In praising Zola, Leo Tolstoy said: "Great misfortunes sometimes are for a purpose: it is for the good of France that she should be put to wrestle with her conscience." And an Italian friend of Gabriel Monod said to him: "Your country is great. How I should love to live there! Only the fools pretend that France is debased and dishonored. She is the only country where there are heroes, where men expose their lives, reputations, and fortunes to defend a poor unfortunate whom no one knows. How beautiful it is to see a struggle that was originally undertaken by two or three men, alone against all, disregarding violence and injury; this devotion of all those who, in a span of three months, succeeded in rousing the entire world for the cause of justice; and who finally united in their ranks all the best, most honest and intelligent among their people. I should be proud to be a Frenchman!"

In the meantime, Zola appealed his conviction.

Part Three

TRUTH ON THE MARCH

18

IN THE TIDAL WAVE of anti-Semitism that swept over the country, many towns organized boycotts on Jewish shops. Petitions to expel from France the Jews and all those who defended them rained down on the Government. Laws were demanded to deprive the Jews of the vote. The nationalist press incited employers to dismiss Jewish workers. In Algiers, popular meetings and the press urged that Jewish children be excluded from schools, Jewish employees thrown out of the civil service. Even the medieval charge of ritual murder was rehashed.

The Catholic press went straight to the heart of the matter. The Great Revolution was described as an insurrection of man against God and was called the original sin of the century. Gleefully it rejected the Rights of Man and mounted an offensive on intellectual freedom. At a college festival presided over by a general, a Catholic priest pleaded for authority through power:

> When I speak of the necessity for a nation to arm itself with power I mean the material power that does not reason, but imposes itself—the power of which the Army is the most forceful expression, the power of the cannon, which is the ultimate argument of statesmen and of nations. . . . The enemy is intellectualism which professes to disdain power. Turn the point of the sword against it. Woe to the government that veils its weakness behind a supposed insufficiency of legal powers and lets the sword drop. The country in the grip of anxiety will reject those who refuse to save her even at the price of bloodshed.

A poet, asked to write a poem to celebrate in the Pantheon the centenary of the historian Michelet, was made to strike out the lines in which his poem appealed to France to show the world that she still was the champion of right and justice.

The left-wing intellectuals sounded the tocsin for battle. They revived the Society of the Rights of the Man and of the Citizen. On the Right, Paul Déroulède resuscitated his League of Patriots, dissolved when Boulangism ebbed.

The atmosphere grew even tenser when a humiliation was inflicted on France by the British. A young French officer named Marchand started out to explore Africa from west to east, with a task force of a couple of engineers and 120 Senegalese soldiers. They operated a diminutive steamer that carried them across the rivers, while they carried it on wheels from port to port. A success for them would have extended French sovereignty from the Atlantic to the Red Sea and cut the Cairo-Cape line of the British.

The French public had followed the bold venture with enthusiasm. For many months the *voyageurs* seemed lost in the jungle. Then unexpectedly they made their appearance on the Upper Nile and hoisted the tricolor over an oasis. Possession of the Nile at its source would have meant the control of Sudan and of Egypt.

A few days after the event a small British fleet steamed up to the spot, called Fashoda. It was commanded by Lord Kitchener. International law was on the side of the French as the first nation to take possession of an unknown land. But the British relied on force, not law, and demanded that the French quit the oasis. The victory for French boldness, energy and resourcefulness had been a heartwarming consolation for Sedan. But the British fleet put to sea and made menacing gestures against France's Atlantic harbors. Nor was France's ally any help. The Tsar of all the Russians refused to support the African venture. France was isolated and had to capitulate, and Britain did nothing to help her capitulate with dignity. "A second Sedan," William II, the German Emperor, commented with satisfaction.

A new general election was held in May 1898. No party raised the Dreyfus case as an issue. But Paul Déroulède appealed to all voters to reject candidates who had been for the revision of the Dreyfus verdict. The appeal was not needed. No deputy who had been active on Dreyfus' side was re-elected.

Jean Jaurès faced a resolution adopted by a Committe for Repub-

lican Action in his constituency that expressed profound contempt
for him. Jaurès did not mention Dreyfus, but nevertheless warned the
electors: "Our ancestors of the Great Revolution saved the country by
demanding that all leaders obey the laws of the Republic; it is for us,
too, to make France strong and great by instilling into her the spirit
of justice." Jaurès lost his seat. Drumont was elected in Algiers. An
immense crowd greeted the "rabbi of anti-Semitism" when he arrived
in Paris. His cab was drawn in triumph from the railroad station to
his office. Joseph Reinach, one of the leaders of the revisionists, was
prevented from speaking in his constituency. The *gendarmerie* had to
rescue him from a mob. Another Jewish candidate, a certain Klotz,
sought to disarm opposition by declaring that he had been against the
revision of the Dreyfus verdict all along. He condemned the "odious
campaign against the Army."

The Radicals on the republican side, as well as the nationalists of
all shades—authoritarian republicans like Déroulède, Césarists, as the
former Boulangists were now called, and Drumont's anti-Semites—
emerged strengthened, but the balance of the parliamentary forces
remained substantially unchanged.

The elections taught the extremists a lesson: the Republic could
not be overthrown by legal means. There was, however, one issue
that would sweep the entire electorate along with it, even those who
had faithfully supported the republican parties through all vicissitudes. The efforts of the Right must be concentrated on that issue: the
Dreyfus case.

Royalists, Catholics and authoritarians began preparing for a civil
war. By this action of the Right, the strange phenomenon of the "Drey-
fusian revolution" was set in motion. For that is the accepted name of
the unrest which from 1898 onward almost brought to a standstill the
pursuits of public and private life in France, substituting for them
meetings, demonstrations, brawls, debates, the organizing of *coups
d'état* and of forces to forestall them. Families and friendships broke
up forever, new human relations formed.

Léon Blum in his reminiscences compared these times to the Great
Revolution: the individual's life ceased to matter. He was ready to be
sacrificed without hesitation for the cause of truth and justice, nor
would he have hesitated to sacrifice the lives of his opponents. And
his adversaries in their turn burned with equal eagerness to defend
what they considered the nation's vital interests, no matter who died.

People of all persuasions were out "to look beyond the pursuits of life towards the Ideals, or towards the Chimaera—but to something that transcended their own daily interests," as a contemporary English periodical put it.

Curiously, it was a happy life, not only because it became elevated and meaningful but because one lived with and among friends who held the same opinion on the case. Family ties were not strong enough to stand the strain of diverging opinions, and agreement made intimate friends of people who otherwise fitted ill together. Elegant aristocrats hailed the butcher boys of the Anti-Semitic League at mass meetings and conservative academicians shared the platform with revolutionary syndicalists. Melchior de Vogüé's words may be accepted as true: "Above shrewd interests and criminal passions, the bravest hearts of France rushed upon each other in the dark with equal nobility of sentiment, exasperated by the awesome conflict."

The question had come into sharp focus. Clemenceau denounced nationalism and contrasted it to patriotism: "Patriotism requires a *patrie* which cannot exist without justice." The nationalists answered: "Justice cannot exist independently of a society. Societies have existed without justice, but justice has never existed without a society." In this particular instance, the nationalists said, the nation had taken its stand. Déroulède in his own simplicity summed up the feeling of the masses: "It is improbable that Dreyfus is not guilty, but it is certain that France is innocent."

Thus the controversy was clear on all levels: Rights of Man versus reasons of state. Many people of high intellectual standing rallied to the nationalists. They did not actually believe that the bulk of French society served France's vital interests in opposing the Rights of Man. But the fact that the country by an overwhelming majority refused to accept revision of the Dreyfus verdict seemed to them to make it vital to give in. If revision prevailed, the nation could not recover. Its trust in the Army would be shattered and Germany would wax unopposed. To others the Dreyfus affair was a short, dramatic interlude in the eternal struggle between faith and reason, with reason on the side of the nationalists, faith on that of the revisionists.

The stubbornness with which views were upheld in the face of adverse fact and evidence can be measured by the statements of two university professors at a later time when it had become difficult to insist on Dreyfus' guilt. The one said: "All right. So it was not Dreyfus who wrote the *bordereau*. He was the more the traitor. He conspired with Germany to have himself wrongly convicted in order to harm the prestige of the General Staff." The other said that even if Dreyfus were acquitted, he and his entire race would nevertheless remain the object of hatred for the French and be cursed forever. "I like to stick to the thought that I shall yet see him pierced by twelve bullets." This was Jules Soury, a professor at the Sorbonne.

Jean Richepin, the poet, broke with his friend and godfather; they were not on speaking terms for eight years because of their disagreement on the affair. The literary salon of Mme. de Caillavet splintered when Anatole France became one of the leaders of the revisionists. It had been possible in 1897 for Emile Zola and Maurice Barrès to meet and talk quietly of matters pertaining to literature if they agreed in advance that the Dreyfus affair would not be brought up. But now it was impossible. The Caillavet salon now entertained Jaurès and other Socialists. They mixed there with the old habitués—the Comtesse de Noailles, Marcel Prévost and the young Marcel Proust, Dreyfusards all. At Mme. de Loynes's salon, Maurice Barrès, Charles Maurras, Léon Daudet, theorists of nationalism, met Jules Lemaître, the literary critic, and even old Rochefort, who had now definitely landed on the right wing after a long life spent in revolutionary opposition to all constituted authority. The scientists lined up almost to a man on the revisionist side. Professors of the humanities and writers were divided, with the majority favoring the nationalists.

Lectures at the universities became a problem. They were interrupted by demonstrations by the members of the Anti-Semite Youth; or of the Committee of Royalist Youth; or by Jules Guérin's anti-Semitic shock troops; or else by the Socialist Youth. The demonstrations usually ended up in street fights.

The revisionist youth set up headquarters in a bookshop run by the poet Charles Péguy on the Rue de Cujas in the Latin Quarter. Serious young men gathered there who wished to broaden the fight for justice in the Dreyfus case into a fight for justice to all. Christians, or humanitarians, they eventually became Socialists, followers of Jaurès, who, as they earnestly hoped, would lead them, not into class struggles but toward social reform based on a moral renascence. Some began by fighting the depraved General Staff only to become antimilitarists or pacifists.

The Dreyfus Affair was omnipresent. In the theater Ibsen's *An*

Enemy of the People caused a free-for-all. One sentence sounded as if it were an allusion to Zola. The play was withdrawn. Jules Renard in his diary mentions a young man whose family desired him to marry a certain young girl. He requested her parents to let him have her photograph and also to inform him of her views on the Dreyfus Affair. A French expedition to the Arctic wintered on an iceberg and was feared lost. In the spring they were found safe and sound. Their first question to the rescuers was "What about Dreyfus? Is he free?"

Scores of duels were fought between former friends on account of the affair. The publisher Stock mentions thirty in the circle of his acquaintance. A number of suicides were committed in this context, not without a suspicion of murder arising on one side or the other.

The battle was carried on in hundreds of pamphlets. It seemed that almost everybody wished to make a public declaration of his stand. There were devastating cartoons. The greatest hit was scored by a picture in two sections. The first showed a large and happy family gathered round a richly laden dinner table. The caption read: "They have not yet spoken of *it*." The second showed the same place turned upside down in fiendish disorder, everyone gesticulating, hurling insults. The caption ran: "They spoke of *it*."

The letters of the unfortunate Dreyfus to his wife were published in a series in *Le Siècle*. "These letters are admirable," Zola wrote to Brisson. "I know of no more elevated and eloquent pages. It is the sublime in suffering. When our writings have sunk into oblivion, they will still stand as an imperishable monument. The man who wrote these letters cannot be guilty. Read them, M. Brisson, read them one evening, at home with your family. You will be bathed in tears."

They were a long cry in an endless, mute night, these letters, a clamor for justice forever repeated. They touched many sensitive hearts. Women's clubs sent their sympathies to Mme. Dreyfus. But those who believed in Dreyfus' guilt remained unaffected, shielded as they were by a wall of prejudice. The Minister of Colonies, who read all the letters, saw only a ruse in them. The lack of hatred proved to him not humility of spirit but pretense and insincerity.

After Zola was sentenced, Lucie Dreyfus had renewed her request for permission to join her husband on his rock in the south Atlantic. Again the request was denied.

Zola had appealed his conviction on various legal grounds. One of them was that the Minister of War had had no right to *order* prosecution of Zola. That had been the sole province of the military court itself. The High Court of Appeal conceded the merits of this point and annulled the sentence against Zola. A new trial was ordered.

Not even the justices of the High Court of Appeal were spared by the nationalist press. Their judgment enraged the press. They accused the court of obeying the orders of rich Jews and attacked the chief justice, alleging German and Jewish origin. The prosecutor of the High Court became a special target. He was a republican of the old school. He had condemned the anti-Semitic excesses as "unworthy of France, an outrage to the precursors of the Revolution, to Voltaire, the emancipator of human thought." Further, he had rejected the thesis of the trial court on the basis of which all questions had been ruled out of order if they touched on the Dreyfus case.

Had the Government followed its own wishes, it probably would have voided the indictment against Zola. But the nationalist press would have none of that. So a new prosecution was decided on. Where, in the first trial, Zola had been indicted for fifteen lines of *J'Accuse!*, he was now indicted for but three lines: "A court-martial dared to acquit, by order, one Esterhazy—a supreme slap at all truth, all justice."

The new trial was moved to the court at Versailles to prevent disturbances. The courtroom there was too small to hold a crowd. Zola appealed against this move. He and Labori were well aware that the Government had the right to assign the trial to any court on whose territory the issue of *L'Aurore* containing Zola's *J'Accuse!* had been sold. However, they were sparring for time, hoping that in the interim a new government would take over, more sympathetic to the revisionists.

The appeal against the new venue was rejected. The trial at Versailles was to begin on July 18, 1898. A few days earlier Zola had been condemned to two months in prison and a fine of 2,000 francs for libel committed in *J'Accuse!* on the three handwriting experts. He was also to pay 5,000 francs damages to each of them. Zola's lawyers persuaded him he would be of more use to the cause if he did not go to jail just then and appeared in court at a more propitious moment. Clemenceau, meanwhile, promised to explain to the public the reasons for this decision in an article over Zola's signature. The pressure on Zola was great. He had no time to consult other friends. At night, he boarded a train alone for London. He did not even take a spare shirt into exile with him.

Perhaps it would have been wiser for Zola to go to prison. But Labori's arguments were sound and Clemenceau could not be expected to urge another man to choose prison against the advice of his attorney. Zola saw hard times in England. He remained in hiding, first in London, then in the country. Eventually his wife joined him. She made a temporary home and he started working again. "Work always has saved me," he wrote.

The public, of course, could hardly be expected to understand the motives that dictated Zola's flight. But the time which followed was so hectic and so full of astounding events that the episode was soon forgotten.

19

THE CHAMBER RECONVENED. The Radicals were determined to bring the Moderate Cabinet to an end. They moved that henceforth the Government should be composed exclusively of republican parties proper. This was in open conflict with Méline's principle of accepting for allies all who were prepared to pay lip service to the Republic.

The Radicals enlisted the support of the nationalists, bribing them with a promise to appoint Godefroy Cavaignac Minister of War. Cavaignac came from a family of republican soldiers. His grandfather had voted for the execution of Louis XVI; his father had been deported by Napoleon III. Yet Cavaignac, who was himself a graduate of the Ecole Polytechnique, never ceased to hit out against the revisionists. With equal fervor, he criticized the Government for its awkward handling of the Dreyfus case. He firmly believed not only in Dreyfus' guilt but also in the existence of the Jewish syndicate, and had said in public that he would know how to break it up. His idea was to bring all the secret documents out into the light of day, and thereby prove Dreyfus' guilt conclusively. If some ill-willed persons then still indulged in their nefarious criticism of the Army, he would have them declared traitors.

Méline was defeated and a good republican, Henri Brisson, took his place. As expected, he issued a strong declaration against the participation of the Church in politics: "We are resolved to defend with energy the independence of the lay society and the supremacy of civilian power against any attempt at encroachment." He did not touch on the Dreyfus case. He was not in favor of a revision, and his party was even less so.

Cavaignac, now Minister of War, began an intensive study of the Dreyfus documents to make good his election promise. The policy of closed doors was replaced by one of bold publicity. The file which had so amazed Picquart in 1896 by the meagerness of its contents had in the interim swollen to a collection of some 300 documents. General Gonse and Lieutenant Colonel Henry, in order to make examination of the files more difficult, had fattened them with sheafs of irrelevant documents.

The nationalists were looking forward with enthusiasm to Cavaignac's speech in the Chamber. But the General Staff had forebodings.

General Boisdeffre developed poor health and made known his wish to retire. Henry talked freely of getting tired of paper work and longing to get back to the troops. When asked whom he would recommend to take his place at the head of the Second Bureau, Henry proposed Major du Paty. The marquis declined the dubious inheritance. He too expressed a wish for a rest from the excitements of the General Staff. The new War Minister seemed to all a bull in a china shop.

Meanwhile Henry had become incensed at the marquis. Du Paty had always regarded Henry's forgeries as clumsy; it was plain he was no man to rely on in a crisis. To forestall a stab in the back, Henry began to try to shift the responsibility for his own crimes to the marquis. He adroitly planted rumors, and, coming as they did from that large hunk of peasant simplicity, loyalty and honesty, they were believed.

Cavaignac had his own views as to the true story of the Dreyfus case. He distrusted Esterhazy and had it in mind to throw him to the wolves of the revisionist cause, in return for which he expected them to stop protecting Dreyfus and Picquart. Of the conflicting versions of whether the *bordereau* had been written by Dreyfus or by Esterhazy, written by the former in imitation of the handwriting of the latter, or written by the latter at Sandherr's request before returning the original with the marginal note of the German Emperor to the German Ambassador, Cavaignac subscribed to none. For some reason, he believed the two men were confederates in treason. In fact, he had persuaded himself that Dreyfus and Esterhazy were simply accomplices. Yet he felt that in believing this he might be falling into the trap of the "syndicate" (in the existence of which he blindly believed) and be substituting a Gentile for a Jew. So he intended to have Esterhazy jailed on lesser charges. At the request of the General Staff he refrained from identifying the two military attachés—Schwarzkoppen and Panizzardi—when he finally announced the text of the documents Henry had forged. Henry was grateful. He had feared that the attachés might issue convincing denials.

Another firm belief of Cavaignac's was that Dreyfus had confessed to an officer of the Republican Guard on the day of his degradation. He found no evidence to the contrary. For Du Paty's report on his unsuccessful visit with Dreyfus at the prison of Cherche-Midi and Dreyfus' letter written after this episode to War Minister Mercier were not on file. They had disappeared, and with them the memorandum of the interrogation of the officer who had started the rumor in the first place, and then had admitted, red-faced, that he had only been in a tavern and drunk too much.

The process of providing the occasion for Cavaignac's eagerly awaited speech was this: a question would be put from the floor of the Chamber and the War Minister would rise to answer it. By a queer coincidence it was Deputy Castelin again who was chosen to put the question. It was Castelin's question and the Government's desperate anxiety to answer it with a *fait accompli* that had precipitated Henry's decision to fill the gaps in evidence by forgeries.

Finally Castelin was advised that he might ask his question. Cavaignac was prepared to answer it definitively, conclusively and forever. Castelin duly rose in the Chamber and asked the Government to state the truth about Dreyfus and restore the country's faith in the Government's capacity for dealing with the matter. Nothing novel in the way of proof was expected by anyone, least of all by Castelin. It seemed clear to everybody that an abundance had been produced already, sufficient to prove the guilt of a dozen Dreyfuses. What was wanted was forceful action against the Dreyfusards—even if, Castelin's question stated—new legislation was needed to accomplish it. Castelin wanted in particular to see Mathieu Dreyfus in jail for having criminally libeled Esterhazy, and Picquart for having "disclosed secret documents" to Leblois and, through the attorney, to the entire syndicate.

Cavaignac rose to deliver his answer. He was dry, forceful and had the impact of sincerity. He said he had absolute certitude of the crime of Dreyfus. Lacking such certitude, he would never lend his hand to keeping an innocent man in prison—reasons of state or no reasons of state. Then he read the documents, three chosen out of "a thousand pieces of correspondence exchanged for six years between people active in espionage." The documents, where genuine, did not refer to Dreyfus. But where they were Henry's forgeries, they implicated the captain directly. The Chamber ignored the fact that General Pellieux had produced the identical incriminating documents only six months before and that they had been denounced then as forgeries by Scheurer and Picquart. "This is a French and a republican speech!" exclaimed the left-wing deputies, while Déroulède shouted, "Thank you in the name of France!"

Then Cavaignac turned his attention on the revisionists. The silence so far observed by the Government, he said, or possibly criminal maneuvers, had led this group astray. But they represented a distinguished section of French thought. The threat of a misunderstanding between them and the Army had arisen, which was the more serious since it was the mission of the Army at all times to defend the heritage of France, the moral and intellectual heritage as well as the material one. The nation's resentment at the provocation to which the Army was subjected had reached such a pitch that at times he felt inclined to enforce respect for the Army by repressive measures. But this would not be the kind of respect which was the Army's due. "The Army honors justice and accepts the supremacy of civilian power. There is no reason to create the impression that the Army is in need of defending itself against the truth by invoking reasons of state."

The speech was hailed as that of a soldier-statesman. The Chamber unanimously voted to have it publicly displayed in the 36,000 communities of France. Fifteen Socialist members abstained from voting. So did Méline, the former Premier, who had consistently held that the only safe policy for the Government to follow was that of the "adjudged case."

The speech certainly confirmed the nation in its convictions. But at the same time it was a fresh breeze to the revisionists, giving them new vigor. Cavaignac had not only accepted most of their arguments but had acknowledged their good faith. He had discarded the reasons of state and played down the *bordereau* as evidence. In fact, Cavaignac had retained nothing but the alleged confession and the forgeries.

Demange, who had defended Dreyfus, was in a position to destroy the allegation that a confession had been made. He had knowledge of Du Paty's report to the contrary and possessed a copy of Dreyfus' letter to the War Minister telling of Du Paty's vain attempt to squeeze a confession out of him. But only Picquart could prove that the documents in question had been forged.

Picquart had no illusions as to the impartiality of the courts. He knew that the step he was about to take might lead him to prison or worse. It would amount to outright provocation of the Government, the parliament, the public and the Army. Yet he decided to take the step. He wrote a letter to Prime Minister Brisson which was published immediately by the press:

Up to the present I did not feel free to give an account of the secret documents on the strength of which Dreyfus' guilt was allegedly established.

The Minister of War quoted three of these documents from the speakers' stand in the Chamber. I consider it my duty to let you know that I am in a position to establish before judicial authorities that the two documents which carry the date of 1894 do not refer to Dreyfus, and the one that carries the date of 1896 has all the characteristics of a forgery.

It will then become apparent that the Minister's good faith has been abused, as well as that of all who believed in the validity of the first two documents and in the authenticity of the third.

Cavaignac's answer was the decision to have Picquart prosecuted for his alleged revelation of secret documents to his attorney. At a gala reception in the Elysée, Cavaignac was the hero of the evening. From it the news spread that Picquart was to be arrested. Picquart heard it at Trarieux's house, where he was visiting with the former Minister of Justice. Other friends were urgently called to come and shake hands with the colonel. He never lost his quiet smile.

That same night the news was released that Esterhazy had been arrested. Esterhazy had been warned by his attorney that Cavaignac was after him. But he did not heed his attorney's advice to flee. Instead, true to type, he asked for an interview with that "maniac of honesty" but received no reply. Then he went over to the offensive. La Libre Parole, as of old, took up the major's cause and made it clear that the project to make Esterhazy the scapegoat, while letting off his protectors, could backfire. The paper asked:

Did the investigating judges find that Esterhazy had acted on his own without advice or directives from others? Did the initiative with respect to certain acts that are laid to his door come from him personally? . . . Would Esterhazy be thrown over to gratify the Jewish and German Syndicate, the campaign organized by two spies, Von Schwarzkoppen and Panizzardi? . . . After Esterhazy, it will be the turn of Du Paty de Clam, after Du Paty that of Henry, Lauth and Boisdeffre, after Boisdeffre, that of Mercier. In abandoning their unfortunate comrade, the representatives of the Army would abandon their very selves.

In spite of all this, Esterhazy was arrested. Before a military court a charge was laid against him of moral conduct unbecoming an officer. Esterhazy called witnesses to prove that officers of the General Staff had assisted him in writing insulting letters to the President of the Republic and in preparing his trial on the Mathieu Dreyfus charge. He clashed with Du Paty, who, on the witness stand, refused to involve members of the General Staff. Esterhazy finally embarrassed the officers who formed the court with astonishing revelations. He maintained that even the letters sent to Picquart, when that officer was in Tunis, had been fabricated by the General Staff. The political campaign against the Government at that time had also been directed by the General Staff, through Pellieux; he, Esterhazy, had acted only as its agent. Most of this was true, but the verdict of the court was to put Esterhazy on the retired list. The decision ruined him in the Army, but it was his own testimony that destroyed him with his followers.

Cavaignac's next step was to deal with Picquart, who had maintained in his letter to Prime Minister Brisson that Panizzardi's note addressed to his German colleague, advising him to deny—as he himself would—that Dreyfus had worked for them had all the characteristics of a forgery. The Premier, however, wanted to reassure himself of the authenticity of all important documents in the Dreyfus file and assigned Captain Cuignet to examine the lot with utmost care and report to him personally.

Cuignet worked away in one of the offices of the General Staff. Time and time again he went over the documents, working late into the night. On one occasion, when examining once more Panizzardi's "Liberator" letter, he noticed that the lines on one part of the sheet were slightly different in color from the rest. He lifted the sheet, holding it closer to the light, and turned it over. There could be no doubt. Two letters had been glued together expertly. The letter was a forgery. Cuignet was aware that it had reached the Second Bureau in 1896 by way of Henry, Henry alleging it had come via Mme. Bastian. It was obvious to Cuignet that something very irregular had taken place.

The two officers had been friends. But Cuignet seemed to have no grasp of all the implications of this "irregularity." Perhaps he was a man of little imagination. Later remorse would make him writhe for it to the outer edges of his sanity. He would make the most frantic efforts to undo what he had done. But now he acted without hesitation. He walked over to General Roget and asked him to hold the sheet against the light. Roget saw that it was a forgery but said that the matter probably would be cleared up by Lieutenant Colonel Henry, who was on his annual leave. He always took it at the opening of the hunting season.

That was on August 13, 1898. On the following day both officers called on the Minister of War. It must have been a cruel blow for Cavaignac to accept as a forgery the document he had referred to as irrefutable proof in his great speech, still on display in every village and town throughout the length and breadth of the country. Roget advised him to have Henry immediately recalled from leave.

Resentment overwhelmed Cavaignac. A burning hatred for Henry seized him. The man had exposed him to ridicule and he was determined to get him for it. He decided that if Henry were told to interrupt his leave, he might smell a rat. So Cavaignac played it close to his vest. He ordered Cuignet to prepare a dossier of the forgery so complete that Henry, faced with it, would be incapable of denying his crime. He ordered the strictest secrecy. He did not even inform the Prime Minister. Then, coolly, he went on a speaking tour that had already been advertised. He did not hesitate to address audiences from stands adorned with the poster of the speech that had so heavily relied on the forgery. Incredibly enough, Cavaignac was so strongly convinced of Dreyfus' guilt that it never occurred to him that the loss of one piece of evidence, dated after the captain had been convicted, might endanger the case.

On August 30, Henry returned to Paris. In the meantime Cavaignac had informed Generals Boisdeffre and Gonse of the discovery. No one now tried to tip off the man who had been so indefatigable in doing his superiors' dirty work. But actually no one really thought he was in any very great trouble. There was a general conviction that

Henry could explain the matter away. General Gonse took him to the War Minister. Boisdeffre and Roget were present, the latter taking down a record of the hearing.

Henry, presented with the evidence, denied it. Looking around, he saw Boisdeffre avoid his glance and he became aware of the danger. "I remind you," said the War Minister in a cold, hard voice, "that nothing is more grave for you than to offer no explanation. Tell me what happened. What did you do?"

"What do you want me to tell?" asked Henry.

"I want you to give an explanation of what you have done."

After much wrangling Henry conceded that he had arranged a few sentences but denied that he had fabricated the text.

"It is not true," Cavaignac said, "that you fabricated the text?"

"I swear I did not." Then Henry added, "I wanted to give more weight to the document."

"Which are the words you fabricated?"

"I do not remember. The last sentence, part of it."

"You fabricated the whole piece."

"I swear I did not."

He stuck to his denial, then conceded one step. "My superiors were disturbed; I wanted to calm them. I said to myself: Let us add a sentence that can pass as proof in the situation in which we are. . . . I acted alone and in the interest of my country."

It was obvious that Henry had copied onto the document the signature "Alexandrine" from an intercepted innocent letter by Panizzardi. Still he denied it.

Then Cavaignac decided the time had come to reveal to Henry the proof. "The lines on the paper are of different coloring in one part than in the other," he said.

"Which parts are inserted?" Henry asked.

"I do not ask you to put questions, but to answer them. Did you fabricate the entire letter?"

"I swear I did not."

He looked again at Boisdeffre and Gonse. They were pale and silent. The War Minister said, "Then, this is what happened: you received in 1896 an envelope with an insignificant letter inside. You suppressed the letter and manufactured another one. Is that so?"

"Yes," Henry said.

It had taken an hour for Cavaignac to squeeze it out. Roget led

Henry to the next room. General Boisdeffre sat down at a desk and wrote his resignation:

MY DEAR MINISTER:

I have acquired proof that my trust in Colonel Henry, chief of the Intelligence Service, was unjustified. That trust was absolute and led me to the mistake of declaring a document to be genuine which was not, and of presenting it to you as such. In this situation I must ask you to relieve me of my duties.

Cavaignac tried to make the Chief of the General Staff change his mind. After all, anybody can make a mistake. "Yes," Boisdeffre replied, "but it was not anybody who testified before a court and stated that the document was genuine." He left.

Henry thought that it was Esterhazy who had talked. "I never did harm to anyone," he kept saying to himself. "I always did my duty. What rotten luck to run up against such a scoundrel!"

A major from the office of the Military Commander of Paris escorted Henry to the fortress of Mont Valérien. He took Henry first to his home. He showed calm when he talked to his wife: "You know that I am an honest man. Everything is going to be cleared up. Now the Minister wants me to go to Mont Valérien. I go." He packed some shirts in a suitcase and whispered to the officer, "Let's go quick. I can stand no more." They got into a cab. He again talked to himself: "It is inconceivable. It is to go out of one's mind. What I did I would do again, for the country and the Army. My poor wife and my poor little boy. Everything crumbles away."

He was given the same room which Picquart had occupied not long before.

A short communiqué was released to the press: "Today, in the Office of the Minister of War, Lieutenant-Colonel Henry was recognized as being, and himself confessed to be, the author of the letter dated October, 1896, in which Dreyfus was named. The Minister of War immediately ordered his arrest. The Lieutenant-Colonel was taken to the fortress of Mont Valérien."

Henry, up early, asked for newspapers and read the news. Nowhere did he find words of indulgence. The General Staff's favorite newspaper, *L'Eclair*, threw the first stone at him: "This officer committed a most abominable crime." He was abandoned by his colleagues as well as by his fellow nationalists. The game was up. A Dreyfusard

War Ministry was in view. Everything he stood for would be turned upside down. Court-martials, humiliations, prison.

He wrote letters, to General Gonse to come and see him; to his wife:

My adored Berthe, I see that but for you, everybody is going to abandon me. . . . My letter was a copy and there was no question of a forgery: it only confirmed the information I received a few days previously. I am absolutely innocent, they know it, and everybody will know it later, but at this moment, I can't talk. Take care of our adored little Joseph, love him always as I love him and love you.

It was a very hot day. The sun poured into the room. Henry began another letter to his wife. He wrote that he was going to take a dip in the river which he saw from his desk curving around the fortress. He did not finish the letter. He lay down on the bed, took his razor and cut his throat.

His body was cold and had bled white before the guard found it.

20

THE COUNTRY had not recovered from the shattering effect of Lieutenant Colonel Henry's arrest when the news of his suicide struck. Then another blow fell. General Pellieux, indignant at having been deceived by Generals Boisdeffre and Gonse into misleading the jury in the Zola trial, wrote out his resignation and sent it to Cavaignac:

Having been the dupe of men that have no honor, having no hope of retaining the confidence of my subordinates without which it is not possible to wield command, having lost confidence in those of my seniors who caused me to deal in forgeries, I have the honor to request you to order my retirement. . . .

At the insistence of the Military Commander of Paris, General Zurlinden, Pellieux retracted his resignation. Boisdeffre was replaced by General Renouard.

A retrial of the Dreyfus case now became inevitable. Overnight everybody seemed to have turned revisionist. The press commented:

The Dreyfus trial has to be re-enacted—and not in the darkness of a cave. We want to know everything. Did General Mercier violate the law? . . . If

Dreyfus is guilty then he will be sent back to Devil's Island; that is the extent of the risk we take. Revision is the one and only solution.

Everything has changed. Revision is imposed on us. It is now being desired even by most officers in the Army. The government in a few weeks can by this means put an end to the unfortunate affair. The abscess has burst open. If it is necessary to cut into the flesh, it will be done. Open wounds heal fast.

The entire documentation has been thrown open to suspicion. Anything that went through the hands of Henry.

To what purpose is it now to assert that Dreyfus was rightly convicted? Doubt found its way into the minds and hearts of many. A link in the chain has broken. . . .

A revision boldly provoked by the government is preferable to one belatedly extorted by the scruples of jurists or by the interests of one particular person.

The case should be finished and done with this time by a sentence issued in the full light of day with all the safeguards that the defendant possesses in a free country.

If anyone knows of another way to put an end to the agitation we would be glad to hear of it. As far as we go we do not see it.

Only *La Libre Parole* and *L'Intransigeant* dissented. But even they were in considerable embarrassment at first. "If the unfortunate Henry had wanted to serve the Dreyfusards he could not have done better. His action was both stupid and criminal," *La Libre Parole* declared. Rochefort, in *L'Intransigeant*, wrote that he could not understand Henry. The forgery could have no influence on the traitor already condemned. "The other documents in the file are absolutely authentic: the exception only confirms the rule."

Such also was the opinion of Minister of War Cavaignac: "I would accept a revision now less than ever," he declared.

The Government deliberated night and day. Premier Brisson now was determined on a new trial. He dispatched a friend to Mathieu Dreyfus advising him to petition for one. Demange, whose large practice had crumbled away, his clients having deserted him for his defense of Dreyfus, immediately complied.

But Cavaignac put up resistance. He was bent on getting Picquart away from civilian jurisdiction and putting him before a court-martial. He was to be accused of having forged the *petit bleu*, the special-delivery card from Schwarzkoppen's lady friend to Esterhazy, in order to substitute Esterhazy as a traitor in place of Dreyfus. Cavaignac proudly claimed the glory of unmasking Henry's forgeries. "I was the only one to prove that the document was forged," he said in the debate. "But how prevent the revision now?" some Cabinet ministers objected. "By doing what I proposed to do three weeks ago," Cavaignac replied. "Have all who meddled with the Dreyfus case arrested and accused of high treason." His colleagues in the Cabinet seriously believed that the tower of simplicity which was Cavaignac had lost his balance. His suggestion found no takers. Cavaignac left the cabinet meeting and resigned. "I remain convinced of the guilt of Dreyfus," he announced, and he prepared to rally the bedraggled anti-Dreyfusards and take over the Government.

The nationalist and Catholic press showed signs of a quick recovery. "The War Minister's opinion stands intact. His views have been reinforced by his close study of the documents. Only one of them was found to have been forged. This is one more proof of the authenticity of the rest. The guilt of Dreyfus is more evident than it has ever been."

"Tell this to the public, ceaselessly and day by day, so that public opinion will not be misled," the press urged.

The Cabinet kept deliberating. Although the Government had received an invitation from the Tsar to join all European powers in getting up an international court to arbitrate disputes between nations, and so eliminate wars—a suggestion that resulted from the Fashoda incident—nothing but the Dreyfus Affair was dealt with.

Premier Brisson decided to appoint a new Minister of War. He refused to take over the post himself, as many suggested, being of the opinion that a general would be in a better position to hold the military in check in such critical days. There were numerous refusals of the post, but finally General Zurlinden accepted. He made one condition —that he might study the Dreyfus file before sending a request to the Minister of Justice for a retrial of the case. Zurlinden visited the General Staff to confer with General Roget, who convinced him that it was Picquart who had set the whole affair in motion by forging the *petit bleu* to involve Esterhazy and free Dreyfus. The extremist press did its best to intimidate Zurlinden. Rochefort wrote: "Now in the end, a general was found who is willing to betray the Army. . . . His defection is no less odious than that of the rabble whose protector he is."

Esterhazy, when the news of Henry's suicide reached him, felt

that he could not afford to stay in France any longer and hastened to
look for "more favorable skies." He fled, without luggage, taking a
local train from Paris in order to remain undetected. Then he walked
across the Belgian frontier. Finally he arrived in London as a Monsieur
de Bécourt. The time had come for him to confess and take revenge
on his accomplices for deserting him, and make money out of it.

While the revisionists feared that Lieutenant Colonel Henry had
carried the evidence against the General Staff to his grave, and suggested that he had been murdered by the generals, some Catholic
papers wondered whether Henry had not been murdered by the Jews.
The royalist Charles Maurras launched a campaign to vindicate Henry,
to make him out a man of honor, even a great man. "Colonel," he
wrote, "there is not a drop of your precious blood that does not pal-
pitate in the heart of the nation. . . . Before long, expiatory monuments will be erected for you springing from the soil of the father-
land, in Paris and in your own home town, monuments that shall point
to our own cowardice. . . . In life as in death you were our leader.
Your unfortunate act will be counted among your finest achievements
in war."

The recovery of the nationalist and Catholic press made astound-
ingly rapid progress. With one voice they now said that Henry had
forged a document for the sole purpose of not being compelled to use
another, a genuine one. To divulge the genuine one would have meant
war while the Army was unprepared. It would have spelled *débâcle*.
Allusion was made to the by this time notorious marginal note of the
German Emperor. The *Koelnische Zeitung,* inspired by the German
Foreign Office, hastened to publish an article, saying, "They may publish everything and anything: the Emperor who would not exchange
letters with a spy will not declare war on account of an inept forgery."
It was to no avail. The nationalist press insisted this was but a trap.
War would most certainly follow the publication of a document which
proved that the Emperor had lied when denying that he had written
the note.

La Libre Parole, having first given its pernicious treatment to the
new Minister of War, announced with satisfcation that Zurlinden
would rather resign than be an instrument of the revisionists. Their
information carried authority. For days on end the Cabinet had dis-
cussed the matter of revision and remained divided on the issue.

The nationalist press kept urging the President of the Republic to intervene. He did so by supporting Zurlinden's opposition. But Premier Brisson stood firm and the majority in the Cabinet followed his lead. The revisionists had won. Then Zurlinden resigned. "Thorough examination of the judicial files of Dreyfus," he wrote, "has so strongly convinced me of his guilt that, as Chief of the Army, I am unable to accept any other solution than maintenance of the sentence in its entirety."

Brisson had to look for another general. He picked General Chanoine, putting heart into him by telling him that he need take no stand for a revision since that had already been decided on. Chanoine accepted the post.

Zurlinden resumed his duties as Military Commander of Paris, but not before having ordered the retirement of Du Paty de Clam. The marquis, principal target of the Dreyfusards, had never been of any real consequence to the military. Now he was a liability. Zurlinden had left one further bequest to his successor—a request to the civilian court to transfer Picquart to military jurisdiction for prosecution on the charge of having forged the *petit bleu*.

The legal requirements for this transfer were such that Chanoine had to act quickly if at all. It was obvious to Brisson why Picquart's prosecution was being insisted on by the military. If Picquart were convicted of forgery, the prospects for a retrial of the Dreyfus case would be reduced substantially. And, even if there were a new trial, Picquart's testimony would be discredited and Dreyfus would be convicted all over again—a consummation most prayerfully desired by the General Staff. It was bad enough to convict a guilty man on false evidence. How much worse if the man had been innocent all along! Yes, Picquart's head on a plate was something the generals wanted, and Brisson, even though he was all out for revision, had to yield. He could not afford to lose yet another Minister of War.

Picquart was acutely aware of the danger he was in. Would men who had not stopped at forgery stop at murder? It was something to think about. When Henry had cut his throat, his whole damning story had remained untold. It seemed to some quite a coincidence. And there was the man who had entered history under the last of his many aliases —Lemercier-Picard. This was the unsavory little crook who had done the actual forging of "The Liberator" for Henry. He had attempted to profit from it. Blackmail was one of his means of making a living and one day Lieutenant-Colonel Henry's adjutant had visited him in his dingy little room. The same day Lemercier-Picard had been found hanged in the same room—a fact with which Picquart was well acquainted.

The question of jurisdiction, whether military or civil, was argued in court by Labori for Picquart. The law was on the side of the military and, when this became apparent, Picquart walked forward. Looking directly into their faces, he addressed Generals Gonse and Pellieux, sitting side by side:

Tonight I shall probably go to the Cherche-Midi [the military prison]. Perhaps this is the last opportunity for me to speak in public, before the secret investigation there. I wish everyone to know that if the rope of Lemercier-Picard or the razor of Henry should be found in my cell it will denote murder. For a man like myself would never consider suicide. I shall face this new accusation with serenity, as I faced the others. This is all I wanted to say.

He spoke in a calm voice. Then he turned around and the military guards moved forward. "I am fine here," he wrote from Cherche-Midi, "at peace with myself."

What Esterhazy had been to the nationalists, Picquart became now to the Dreyfusards—hero and martyr. But what a difference! Here was a man of dignity and probity who had been on his secure way to becoming the youngest general in the Army. Dreyfus was a martyr, to be sure. But it was difficult to make a hero of him. Almost no one knew anything about him as a man. Zola was a hero, yes, but not really a martyr. His fame was greater than it had ever been, and he had never gone to prison. But Picquart had given up everything and was in prison.

After a visit with him at Cherche-Midi, Octave Mirbeau wrote:

In the semi-darkness, one could distinguish only his eyes, his clear eyes, limpid and happy: they receive you amiably. Not the slightest weariness or nervousness. A little pale, not the paleness of suffering but that pallor peculiar to people who do not go outdoors. We talk of Carlyle, of Michelet, of Wagner and of the primitives in music—of everything. And I feel how large, how cultured his mind is and that it has been growing and enriching itself. It is surprising that no rancor slips into his philosophy; on the contrary his mind is open to all great conceptions, social and human alike. The silence and the solitude make his thought more active and profound. . . . He himself is astonished that he has no hatred. He is a man! Humanity is led toward death by its heroes. It is given life and vigor by a man!

Picquart certainly possessed one thing that makes for greatness in a man: courage.

"There is something entrancing in the contemplation of an ordeal nobly borne, something that exalts courage," H. Villemar wrote in an essay on Picquart. "He who knows how to conquer himself reveals to others the secret of his triumph. He gives them also the desire to follow him. He teaches by his own example that, if the first virtue to cultivate is to master one's self, the only aim to pursue is peace of the mind."

The revisionist fold kept growing. The machinations of the General Staff unveiled by Henry's arrest and death alarmed the left-wing republicans and the Socialists. They realized to what extent the Church and the Army had encroached on the field of politics and public life under the pretext of concern for national security.

Jaurès, whose eloquent and warm humanism had been direly missed in the Chamber, published his book *The Proofs*, a penetrating guide to the labyrinth of the Dreyfus case. He called public meetings on "the Dreyfus Affair and Socialism." They ended, as a rule, in pitched battles between Socialists and nationalists fought out in the streets. The police arrested Socialists only. The revisionists organized demonstrations along the Champs Elysées to reclaim the streets that for so long had been the exclusive domain of the nationalists.

Revisionist republicans, Socialists and anarchists spoke from one platform with priests who were Dreyfusards. In that fraternal front the cause of justice for Dreyfus began to broaden into the cause of social justice. On the other hand, the patriots, who dreaded a disintegration of the Army, shared their meetings with rabid anti-Semites, Césarists, who were on the lookout for a general whom they could make a dictator, royalists, who hoped to see a king recalled to surmount public anarchy, and the clericals, who clung to their grip on education and the Army.

The mass movement made its imprint also on the revisionist press. In place of lucidity and irony, there were now rude and sharp attacks. On Picquart's arrest by the military, Clemenceau had made short shift of Prime Minister Brisson, who, though a good republican, was anything but a strong man:

"What of Brisson, who bemoans his destiny of having to lead us into a catastrophe? Is he stupid rather than cowardly or cowardly rather than stupid? Both. Cowardice and imbecility are not necessarily mutually exclusive," Clemenceau went on. ". . . Brisson, Sarrien, Bourgeois, the whole gang of radicaldom are Jesuits of a deeper dye than the whole Jesuitry. . . ." Clemenceau preferred the traitor Bazaine to his fellow radical Brisson. "He, at least, would fight for his honor," unlike Brisson, "who kneels on the sword and sighs in melodramatic tremolo, begging in turn for the favor of the friends of truth, and for that of the partisans of the lie."

Jaurès wrote: "This last crime was foisted upon us only by the Ministry of War, and by Faure, President of the Republic. Faure was not surprised as was Brisson by the abominable machinations."

Paris in those days was in the throes of constructing a subway. The *Métro* was to be completed for the World Exhibition of 1900. The workers involved in the construction went on strike. The Government called out the Army, in fear of sabotage and disturbances. The streets took on the look of encampments. Wild rumors of a revolution appeared in the papers abroad. In France, inspired reports flew about: conspiracy between the striking workers and the Dreyfusards; general plans for a *coup d'état*; Dreyfus back, held at Mont Valérien; Dreyfus dead; Esterhazy hanged. The reports were printed in the nationalist press. *L'Aurore* presented its readers with the version that Henry had not committed suicide: the Jesuits, the paper said, had put a razor in his hand. He had been made to choose: degradation and deportation or else suicide with a pension for his widow and the Dreyfus revision buried.

Truth had a thorny path to travel. And the end was still years away.

21

A PETITION for the revision of the Dreyfus verdict was before the High Court of Appeal. But the nationalists had recovered from the body blow of the Henry suicide and were resolved to prevent revision by any manner of means, legal or illegal.

Brisson was to present his Cabinet for approval by the Chamber of Deputies on October 25. The League of Patriots launched an appeal to the people to mass in front of the Palais Bourbon at the opening session of the Chamber to demonstrate "their trust in the Army and their aversion for the traitors." The Anti-Semitic League made its own appeal for demonstrations in front of the Chamber. The appeal ended: "Down with the Jews! Long live the Army! Down with the traitors!"

The royalists, however, did not succeed in enrolling Déroulède into a united front with the Anti-Semitic League, which they kept entirely under their control. Déroulède still stood for the Republic and for equality. He rejected liberty only for the sake of authority and strength. Guérin, on the other hand, promised his royalist sponsors that he would mobilize his shock troops, numbering five thousand, who were on the pay roll of the League, and he also expected a large mass of sympathizers from the labor unions. His tactical plan was to infiltrate Déroulède's League of Patriots in a peaceful way and, at the decisive moment, stampede them into action.

Guérin's strategy was not without basis. He had made inroads on the railroad workers' union and its twenty thousand members. The union was ready to take part in the demonstration, marching under its own slogan "to teach the inhuman capitalists a lesson on what the people could do if they only chose."

The strike of the workers on the World Exposition projects had been on for some time without leading to incidents. Now there was violence—arranged by Guérin's hirelings and *provocateurs*.

The parties of the Left renounced counter-demonstrations for fear that a clash of the opposing camps might offer a pretext to the nationalists for a *coup d'état*. The League of the Rights of Man warned the republican public to keep off the streets "in contempt of the perfidious meetings of an association of criminals." The Socialists resolved to be on the alert but to intervene in the streets only if the situation turned grave.

The Government had the railroad stations occupied by the military. The rails were guarded by sentries.

Such was the atmosphere in which the Chamber met to accept or reject Henri Brisson and his Cabinet.

No sooner had he finished the speech in which he introduced the new Government when, to Brisson's complete surprise, General Chanoine, his Minister of War, rose to make a declaration:

I believe that I have a right to my own opinion on the unfortunate Affair ... it is the same as that held by my predecessors who stood in this place before me. Now that the Chamber has reconvened, I declare before you, representatives of the people, that I remit to your hands the trust confided in me to guard the interests and the honor of the Army. I herewith tender my resignation as Minister of War.

It was a conspiracy joined in by the General Staff and it succeeded. The Cabinet fell the same day, rejected by the combined anti-revisionist forces on the Right and on the Left.

The President of the Republic, Félix Faure, designated as Premier the man who was heading the Government at the time of Dreyfus' arrest, Charles Dupuy.

The Brisson Cabinet had been formed under the tremendous impact of the shock which the arrest and suicide of Lieutenant Colonel Henry had caused the country. With Charles Dupuy as Premier, the shock backfired.

But the revisionist front no longer consisted merely of intellectuals, anonymously supported by a subdued and unorganized minority. The Henry suicide had given the leadership confidence. It had encouraged the tacit supporters of the front to become vocal, and those whose eyes had been opened only by the gruesome event to line up and close ranks.

The anti-revisionist government notwithstanding, the case of Dreyfus was still before the High Court of Appeal.

The High Court was under heavy fire from the nationalist press. One paper wrote that the court had only one thought in mind: to find the best means to open France's frontiers to the enemy. The way was easy: the court would receive the secret documents in evidence; according to the rules of judicial procedure, they would be shown to counsel for the defense. From there the secrets would get, within a day, into the hands of the German Emperor. Rochefort, in *L'Intransigeant*, had desperate advice to give: put out the eyes of each member of the High Court to show how France punished her traitors.

The nationalist leaders had no illusions as to the decision an unprejudiced authority would take. The High Court lived up to their worst expectations. On October 27 the Criminal Chamber of the High Court of Appeal considered the petition for the revision of the Dreyfus verdict. With Justice Loew in the chair, Justice Alphonse Bard, a young judge, learned and penetrating, reported on the case. The petition was accepted for hearing. The court ordered that Dreyfus be informed by cable of the decision and instructed to prepare his arguments.

22

REVISIONIST DEPUTIES urged Premier Dupuy to order the military proceedings against Picquart suspended until the High Court of Appeal had completed its hearings in the Dreyfus case. The Premier declined. But the court, on its own initiative, ordered the suspension. Picquart, however, remained under arrest.

One day the door of his cell opened and he was escorted to the High Court of Appeal to testify. For the first time he was before a court that heard without passion or prejudice his careful, precise testimony, delivered in measured words.

The court called previous witnesses to repeat their earlier statements. The generals on the stand unanimously refused to answer questions about the secret papers communicated to the military court that had convicted Dreyfus. "They are not part of the judicial procedure" was General Mercier's argument, and the generals, as witnesses, adhered faithfully to his dictum.

The High Court dispatched a request to the Government to transfer to it all the secret documents involved. General Zurlinden, Military Commander of Paris, ordered the General Staff to refuse the request.

Simultaneously, the nationalist press went into high gear with its campaign: Letting the court look into those documents would be equivalent to revealing to Germany the military secrets they contained. They hurled remarkably unbridled insults at the High Court of Appeal, calling it the apotheosis of treason.

There are three chambers in France's highest appellate court. It was the Criminal Chamber, to which the Dreyfus case had been appealed, that was singled out for vilification. Its president (as the French call their chief justice) was declared to have a brother in the Prussian civil service. It was stated flatly that the members of the court had been bribed.

The new Minister of War, Charles Freycinet, a civilian, was brought under pressure from the Left to order the documents transferred to the court. The Right and the Center brought equal pressure to keep him from transferring them. He came out of the jaws of this vise with the ambiguous statement that he would not transfer any document which might endanger the security of the state.

But the time was past when the revisionist deputies were afraid to fight. Alexandre Millerand, Socialist deputy, wrote: "How can the High Court of Appeal be told that it will be put in the position of not seeing all the relevant documents? How can the people accept the Court's verdict if it is not arrived at by weighing the evidence?"

In the end the Government had to yield to the High Court. The documents were transferred, but there was a proviso: the court was not to make any of them public without previous consent from the Minister of War.

A total of 373 documents were dispatched together with a note saying that these were all the Dreyfus file contained. There was among them not a single piece of evidence against Dreyfus. About fifty were incredibly crude forgeries, or notes and letters, intercepted or stolen by the Second Bureau. They contained clues to or inferences of espionage activities. But there was nothing in them to indicate why they belonged in a file on Dreyfus. The remainder were not even that relevant. For instance, there was a bundle of letters stolen from the German military attaché, written to him by the wife of a Scandinavian attaché. These letters had aroused the Second Bureau's suspicion. A Chinese had been repeatedly mentioned in them. Who was he? It appeared likely that "Chinese" was a code name. The Second Bureau carefully preserved the letters and deposited them in the secret Dreyfus file. If it were treason, and there was no one else to blame, Dreyfus was the one. But it was not even treason. Many years afterward the secret of the "code name" was broken. In 1904 a patent investigator, Captain Targe, had an inspiration. He arranged the letters according to their dates. "Yesterday I was visited by the Chinese," the lady wrote in one. "If you are free, come tomorrow because I expect a visit from the Chinese," she said in another. Captain Targe's inspiration was finally rewarded. There was a lunar cyclicity in the recurring event. This was no treason. It was a biological occurrence.

After the documents had been transferred, a new tack was tried. This was to have the Criminal Chamber of the High Court discredited to such an extent that another chamber of the same court would have to be entrusted with the hearing. The Civil Chamber was known to have an anti-Dreyfus majority among its judges. Accordingly, a campaign began to entrust the hearing to this chamber.

The campaign had a dramatic start. One of the justices, Quesnay de Beaurepaire, sent his resignation to the president of the High Court of Appeal declaring that the Criminal Chamber had shown special favors to Picquart when hearing him as a witness.

A day after his resignation, Quesnay's name appeared on the masthead of *L'Echo de Paris*, the General Staff's spokesman. He was the paper's new editor. He immediately demanded that the Government investigate the members of the Criminal Chamber, including its chairman. He insisted that either another chamber of the High Court of Appeal be entrusted with conducting the trial or else that the justices of all the chambers should adjudge the Dreyfus case together.

Quesnay had been the public prosecutor in the Panama scandal. He had shown unusual skill in protecting the republican deputies, senators and ministers involved. In 1898 a Socialist deputy had made a motion to have Quesnay censured by the Government for having frustrated the investigation of the Panama affair. The motion had put the republican parties in a quandary. To vote for it would be ungrateful. To vote against it would endorse publicly the fact that the prime movers of the great scandal had got away unpunished. They voted for the motion. Quesnay had never forgiven their ingratitude and now he was taking his revenge.

The president of the High Court of Appeal investigated the charges within his own jurisdiction. All turned out to be based on sheer gossip. His report gave, nevertheless, support to those who asked that another chamber should try Dreyfus. It read: "Neither the good faith nor the integrity of the Justices of the Criminal Chamber was in question. Yet, in view of the exceptional gravity of the crisis through which the country is passing, it would be prudent not to let the responsibility for the final verdict rest upon the Criminal Chamber alone."

Three professors at the Sorbonne who subscribed to the nationalism of Barrès and Maurras took charge of the campaign on a more dignified level. They founded a new organization, the League of the French Patrie. Its chief mouthpiece, the literary critic Jules Lemaître, stated that the question that divided France in the Dreyfus Affair was not a moral, but a judicial one—namely: Was Dreyfus innocent or guilty? It was, thus, up to the court to decide. However, the national importance of the matter demanded that the High Court in its entirety should back the decision, thus lending it a unique prestige. Only such a verdict could be accepted by the nation as a whole.

The new movement rapidly gained support from the anti-Drey-fusard conservative public. A nationalist deputy brought a bill to the Chamber to pass exceptional legislation for the case in question, i.e., to disqualify the Criminal Chamber of the High Court of Appeal and qualify the High Court in its entirety to sit in judgment on Dreyfus.

While a committee deliberated the bill, the nationalist press re-sumed its onslaught: "The rogues of the Court have heaped up so much dirt and such untold infamies that even the Minister of Justice, who has a strong stomach, has had enough of it." . . . "The Cabinet has publicly acknowledged the indignities perpetrated by the prosti-tutes of the Court." Quesnay wrote in his paper that two days after the justices had examined a certain secret document it passed into the hands of an agent of the Triple Alliance (Germany, Austria, Italy). *L'Autorité* went even farther. It stated that the nation would not ac-cept the Dreyfus verdict's being declared void even if the entire High Court should order it.

The Socialist Millerand gave voice to the feeling that matters were rapidly moving toward anarchy. "You are killing the very notion of justice," he told the Right. "In the future a journalist may disqualify any court. The bill before the Chamber is simply a premium paid for calumny. In the editorial offices they are already setting up lists of pro-scriptions on other courts, to have judges excluded because this one is a Jew, the other a Protestant, the next one the brother of a revision-ist. . . . A Caesar may despise the law and debase the judges; but the honor and the strength of democracy lies in not tolerating arbitrary power."

The bill was unconstitutional. The Criminal Chamber was expressly named as the court of jurisdiction in such a case as Dreyfus'. But the Minister of Justice replied only: "You had better look to your con-stituencies."

The bill carried the Chamber of Deputies by a big majority.

23

THE FINAL EMERGENCE of the documents brought to light many strange facts. It showed some mysteries to have been deliberate mysti-fications. But not all the mysteries were cleared up. One such con-cerned the spy on the General Staff. Documents did not cease to "fly away" from the staff after Dreyfus' arrest. This alone would have indicated, if the staff had been interested, that someone else was the traitor. Esterhazy had faithfully provided the German attaché with material after the Dreyfus trial and had been rewarded for it. From whom on the General Staff did he procure the secret documents? The guilty man was never discovered.

Esterhazy, from his vantage point in London, published his side of the story for a good price. It was also printed serially in Paris. He certainly knew how to hold an audience. His language was vivid, strong, full of metaphors. The late Colonel Sandherr, he insisted, had briefed him to become an agent of the Germans, to sell them secrets of no consequence, to gain their confidence and give them garbled versions of secret documents to mislead them. His mission had been to gain access to German secrets, he said. Esterhazy bestowed friendly words only on the two corpses, Sandherr and Henry. The Chief of Staff, Boisdeffre, and all others still alive were in a position to expose his lies and so received their full share of invective as cowards who had conspired to save their own skins and sacrifice the lesser fry—that is, Henry and Esterhazy. Henry, he said, had been forced to kill himself. Henry knew too much, so he had had to die, while he, Esterhazy, had had to flee for his life.

Esterhazy's articles were filled with lies, some of them told in pure malice. But sometimes he told a truth for the same reason, out of malice. It was true that someone had had to furnish Esterhazy with secret documents that he could sell to Schwarzkoppen. Had it been Henry? Esterhazy was the only man who knew, and trying to find out anything from him was like trying to find it out from the wind.

Undoubtedly, Major Henry had forged, falsified and perjured himself time and time again to bury Dreyfus under an ever increasing heap of "proofs." Had he been only the lackey doing his master's dirty work, or had there been something more to it? Picquart, who had every reason to hate this unscrupulous giant, refused to believe that Henry had been a traitor. However, Picquart was anything but a judge of the human heart.

There was news from informed sources abroad which seemed to indicate that Henry had been the real traitor and Esterhazy only his tool. It was precisely the fact that Henry had stood behind Esterhazy that made the latter so great an asset in the eyes of the foreign embassies, the London *Observer* reported. And Joseph Reinach came to the same conclusion in *Le Siècle*.

On the day Reinach's revelations appeared, the civilian judge Paul Bertulus, who had aided Pellieux in his investigation of Esterhazy, appeared before the High Court. He testified to Henry's breakdown under investigation. He told the High Court that Henry had begged him to save him and the honor of the Army and that he, Bertulus, had then begun to suspect that Henry might have actually participated in the treason. However, it was no more than a suspicion. Henry's moral collapse may very well have been due to his own psychology. His trouble from the very first had been that he was all uniform and no soul. Now he could no longer be even a uniform.

Reinach's articles aroused lively interest among the revisionists. Zola, in a letter, congratulated the author, though he made strong reservations. On the nationalist side indignation reigned unconfined. Henry's widow was brought in from the countryside to protest. She singled out one Reinach statement: "It was during that year [following Dreyfus' conviction] that the two traitors and Von Schwarzkoppen hauled in their biggest crop—Von Schwarzkoppen in information, Henry and Esterhazy in cash—amounting to nearly one hundred thousand francs." "If you cannot prove that my poor husband received this amount from abroad, you are the most criminal, the most odious and cowardly calumniator," she declared, and threatened to sue Reinach for libel.

Drumont pointed out in *La Libre Parole* that the widow did not have the money to sue Reinach. The paper started a subscription to collect the funds for that purpose. A huge canvas streamer was hung from the balcony of the editorial office: "For the widow and the orphan of Colonel Henry against the Jew Reinach." For an entire month, from December 14, 1898, to January 15, 1899, the solicitation of subscribers continued. "No matter how small the contribution, it will be a slap at the dirty face of the ignoble Reinach," the paper declared. Contributions came from Paris as well as from the countryside, mostly in small amounts. The sum of 130,000 francs ($26,000) was donated by 15,000 signatories.

The list of contributors was published daily. It included four active generals, twenty-eight retired generals, nine colonels, about a hundred senior officers, four hundred retired officers, and numerous priests, some of whom withheld their names. The aristocracy almost to the last man put their illustrious names on the list. It was also signed by a number of politicians, professors and such writers as Barrès, Lemaître, Maurras and even the young Paul Valéry, the latter "with some reluctance."

Many contributors also wrote down their reasons for contributing to the fund. A group of officers on the frontier stated they were eagerly waiting for the day on which the order would be given to try out the new explosives and guns on the 100,000 Jews who were poisoning France. Abbé Cross wanted a Jew's skin in front of his bed to trample on mornings and evenings. Another priest wrote that Christ still loved the Franks and would give them faith and courage to chase the Jews from France. Still another had it that the mercy of God stops where the Jew is concerned.

Many gave advice about what to do with the Jews. A Saint Bartholomew's night was most popular. One contributor wrote that he was training his dog to devour Jews. Another advocated impaling all Jews. Others wanted them driven into the Sahara, thrown into the sewers, bathed in vitriol, their legs cut off, their eyes put out, their skins tanned. Burn them alive was one prayerful plea. Poison them with strychnine was another.

The schools conducted by religious orders as preparatories for the military schools subscribed *en bloc*. In the famous Jesuits' preparatory school for the Ecole Polytechnique, one student refused to contribute. He was advised to leave the school.

Not all the incitements to murder were directed against Reinach or the Jews. Thirty-six were aimed at Brisson and Zola; 41 at Bard, the reporting judge; 43 at Picquart; 48 at Loew, president of the Criminal Chamber of the High Court of Appeal; 58 at Clemenceau. Lieutenant Colonel Hubert Henry was hailed as a martyr and hero who had given his life for *la patrie*.

This exhibition of demented hatred, rancor and spite made a deep impression. Yet it was not an indication of strength. It was a frenzy on the part of those who felt that their front was irremediably dented. Henry's arrest, his suicide, the fact that he had been officially declared to have forged the document that had been publicly exhibited as conclusive proof of Dreyfus' guilt—all this had opened a breach in the wall which separated the public from the truth. Reluctantly many had begun to realize that something must have gone seriously wrong with the generals. These generals had begun to present the repulsive spectacle of crooks falling out with one another. It was an exasperating revelation, humiliating and painful. It made some turn in renewed hatred against those who had forced the cruel facts on them.

The ordinary people, the core of France, were terrified at the apparent collapse of all constituted authority. The feverish efforts to uphold the Army's prestige undermined the authority of the institutions of the Republic. A sustained, destructive daily campaign was being carried on against the Government, Parliament, the judiciary, and in general against all constituted authority. The cemeteries of French history were opening up to claim the living nation as their own.

Those dedicated to a rebuilding of the authority of republican institutions recognized the enemy. They had had to face it ever since the Great Revolution. Clemenceau sounded the old battle cry: "France shall find herself again; we, her children, shall save her from the hands of the Church, and from you, her traitors."

Abroad, some degree of astonishment prevailed over the French Church's lack of restraint in the Dreyfus Affair. It was thought to go counter to the Pope's general policy of seeking a *modus vivendi* with the established order of things. Friendly misgivings were voiced by Irish and American Catholic circles. But the Vatican exerted no moderating influence in France. In the Dreyfus Affair it simply endorsed the position taken by the French Church. It took no exception to the Jesuit *Civilità Cattolica's* challenge to the traditions of the Great Revolution nor to the berserk anti-Semitism of the Assumptionist press. Quite the contrary. A liberal-minded priest censured *La Croix* and argued that "to drag the thrice holy notions of charity and love through the mud by invoking them in the wrong places is contrary to public morality, for it amounts to making Christ share responsibility for the false apostles." The Secretary of State of the Vatican, however, in the name of His Holiness, the Pope, sent an encouraging message to the Assumptionist Order: "You will be able to maintain and further to increase the high esteem in which your Order stands, an esteem that accrued to it by virtue of its accomplishments."

The Princes of the Church of France, at this juncture, succeeded in convincing the Vatican that the time had come for the Church to prevail over the heritage of the Revolution; that the Church and republicanism in France were principles that excluded each other. Those who called for moderation went unheard. In 1898 Paul Viollet, a liberal Catholic, appealed to the papal nuncio "to warn the papers that their monstrous attitude will bring painful retaliation to the Church, and that with some justification." Not until 1899 did the Vatican give a pointer that could be read as disapproval of the fanatical anti-revisionist campaign. An article in *Le Figaro* by Boyer D'Agen described an imaginary talk with the Pontiff. It was neither confirmed nor denied by the Vatican. The general trend was a query by the Pope concerning the passions that were rending France in twain. What has become, so the Pope's soliloquy ran, of the generosity of your race, in this cutthroat struggle of the parties? After all, the unfortunate affair has in the end found the tribunal that is to give it a fair trial. Not only has the accused been given the opportunity of this hearing, but your Parliament gave him the exceptional right to be heard by a plenary court of the highest judicial authority in the land. . . . Yet the arms are not laid down even in sight of this grandiose and reassuring machinery of jurisdiction. Do not think that this issue between the parties can be made a religious issue. Our religion has already hallowed several millions of martyrs who were dedicated to the just cause.

The result was a campaign among the faithful to implore God to enlighten the Pope. But the Pope's oblique warning came too late to avert the consequences of the Church's anti-republicanism. In the French Chamber, bills had already been introduced to enact the separation of Church and State and to bar the Church from the field of education. Though the Chamber was still dominated by moderates and rightists, the republican parties were sufficiently united to take action against the Church in politics. A commission was appointed to study the question of lay education.

There were, of course, active dissenters in the Catholic camp. Paul Viollet joined the League of the Rights of Man, and left it only when the majority of the League voted to disqualify the members of religious orders from teaching. He then set up the Catholic Committee for the Defense of Right and Justice. Two hundred Catholics joined the organization. It is also worth noting that not a single bishop subscribed to Drumont's collection for Lieutenant Colonel Henry's widow, and no more than three hundred out of fifty thousand parish priests appeared on the lists. Thus, the hierachy of the Church refrained from being directly involved in the affair. They merely refused to call a halt to the Catholic press campaign against the republican institutions, against the truth and against the victims of the miscarriage of justice.

Abbé Pichot published a pamphlet on "The Christian Conscience and the Affair," reproaching *La Croix* and other papers connected with it. "If you only love your friends," he wrote, "you are no better than the heathens. . . . If your justice is no better than that of the Pharisees you will not enter the Kingdom of Heaven." Abbé Pichot was ostracized by his flock and eventually found sanctuary with the Prince of Monaco, who invited him to his diminutive principality.

The Prince of Monaco was deeply stirred by the Dreyfus Affair. He made the good Major Forzinetti a state functionary of the principality when the director of the prison of Cherche-Midi, who had recognized from the first that Dreyfus could not be a traitor, was discharged. In Berlin, the prince paid a visit to the Emperor and asked him frankly whether Dreyfus had been in the service of Germany. The Emperor denied it. The Prince then called on the President of the Republic, Félix Faure, on February 16, 1899.

Faure liked to be agreeable to heads of state. Of humble origin, the hide merchant from Le Havre found pleasure in being among royalty and in boasting of it when talking to simple people, soldiers of his palace guard. Perhaps the visit with the Tsar of all Russians had gone to his head. He became an out-and-out snob. He liked to ride out in gala with his adjutants. When he went to the opera the staircase was lined by the Republican Guard. Imitating the Tsar, at receptions he shook hands with the envoys but not with the accompanying secretaries of the embassies. Faure had increasingly sided with the generals and the aristocracy, and was a decisive force in keeping antirevisionist Premiers in office. But censure of his personal life and lax morality, coming first from the Right, then from the Left, had made his tenure of office anything but easy.

He had a long and heated discussion with the Prince of Monaco. It brought him no nearer to condoning a revision.

After the prince left, he worked a while, then retired. An hour later cries were heard coming from the President's suite. Faure was found in agony. A woman was present, the wife of a painter, whom he had met at the Army maneuvers. The lady was spirited out a side door in a hurry. The room was tidied and the President's wife informed. Only after that were the official physicians called. Faure fell into a coma. He died from a brain hemorrhage that night.

His death was a great loss to the anti-revisionists in what seemed to be a decisive hour. Drumont wrote that "the scent of murder exhaled from that coffin." Déroulède's paper spread the news that the Jews had killed the President. According to *La Patrie* they had poisoned him. Another rumor was that the Prince of Monaco had given him a poisoned cigarette.

Under the Constitution, a Presidential election had to be held immediately. In a surprisingly short time, the republican parties of all shades agreed on Emile Loubet, President of the Senate, as their candidate. A provincial lawyer, he was known to have been for the revision of the Dreyfus case. He was handicapped only by the fact that he had been one of the deputies involved in the Panama scandal, at least to the extent that he had helped drag out the investigation.

The royalists recognized that they would miss their chance for a *coup d'état* forever if they remained inactive. They hoped for Déroulède's support, but "the man with the big heart and small brains" would not abandon the tricolor. He declined even to receive the royalist emissaries, with their white *fleur-de-lis* flag.

Nevertheless, royalist proclamations were posted all over the country. The Duke of Orléans recalled his promise that he would come when the hour demanded it. It now seemed to have arrived. He would not be caught napping; a list of his future state officials was drawn up. Guérin's anti-Semites made preparations to take control of the streets of Paris.

But the republicans in the Assembly did not scare. It only helped them close their ranks against the mob. The nation was backing them solidly, and Paris street mobs could no longer impose their will on the country. Times had changed: Déroulède and Drumont were shouted down in the Assembly at Versailles. Loubet was elected President on the first ballot.

The journey of the newly elected President from Versailles to Paris was, however, marred by well-organized demonstrations. The Cabinet did nothing to prevent them. Instead of riding directly from Versailles, as usual, the President was advised to take the train. Royalists, anti-Semites and Déroulède patriots lined the route from the railway station to the Elysée and hurled insults at the President.

Roofs and windows along the streets where the President's coach passed were packed with young people yelling "Panama! Panama!" The police did nothing to push back the spectators whc were insulting the President at arm's length. Prime Minister Dupuy sat at Loubet's left and seemed not too much put out by the demonstrations.

The same day Déroulède spoke to the populace at the statue of Joan of Arc. "Today's elections," he said, "were a provocation. . . . It was up to the people to elect a President, and not to the few who sat in the Chamber. We shall get rid of the newly elected President whom I do not consider the head of the French nation. We shall overthrow this Republic to erect a better Republic in its place. Long live the better Republic!"

The huge, enthusiastic meeting urged Déroulède to march on the Elysée. The sympathetic indifference of the police encouraged immediate action. But, in the Elysée, Faure's body was lying in state. Déroulède postponed the coup to the day of Faure's funeral. He singled out as his candidate for dictator General Pellieux, who had caught his imagination at the trial of Zola when the general had impressed the court and the audience with his towering anger. His plan was to persuade Pellieux to march with the troops on the City Hall, the traditional site of republican *coups d'état*, and from there, swelled by the huge following of patriots, on to the Elysée.

Déroulède had a proclamation printed for The Day: "We are the guardians of the ballot-boxes, we are the sentries of the country. . . . We shall vigilantly maintain order and defend our reconquered liberties. Long live the plebiscitarian Republic." The place for the signature on the proclamation was left blank. He needed a general to seal the alliance between the people and the Army and make his ambition a reality.

Déroulède's League was ordered to mass at the Place de la Nation, near the cemetery. His followers were to hail Pellieux when he rode by leading the troops back from the funeral. They were to mingle with his troops and sweep them along in a frenzy of patriotism. At the same time, the royalists mobilized Guérin's anti-Semites, who in their turn were to stampede Déroulède's masses into going in their direction. They hoped to make up for their inferior numbers by boldness and vigorous brutality.

An impressive multitude joined in the funeral procession. The President, members of the Government and high state officials marched in front. General Pellieux led the troops. However, before the troops were to march back to barracks Pellieux had a word with the Military Commander of Paris, General Zurlinden. He had been informed of Déroulède's plot and asked Zurlinden for permission to transfer command to another general in order to avoid any demonstrations for his person. Zurlinden consented and assigned General Roget to take over for Pellieux.

Pellieux deployed his troops in front of the catafalque and the new President in perfect order. Another general, however, Kermartin, turned his head away before arriving at the President's stand. At this insult, Zurlinden shouted a command to the general: Eyes to the left, Kermartin! The general immediately complied and saluted the President with his sword. Later he explained that he had made a mistake. He apologized to Loubet. After the march past the President, Pellieux quietly withdrew.

Déroulède and the anti-Semites took up their posts at the Place de la Nation and along the route to the City Hall in expectation of the appearance of Pellieux and his troops on their way back to barracks. Police were concentrated far away, around the Presidential palace. Déroulède's disappointment was great when he noticed that Pellieux was not there and that Roget was in command. But action could not be postponed. Déroulède ran up to Roget, who was on horseback. His patriots swarmed in among the troops. "Follow us, General," Déroulède exhorted Roget. "Have pity on the country. Save France and the Republic. Our friends are waiting. Lead us to the City Hall and to the Elysée."

A band struck up the "Marseillaise." The crowd joined in lustily. The bewildered general, sword in hand, was at a loss what to do. Instinctively, he pushed Déroulède aside and signaled the troops to continue their march. The patriots tried to turn the soldiers in the opposite direction. General Roget busied himself with his prancing horse. At the barracks he ordered the gates closed in the nick of time. Déroulède and a few of his head lieutenants were already inside. The patriot chieftain knew he was defeated. He felt that the ignominy would be unbearable if he failed even to get arrested. He insisted, and after some hesitation the police complied.

The Government wished to minimize Déroulède's attempt to kidnap a general. But Déroulède desired to be a martyr. He was shocked to find himself accused only of having refused to leave the barracks grounds. Before the jury he demanded that he be charged with high treason. "I was arrested," he boasted, "for having harangued the troops in the courtyard after I attempted to carry them away with me. . . . I am only saddened that I did not succeed in arousing the Army and the people against the parliamentarians."

His witnesses did what they could to support his accusation. Barrès, the author, bragged about having participated in the abortive coup. Another colleague of his in the League de la Patrie exalted "the symbolic gesture" of Déroulède. Even a general professed his faith in the accused: "If war should break out I would not hesitate to look to Déroulède's clarion call to restore the confidence in the Army that is shattered at this moment. His clarion is an instrument of war. I beg of the jury not to break it." The general was gently taken to task for his support of Déroulède. He answered that he had been misunderstood.

The jury acquitted the leaders of the patriots. "Déroulède acquitted means Loubet condemned," *La Libre Parole* commented.

Events were going too fast for Loubet to mark time. A young professor at the Ecole Polytechnique published an article in *Le Figaro* describing his first day of teaching in that school of glorious tradition. "There they were in front of me," he wrote, "more than two hundred, soldiers today, officers tomorrow; taken from the elite of the youth in the four corners of the country, coming from our lycées or from the rue des Postes, Catholics, lukewarm or fervent with a sprinkling of Protestants and Israelites, all profoundly French at heart, the latter no less than all of them." *La Libre Parole* in high anger exhorted the students to demonstrate against the professor at his next class. They did, and the young professor's courses were suspended.

This incident provided a welcome opportunity for the Left to bring about the resignation of the Minister of War.

Meanwhile the nationalist's press and mass meetings continued their onslaught upon the court. The justices were called crooks, gorillas, the court itself a temple of the law turned into a stock exchange.

On June 4, President Loubet attended the races at Auteuil, that meeting place of the aristocracy and the wealthy to which ladies all over the world looked for advance notice of the coming season's fashions. The President took his seat on the tribune among the ministers, generals and diplomats. Next to him sat the wife of the Italian Ambassador. He was greeted by the aristocratic youth and the hired butcher boys of Guérin's Anti-Semite League with wild shouts of: Down with Loubet! Down with Panama! Resign!

An elegant young man, the Baron Christiani, ran up the stairs and before he could be stopped struck the President twice. Loubet held up his arms to shield his head and only his top hat was broken. General Zurlinden caught the baron and threw him back while the President, keeping his poise, apologized to his neighbors for the inconvenience. The assault was the signal for a large-scale brawl. The young rowdies resisted the police and tried to wrest the baron from their hands. The military had to be called out in support of the police. More than fifty youths were arrested.

The police made public the names of their prisoners. It was a roster of the brightest names of the aristocracy. No butcher boys were mentioned. Probably they had been let off. But the news that the aristocrats had dared attack the President welded into one front artisans, merchants and workers. The President was the son of poor people like themselves. The countryside resented the aggression from the feudal classes as much as Paris did. Loubet overnight became immensely popular.

"We are going to give you the treatment, you fine gentlemen," the Socialist *La Petite République* threatened, "that you once accorded your lackeys." And in the Chamber a Socialist deputy hailed the President as a man of honor.

24

THE PRESIDENT of the High Court of Appeal appointed Justice Ballot-Beaupré to report to the full court on the Dreyfus case. Ballot was a judge of high repute and a known anti-revisionist. He ordered a number of supplementary hearings. Several new witnesses were called. One of them was Captain Martin Freystaetter, who had served as one of the seven military judges of the court-martial that had convicted Dreyfus in 1894.

Soon after completing that duty he had been ordered to service in Madagascar. When news of Henry's suicide reached him, in 1898, Freystaetter's conscience began to plague him. He had cast his vote against Dreyfus almost entirely on the basis of Henry's testimony that a man of the highest reputation had assured him that Dreyfus was the traitor who had operated within the General Staff.

Freystaetter began to read the newspapers. It was brought home to him for the first time that considering secret documents in the private chambers of the judges without disclosing them to the accused or his attorney was a violation of the rights of the defendant. He made efforts to get a hearing for his new and changed point of view.

The captain encountered obstacles, but he persisted. Finally he was called as a witness. But a court ruling silenced him as he took the stand, before he could offer any testimony. President Mazeau of the High Court ruled that Ballot's hearings could not invade the privacy of the closed room where the court-martial had deliberated, that the motives of the individual judges in reaching their decisions were not relevant to the inquiry.

But the attorney for the Dreyfus family found a way to help Freystaetter ease his conscience. He succeeded in asking the following questions: "Was the existence of the document which contains the phrase 'the Scoundrel D——' mentioned at the hearing of the court-martial?" The captain replied that it had not been. Nothing but the *bordereau* had been produced in the presence of the defendant, his attorney, the prosecutor and the witnesses.

The next blow was struck by one of the handwriting experts, now fatally ill. He had attributed the *bordereau* to Dreyfus. Now he acknowledged that he had been in error.

A clash between the Minister of War and the Minister of Foreign Affairs followed the testimony given by Cuignet. Cuignet was the officer who had chanced to discover the Henry forgery. Since Henry's suicide he had come ruefully to regret it. Guilt-stricken, he now tried to undo what he had done. The Minister of War had assigned him to liaison duty between the ministry and the court. His opportunity to make up to his superiors came when the hearing began to explore the subject of the query that Panizzardi had sent to Rome asking whether Dreyfus had been in the service of the Italian Government, and suggesting that if he had not been, an official denial would be welcome to halt the clamor in the press. It will be remembered that this telegram, intercepted and decoded by the French Foreign Office and delivered by it to the Second Bureau, had been translated incorrectly into French by Du Paty de Clam in a manner to incriminate Dreyfus. Du Paty's tampering with the document had subsequently been exposed. But Cuignet thought he saw a chance to clear Du Paty by shifting responsibility to the Foreign Ministry. He testified that he doubted whether the Italian text, as conveyed by the Foreign Ministry to the Second Bureau, had been correctly transcribed in the first place.

The testimony put Foreign Minister Théophile Delcassé into a temper. Such matters as the decoding and transcription of dispatches were in the province of minor officials supervised by others of only

slightly higher rank. To suspect that routine copying had been falsified was to accuse the ministry of being crooked from top to bottom.
The ministry requested a new copy of the original message from the
postal administration. The message was duly produced, inspected by
all the justices, the witness Cuignet, and Paléologue, who represented
the Minister of Foreign Affairs. The correct translation was then put
on the record.

The press lost no time in publishing the details of the exchange between the two ministers. Cuignet, under pressure from the Foreign
Minister, was relieved from his function of liaison between the court
and the Ministry of War.

The nationalist papers succeeded in obtaining an advance copy of
the report that Justice Ballot-Beaupré was preparing for the court and
published such excerpts as were favorable to the anti-revisionists. A
flood of pamphlets analyzing the hearings began to go into circulation.
They were for the most part heavily biased, written as if the incom-
plete material at hand represented the whole story.

Official copies of Ballot-Beaupré's advance report of the hearings
had been printed in limited number for the members of the court, the
prosecutor and the attorneys. The copies were, of course, secret. But
when the nationalist papers made a mockery of the secrecy, Mathieu
Dreyfus immediately turned his attorney's copy over to the writer
Bernard Lazare, whose pamphlet had been the first to argue publicly
the innocence of Captain Dreyfus. Lazare hired some young Russian
Jewish refugees to make another copy. They worked at it night and
day in deepest secrecy. When it was finished, the original was turned
back to Mathieu.

The revisionists were aware that the Dupuy administration was so
prejudiced that the indulgences given to the anti-revisionists would
never be extended to them. Nevertheless, they decided to publish the
court record, as it revealed their side of the story. For an avenue to the
public, they chose Le Figaro, which, after Henry's suicide, had returned
to the revisionist front. In order to eliminate any traces of the source
of their information, they adopted the comic-opera methods more appropriate to Du Paty and Major Esterhazy. Victorien Sardou, a successful playwright of the time, was planning to write a play about the
affair, and was himself ready to take a part in the real drama. The copy
was sent to him hot, day by day, as the young refugees turned it out. He
in turn forwarded what he received each day to a woman who played a

role very like Esterhazy's "veiled lady." She delivered the copy to the offices of *Le Figaro*. The revisionists were right. Although the administration had greeted with equanimity the violation of the secrecy order by the nationalist press, it was in an uproar over *Le Figaro*. The police were sent, but they were completely baffled. They searched the premises of the paper but did not find any clue to the origin of the installments which appeared daily for a month. *Le Figaro* was fined 500 francs, a small price to pay for the increased circulation and immense interest that resulted.

All the cross-currents of lies, jealousies, self-contradictions and mutual suspicions among the generals came out in the open in *Le Figaro's* columns. Public quarrels ensued, corrections, retorts, amendments, denials, explanations. These were reported in all the other newspapers. Disillusionment and disgust now made inroads even into those who so far had been impervious to the truth. Where Henry's suicide had been the first rock that broke the powerful stream of anti-revisionism, the publication in *Le Figaro* of the report of Justice Ballot-Beaupré was second. *L'Echo de Paris* and *La Libre Parole* were furious. They suspected that one of the justices was responsible for the leak. "A Scoundrel in Ermine Betrays" was a headline.

Prior to terminating the supplementary investigation, Ballot had asked for all secret documents. After the court had examined them, he questioned Colonel Chamoin, who had taken the place of Cuignet as the War Ministry's liaison officer. "Is this all?" he demanded. That was all, Chamoin said. "Where is the piece so often spoken of—the one which could not be produced because it might have caused war?" Chamoin declared that the document did not exist. It was entered into the record that there were no further secret documents. All the evidence was in.

The plenary session of the High Court had been scheduled for May 29, 1899. On that morning there appeared in an English newspaper and in *Le Matin* an interview with Esterhazy.

Esterhazy had spent hardly a day of the intervening period out of the world's headlines. Among his numerous troubles was a suit brought by Duke Esterhazy in Paris enjoining him not to use the title of Count and even the name Esterhazy unless preceded by Walsin, to identify him as belonging to an illegitimate branch of the family. Then he had come before Ballot as a witness, traveling from England under a safe-conduct that granted him immunity from harassment by the law. Did you write the *bordereau?* he was asked point-blank by Ballot. His reply was neither yes nor no. "One military court decided it had been written by Dreyfus," he said. "Another one decided I had not written it."

But to the reporter in England who asked the same question on that May day a short while later, he gave a point-blank answer:

I rendered considerable service to my country [he began]. I was a courageous soldier on the battlefield. And today I am the most abominably dishonored man in the world. Those swine who think this can continue have never had a look into my eyes. . . . I repeat, I am a martyr to an idea which the French, degenerate as they are today, are not even able to understand. . . .

I was employed in counter-espionage, a mission of grandeur and abnegation which is unrecognized in our days. I am a soldier and have always acted as a soldier. I am a man who deserved to live in less cowardly times. In other days, I would probably have had a chance to become a Napoleon. Do you know that I am now starving? You may say that you have seen Major Esterhazy—the "Uhlan," as the idiots or bandits call me over there—crying. . . .

France is perishing from the revolution of 1789 which she could not live down. . . . As to Henry: we were very much attached to each other; nothing remained hidden between us. . . . Do you really think that he committed suicide? Oh, the heroism of that life of simple duty! His guilt? Will they ever understand, these French, that a military information service is bound to be an office of forgeries?

The English reporter persisted. Had he or had he not written the *bordereau?* "All right, then," said Esterhazy. "Yes. I was the one who wrote the *bordereau,* and the generals knew it."

But now that Esterhazy had finally told the truth, nobody believed it except those who had believed it before. He had told too many lies. He had sold out too many times.

In any event it came as an anticlimax. In December 1897, at the investigation preliminary to the trial which had acquitted him as the author of the *bordereau,* Esterhazy had been in a far less cautious mood than when facing Ballot. With his gift for dramatic statement, he had not been content merely to deny having written the *bordereau.* He had sworn that he had never even written on such paper. But Ballot's investigation had uncovered a letter Esterhazy had written on August 17, 1894, the same month in which he had written the *bordereau,* and this letter was on the same kind of thin cream-colored graph paper. Still those who did not believe the truth when they heard it would not believe evidence, either, when they saw it.

Forty-six justices of the three chambers of the High Court of Appeal, with President Mazeau in the chair, sat in robes of red and ermine to deliver their verdict on the petition before them.

The audience in the courtroom was made up of journalists from the four corners of the earth, diplomats, women of fashion, great names in politics, literature and the arts, high functionaries and generals. France and the civilized world awaited a verdict that, it was hoped, would end a nightmare that had already endured for five years.

The audience listened intently as Justice Ballot-Beaupré delivered his report. He began by making it clear that there were substantial legal reasons for annulling the sentence of the military court. However, the petition was not for annulment. Dreyfus wanted a new trial. He desired to have his innocence formally conceded by his fellow officers in the Army.

In a quiet voice, Ballot reviewed the case for one side in the controversy. Then, with equally dispassionate objectivity, he reviewed the case for the other side. He subjected the two conflicting positions to analysis and then finally evaluated them in the light of disinterested judgment. In the end, he reached a conclusion: there was only one piece of genuine evidence—the *bordereau*. Had it or had it not been written by Dreyfus?

He paused. Dead silence filled the room, the silence of held breath. Then the justice resumed: "After the most careful weighing of all evidence, I have come to the conclusion that the *bordereau* was written not by Dreyfus but by Major Esterhazy."

Mazeau did not try to quell the storm of applause that thundered in the courtroom.

Ballot, ending his report, raised his voice: "Before my soul and conscience, I would fail in my sacred duty if I did not solemnly declare that there is in this affair a new fact which substantiates the innocence of the man who was convicted in 1894." He was referring to Esterhazy's August 17 letter written on the same paper as the *bordereau*.

Then J. P. Manau, the chief prosecutor, and Henri Mornard, the attorney for Dreyfus, gave their arguments for a retrial. Mazeau adjourned the session.

The same evening, General Zurlinden, by order of the Minister of

War, had the Marquis du Paty de Clam arrested for forgery and for using forged documents. He was taken to the Cherche-Midi, the military prison where both Dreyfus and Picquart had been held.

Four days later, on June 3, the High Court of Appeal reconvened to announce its verdict. It declared null and void the sentence of the court-martial of December 22, 1894, and ordered Dreyfus to stand a new trial before a court-martial at Rennes.

The court based its decision on two facts: the submission to the judges of the first court-martial of the document which contained the phrase, "the Scoundrel D———," as referring to Dreyfus, although in truth it did not; and the fact that the *bordereau* had not been written by Dreyfus.

Two days later the chief warden entered Dreyfus' cell on Devil's Island and showed him a cable: "In consequence of the decision of the High Court of Appeal, *Captain* Dreyfus has ceased to be subject to the rules for deportees . . . and is again permitted to wear military uniform . . . the guard is to be dismissed, and Dreyfus released from criminal custody. The cruiser *Sfax* sails today from Fort-de-France to return Dreyfus to France."

25

DREYFUS STARED, blinking. Someone had remembered him? Someone knew he was still alive? For a long time Dreyfus had had no word at all from Lucie. The answers to his letters had not been given him. Then suddenly, for no reason that had been explained to him, he had been allowed to walk daily for a brief period outside the two stone fences around his stone tomb. That was when the High Court had agreed to hear his petition. For the first time in two years he had been allowed to look at the ocean. Now there was this.

The captain wrote later that the shock was so great he feared he would not survive it. He was unable to stop weeping. Finally he sent a cable. It was to his wife, Lucie. "With all my heart, I am with you and the children."

The cruiser *Sfax* crossed the Atlantic and was docked at night. Dreyfus was spirited ashore in a driving rain and rushed to the military prison at Rennes in Brittany. Kindly, levelheaded Mathieu came to bring him up to date on what had been happening. Yes, someone had remembered him. Some people had known he was still alive. Governments had fallen. War Ministers had been bowled over like tenpins. There had been riots, pogroms and attempts at revolution, and now the situation was this: if the court-martial found him innocent, France as a nation would be declared guilty; if, on the other hand, the court-martial found him guilty, constitutional government, democracy itself, was likely to be doomed. The nearsighted artillery officer could not comprehend. What had all this to do with him, with the fact that he had been a loyal officer and his superiors had been misinformed?

While the *Sfax* was en route to metropolitan France, the Minister of Justice made a motion in the Chamber that a criminal prosecution be initiated against General Mercier, the Minister of War who had forced the conviction of Dreyfus. There was a stormy session, and the motion had been tabled until after the court-martial in Rennes should act. But a good solid bone had been thrown to the Dreyfusards anyway. Two Socialist deputies moved that the decision of the High Court should be posted in every parish in France. This was adopted.

Zola returned from eleven months' exile in England. He wrote in *L'Aurore*:

My soul is elated but with no feelings of anger or vengeance. If the softness of my heart got the upper hand over my skeptical mind, I would be in favor of a general pardon without further ado. As the only penalty for the criminals, I would leave them exposed to eternal public contempt. . . . Yet, a public pillory must be erected so that people may finally see and understand. Personally, I leave it to Nemesis to accomplish the work of vengeance. I am not going to lend a hand. As a poet, I am satisfied with the triumph of the ideal. There remains only one outrage: the awful fact that Colonel Picquart is still in prison. Not a single day has passed when my fraternal sympathy has not been with him in his prison cell. . . . And if Picquart is not released from jail by tomorrow, then France will never be cleansed of the unpardonable folly of having delivered her most noble, most heroic and glorious son into the criminal hands of hangmen, liars, and forgers.

A few days later Picquart was released. He had spent 324 days in prison. Subsequently, the Criminal Chamber quashed the case against him.

The vanguard of the fighters for truth and justice gathered at the home of Trarieux, the former Minister of Justice. About a hundred people came to celebrate their victory. Heroes and martyrs embraced one another. Zola, whose magic vision had seen the truth behind the curtain of lies, forgery and fraud, and whose challenge had set the truth marching; Picquart, who had discovered the truth and stood by it; Clemenceau, whose piercing intellect had hit out mercilessly against the hypocrites and criminals and who had kept the affair focused on the ideals of the Great Revolution; Emile Duclaux, that skeptic who had fought so valiantly for justice; Mathieu Dreyfus, whose dedicated and noble soul had earned the unqualified respect of that august gathering; Bernard Lazare, who first had dared announce Dreyfus' innocence to the public; Joseph Reinach, who had relentlessly pursued and unmasked the criminals and the instigators of the crime; Anatole France, whose broad tolerance for all human frailty had been suspended by the enormity of this crime; Trarieux, who had fearlessly used both argument and influence to further the truth; and Jaurès, Monod, Péguy—thinkers, poets, fighters. One great man was missing: Scheurer-Kestner, whose conscience had given him no rest until he took up the fight for the innocent victim. The senator lay dying.

On the following Sunday, workers, merchants, artisans and students gathered in the streets of Paris to march to the race track at Longchamps to give their answer to the authoritarians and royalists. All the republican groups of the Left, as well as the Socialists and revolutionary syndicalists, put up posters appealing to the people to show their force and unity in a common stand for the Republic. It was a huge demonstration. More than a hundred thousand people, armed with sticks and clubs, sang the "Marseillaise" and the "Internationale." The boisterous youth of the royalists, Déroulède's patriots and Guérin's hordes made themselves scarce, as did the fashionable frequenters of the races.

"Citizens! With the slogan 'Long live the Republic!' you have reconquered this great city of the Revolution," proclaimed the posters. "You have forced the Césarists and the clergy, not long ago so noisy and violent, to take cover. From now on the streets as well as Right and Justice are yours! You are the guardians of the Republic—which is in our eyes the precondition of Socialism."

To have reconquered the workers for the Republic was the historic achievement of the Dreyfus Affair. The co-operation of the radical wing of the republicans with the Socialists in support of republican institutions had given a solid basis to the Third Republic and would now enable it to endure through the rest of its seventy desperate years.

Premier Dupuy was not idle on the day of the demonstration. Hosts of police had been mobilized. Police courts were set up in the field to deal prompt justice to rioters. But there were no rioters. It was a proud, gay and peaceful demonstration.

The time had come when Dupuy could no longer get away with his partisanship for Déroulède and Guérin. A deputy from Paris called the Cabinet to account for police brutalities that had been committed against republicans. The Chamber passed a resolution to support henceforth only such Cabinets as were determined to defend republican institutions.

Dupuy's entire Cabinet resigned.

The civilized world that had participated in the drama as a warning and often despairing chorus could now settle back in satisfaction. "We must never forget," Gabriel Monod told his friends, "the unanimous movement which awakened the conscience of the whole universe in favor of Dreyfus in one of the finest lessons in human solidarity that the world has ever seen."

At this point, if the Dreyfus Affair had been an old-fashioned morality play, the curtain would have fallen. At the start there had been Mephistopheles, personifying evil. He had challenged God to grant him five years in which to prove that he could reverse the moral order that had been established by nineteen centuries of Christianity. Mephistopheles, to make his success more resounding, had chosen the world's most enlightened people for his test. The scene of the battle had been the high ground of democratic Western civilization. He had been confident that his nefarious work would be made easier to accomplish by the rule of the many rather than by the rule of the few. For it is far less difficult for dissenters to revolt against tyrants and oligarchs than to revolt against a passionately convinced majority. Rebels who defied the majority could be easily crushed and outlawed, and would never be pardoned even if at a future time they should be vindicated.

For his supreme effort against democratic morality the Mephistopheles of our morality play had selected France, at the end of the nineteenth century—the country which, with its clarity of mind and vision, had shown new perspectives to the West so many times in the past, the country which had dazzled the world by the radiance of her arts and literature. Mephistopheles knew that France feared an external enemy. Her hopes of redressing the balance tipped by a crushing defeat were being frustrated. A deep distrust of the ideas that had served her in times of greatness and strength took possession of her. To her shrunken self-confidence these ideas appeared as so many mirages to look at in the sky while the soil was crumbling under her feet. Fear and distrust made France see enemies in those who kept reminding her of the mission to which she had been born as a nation, the great idea of justice for all. Fear made her feel strong in a false unity of ends and means, and those who dissented she regarded as sappers of her strength. They were held to be dupes, even paid agents of the enemy.

Thus there was conformity, and sinister forces within the nation attempted to make conformity serve their own purposes. Through the efficient manipulation of mass-communication media they penetrated the plants, the offices, the barracks, the schools, the homes and even the nurseries. They intimidated the sober minority. But it was beyond their power to prevent a few men of courage and responsibility from offering resistance. What chance of success had these men had? It is always easy to stand up against the few on behalf of the many. They had no institutions to rely on other than those which derive their right to exist from the people. On whose behalf was this handful to speak when the whole people was united against them?

This is an insidious danger inherent in democracy and it was foreseen more than a century ago by Alexis de Tocqueville. Writing of the tyranny of public opinion in democratic republics, he put these words into the mouth of public opinion, addressing itself to the dissenter:

> You are free to think differently from me, and to keep your life, your property, and all that you possess; but if such be your determination, you are henceforth an alien among your own people. . . . You will remain among men, but you will be deprived of the rights of mankind. Your fellow creatures will shun you like a leper; and those who are most persuaded of your innocence will abandon you too, lest they should be shunned in turn.

So it would seem that the dissenters had had no chance. But when, against overwhelming odds, a handful made use of the freedom to commit suicide, and stubbornly published and spoke their protests, their single drop of healing truth permeated the noxious tissue of lies and treachery. They broke the spell of fear. The Mephistopheles of the play, on the brink of success, was now forced to acknowledge defeat at the hands of a few men who were as unconquerable as the flag they fought under: the truth. The apotheosis, a worthy end to a morality play, shone forth in this meeting of the Dreyfusard vanguard. But this was not a morality play. This was a vast human drama called The Dreyfus Affair. And so the fight began all over again.

Part Four

THE PUZZLE OF RENNES

26

BALLOT-BEAUPRÉ is a rascal who will go down in history as an arche·type of human ignominy. What price, we wonder, did he fetch from the Syndicate of Treason?

Such was the tenor of the comments by the nationalist press on the verdict of the High Court. And they were not alone. The verdict also drew the ire of the Army officers. In Paris, a lieutenant colonel cautioned students in the Ecole Militaire against condoning the sentiments it reflected. Enraged because troops marching in the streets had been heckled by passers-by who yelled "Long live Picquart!" he said to the students: "I regret that I did not order those who shouted 'Long live Picquart!' put to the sword. In any such instance, I expect you to make use of your arms against those who insult the Army."

Le Petit Journal applauded this attitude: "At long last the leaders of the Army are holding up their heads and looking straight into the face of the rabble, the *sans-patrie*. Others will follow their example. The Ministers of War, one after the other, have violated the Army's code of honor by deserting their posts for two years in succession; the Army, stung to the quick, has only one recourse left: to be its own defender."

The nationalist, Catholic and royalist press was on the offensive. Guérin wrote: "Let us have done with it. Without a knockout blow we shall never get anywhere. Five hundred men will suffice to seize the Ministry. The day after, the Army will march with us."

Déroulède had this to say about the new trial:

Should Dreyfus be pronounced innocent, no honor will be big enough
to compensate the martyr; no punishment terrible enough, nor too infamous
to be meted out to the ministers, civilians, and officers who accused him. Any
retaliation would be held excusable, all suspicion justified, and France herself
would have to atone for the crimes that her generals and ministers committed. Our people would have to prostrate themselves before the people of
Israel. . . . . Two stand accused today: the one is France—her statesmen, her
entire body politic, and with as good as no exception her entire society, the
whole of her people; the other, of course, is Dreyfus. If he is innocent, then
the generals are criminals. Let, then, this message be spread, and make sure it
gets to Rennes.

La Libre Parole predicted: "The Court Martial will send Dreyfus
back to Devil's Island, and his arrival there will be the signal for the
exodus of all Jews—voluntary or forced."

La Patrie wrote that "Dreyfus declared innocent is a crime against
the nation. Even if seven out of seven officers serving on the Court
Martial were to acquit him, the duty of every patriot would still be to
kill him." *L'Eclair* stated: "The question is not whether this wretch is
guilty or innocent, but whether or not the Jews and the Protestants—
this vanguard of Germany, England, and their allies—are to rule our
country."

However, the Dreyfusards at home as well as abroad remained confident. The new Premier did not share their confidence. It was not a
question of his sympathies. Even at the beginning, while he was still
practicing law, the Dreyfus family had come to Pierre Marie Waldeck-
Rousseau to find a defender.

Waldeck was an able man, a staunch republican of conservative
leanings. His objective was a balanced government made up of a coalition of all the parties that supported the Republic. He offered minis-
terial posts to the Socialists, a tactic that produced surprise and uneasi-
ness among conservatives and liberals alike, and then offered the War
Ministry to General Marquis de Galliffet—a tactic that alarmed everybody.

For the marquis was known as the executioner of the Paris Commune of 1871. Ten thousand had been shot without trial. As a result
the general had become almost the only thing all the factions of the
Left could agree on. They hated him.

Waldeck's bid to the Socialists to come into the Cabinet nevertheless precipitated a crisis that affected the Socialists not only of France but of all Europe. To Jean Jaurès the bourgeois republic was the forerunner of the socialist republic of the radical dream. He argued that Socialists therefore had a continuing interest in preserving it. In short, he was an evolutionary. The Marxists and revolutionaries saw great dangers in accepting even partial responsibility for a capitalist regime.

But Jaurès, together with Millerand and Viviani, won the argument—at least to the extent of swinging the Socialist party to the support of a Cabinet that included Galliffet. The general's prestige with the Army was solidly based. In the war against the Prussians, his cavalry charge at Sedan had been a well-disciplined episode of glory in a welter of catastrophe and treason. It had been on his order that all men, women and even children under the remotest suspicion of having been in the militia when the Versailles troops had wrested Paris away from the communes had been mercilessly executed by firing squads working in relays with hot guns that were not given a chance to cool off. But he had sided with Gambetta in the organization of a Republican Army after the surrender of Napoleon III.

To soothe the Moderate Republicans, Waldeck offered the Socialists only two places in the Cabinet. Galliffet was to soothe the Army and quiet those terrors which had motivated it to enter politics so militantly in the first place. Galliffet, called a "butcher" by the Left and a "traitor to his class" by his fellow aristocrats, understood Picquart's nature well. He had publicly expressed his admiration for the selflessness of a man who had placed truth above his own career, and had become a Dreyfusard on that account.

But being a Dreyfusard was not enough for the left wing of the Socialist party. It broke away from Jaurès and published a declaration to the effect that a party of the class war should not shoulder responsibility for a bourgeois government, as it would have to do if it joined the Cabinet.

The new Cabinet, once it was voted into power, lost no time in purging the Army and the administration of die-hard anti-republicans. Among those replaced were the chief of police and the public prosecutor, and Zurlinden himself lost his job as Military Commander of Paris. As a move against Déroulède and to air thoroughly his abortive *coup d'état*, criminal prosecutions were brought against Generals Roget and Pellieux.

The nationalist press gave Galliffet no rest: "He took orders from the Syndicate—took vengeance on a rival." But Galliffet himself issued an order of the day to all garrisons that was to become famous: "Silence in the ranks!"

The Cabinet presented itself for approval to the Chamber. The reception the deputies gave it was stormier than any Cabinet had ever had before. This certainly is saying a good deal, but it was the considered opinion of many contemporary historians. One deputy called the Government a coalition of knaves and murderers, the murderers being represented by the Minister of War. Galliffet blandly replied: "Murderer? At your service."

Premier Waldeck's fate was the usual one of the man who attempts to please all. He had pleased none. His speech, scheduled to take no more than a quarter of an hour, lasted a full hour because of the interruptions. In vain a Socialist minister warned the Republicans: "This is a government that will defend the Republic. You must choose between it and a government of treason!" The uproar did not subside until Henri Brisson, Grand Master of the Masons, rushed to the podium in despair and shouted, "I do not ask you to vote for the government, I ask you to vote for the Republic!" It was either his intervention or the imminence of the new Dreyfus trial that gave the Cabinet a new lease on life. The Chamber voted to adjourn until November, giving Waldeck four months, by which time it was hoped the Dreyfus case would be settled without the Chamber having had to share responsibility.

Waldeck and General Galliffet favored a general amnesty. Jaurés voiced the indignation of the revisionist vanguard: "Is justice in the Republic to hit only the small people?" The Government had the power to advise the prosecutor in Rennes to limit the trial to the two basic matters outlined by the High Court—the *bordereau* and "the Scoundrel D——" letter fraudulently amended by Henry and Du Paty. The Catholic and nationalist press raised the cry of "Light!" The implication was that the Government was seeking Dreyfus' acquittal by subterfuge. They kept demanding that the Cabinet abstain from interfering with the trial.

More than one threatening cloud hung over the Rennes trial. In fact, the sky was full of them. The debate in the Chamber on the motion for the arrest of General Mercier, who had been Minister of War when Dreyfus was arrested, had only been adjourned. Mercier was a powerful personality and, for a soldier, had an unusually flexible mind. With his own position still in the balance, he prepared himself for Rennes. He let his friends know that he was going to present an unanswerable argument and, if possible, force a showdown. Joy flooded the nationalist press: "The court will have to choose between General Mercier and Dreyfus." So the old dilemma was revived dramatically: condemn Dreyfus or condemn the Army. For Mercier was the Army. Should Dreyfus be acquitted, then Mercier and most of the General Staff must be prosecuted for forgery and the use of forged documents to suborn justice, and many generals and lesser officers must be prosecuted for perjury as well.

The press made no attempt to keep Mercier's plan secret. *Le Gaulois* published an open letter to the general: "You have in your possession a photostatic copy of a document, and you are going to produce it to the court in Rennes." This was an allusion to the photostatic copy of the forged *bordereau*, the one that had on its margin a note from the German Emperor and thus had had to be returned to him to prevent war. This document was so crude and inept that it had long since been removed from the secret files. There is some reason to believe that it never even got into the files, that it was prepared but then was destroyed as incapable of convincing anybody, and that Henry merely gave out the story that it existed. But the nationalist press kept harping on it jubilantly. "Mercier's stunning blow" became a byword. A nationalist poet wrote: "Let us meet the truth face to face, no matter how hideous or terrible it be. If it means war, then perhaps that will be our rebirth and salvation. O, Joan of Arc, pray for us! Even disaster is better than shame." The press reported excitedly that the Government had decided to arrest Mercier on the spot should he produce the document in court.

In spite of the ominous choice that was being hammered out for the seven officers who would sit on the Rennes court—General Mercier or Dreyfus the Jew—the revisionists remained optimistic. However, there were other difficulties: along what lines, for instance, should Dreyfus' defense be conducted? Should he simply present himself as a man convicted in error who now was being given the opportunity to have the error rectified? The latter course was advocated by counsel for the defense Demange, for he had always been against taking the case into politics. The Dreyfus family, needless to say, wished to go in the direction which promised the most satisfactory result. But Labori, who had performed such outstanding services for the revisionist cause, insisted on getting into the act and it was difficult to refuse him. He had been defense counsel for Zola, Picquart and numerous others who had been hounded as Dreyfusards. He was *the* attorney for the revisionists, and he, of course, would not let the affair degenerate from its high level of moral principles to a mere criminal case. The Dreyfus family finally decided to retain both attorneys.

William James, the great American pragmatist, followed the development of the Dreyfus case with penetrating interest. The comments he made on the trial at Rennes reflected the attitude of most foreign intellectuals. On June 7, 1899, the day the trial began, he wrote to Mrs. Henry Whitman:

> Yes, the daylight that now seems shining through the Dreyfus case is glorious, and if the President Emile Loubet only gets his back up a bit, and mows down the whole gang of Satan, or as much of it as can be touched, it will perhaps be a great day for distracted France. I mean it may be one of those moral crises that become starting points and high water marks, and leave traditions and rallying cries and new forces behind them. One thing is certain, that no other alternative form of government possible in France in this century could have stood the strain as this democracy seems to be standing it.

27

RENNES WAS A SLEEPY TOWN in devoutly Catholic Brittany. The invasion of Parisians, disconcerting enough, was as nothing compared to that of foreign journalists with their alien ways and speech. The town ignored as best it could the well-dressed horde who grabbed the choicest available rooms and meals and took over the café terraces, the boulevards and even the churches.

Though not exactly disdaining the unexpected gold that poured down on them (Rennes was on a poor byroad off the main arteries of trade), the Rennois had their misgivings. English and German were thick in the speech of these foreigners. It was an uncomfortable suggestion that the gold came from the "syndicate." Only some ten Jewish families lived at Rennes—quietly, as did their neighbors. So the Rennois had very little evidence of their own to set against the propaganda of the nationalists. If there had been more Jews in their experience of life, they might not have been so ready to believe in the

existence of the "syndicate." As it was, they swallowed the nationalists' scarecrow whole.

The great hall of the *lycée* was the only place large enough to hold
the crowds. The trial was held there. Its acoustics were very poor. A
low voice carried no more than a few steps from the witness stand.
The gendarmerie were present in large numbers, prepared to treat any
gathering as an attempt at riot.

The judges were a good cross-section of a provincial garrison, and
Dreyfus probably got the fairest military court the Army could muster.
The chief judge, who was called the president, Colonel Albert Jouaust,
was about to retire. Presumably he could have no personal ambitions
which would tempt him to show special favors to the prosecution. The
prosecutor, on the other hand, a retired officer of the gendarmerie who
had gone in for law at the age of sixty, was a rude and stubborn man
of rigid, narrow-gauge opinions to which he clung with tenacious
fondness. But a fair military court is not necessarily a fair court. Army
discipline and the prestige involved in the sacred chain of command
weighed on all the judges and tipped the scales heavily toward the
higher ranks. With all else even, if it came to a question of whether it
was a captain or a general who was lying, the general would get the
better of it.

The trial opened at the briskly military hour of 6:00 A.M., and
shortly thereafter Colonel Jouaust ordered Captain Dreyfus brought
in. Avid eyes were fixed on the door to watch the man behind the
legend make his entrance. For years now every person present had
known Dreyfus' name almost as well as his own, had spoken it perhaps more frequently, and had lived a life of emotion on his account.
Yet hardly anybody had ever seen him.

Captain Dreyfus was led in by a sergeant. There were those who
had witnessed his degradation in 1894 on the parade grounds of the
Ecole Militaire. They recognized his jerky, mechanical step, his stiff
military bearing. He bowed to the president. Those up close noticed
his desperate effort to keep his knees stiff under him. Only thirty-nine
years of age, he was now an old man, gray-haired, frail. The eyes behind the glasses were so pale they seemed a ghostly blue. His skin, like
faultily tanned hide, was yellowed and browned, and appeared glued
to the protruding bones of his face. Even in his brand-new uniform
he looked no more than a bag of bones.

Most of those present had read some of the letters Dreyfus had written to his wife while he was on Devil's Island. His appearance shattered even the most determined effort to remain judicial and unmoved. He turned to gaze at the crowd. He was visibly pleased to see people other than prisoners and guards. A writer reported that the audience gaped at him and felt almost spent by the force of the experience.

But, as in the past, he broke the spell as soon as he began to talk. It was still true of him that he opposed any appeal to the feelings of others as not befitting a soldier. He spoke of himself in cold, objective terms. When Labori read out excerpts from his letters he sat as motionless as if he were listening to the exposition of a factual problem, and apparently as unmoved. His voice gave expression to his feelings only in rare, sudden outbursts. Otherwise it remained colorless, deferential and matter-of-fact.

Through an accident of time and place this man had been for five years the symbol of international ideas and national interests which had clashed over possession of his body so violently that the sound and fury nearly drove France to fratricide. But to have responded with emotion to the role foisted upon him would have struck him as indecorous and unmilitary. To feel violated his own deepest feelings. He would not even reveal his physical misery. His weakened condition and loss of self-control became apparent only when his eyes would suddenly stream tears. But he cried like a doll, his face emotionless. It was not really crying; it was simply water gushing from his ghostly eyes. "His heart did not talk," wrote Chamoin in his report to the War Minister, and he voiced the general feeling of the audience.

Military discipline and respect for his superiors were deeply ingrained in Dreyfus. Many of his sympathizers saw with astonishment that he took great pride in being noticed by a general. He listened with profound respect when General Boisdeffre spoke of him at length to the judges—even when Boisdeffre asserted that he was convinced of Dreyfus' guilt. Yet when Picquart, a mere lieutenant colonel, dared belie the generals and assert his belief in Dreyfus' innocence, Dreyfus' eyes took on the stricken and tormented expression of a trapped animal. It is quite possible, in the light of what he did later, that if Dreyfus had been sitting on the court he would have convicted himself.

Clemenceau, asked by his private secretary just how much Dreyfus had understood of the case, replied: "Nothing. He is the only one who has not understood it at all. He stands abysmally below the Dreyfus Affair." A younger Dreyfusard, Léon Blum, wrote that Dreyfus, had he not been Dreyfus but someone else, would not even have been a Dreyfusard. Georges Sorel, the revolutionary syndicalist, remarked that Dreyfus had been a servile socialite, a chauvinist whose heart beat as one with that of the General Staff which was bent on his destruction. Much later, when the president of the League of Rights of Man spoke to Dreyfus about his historic part, Dreyfus protested, crying, "No, no. I was only an Artillery officer prevented by a tragic error from following my career. Dreyfus, the figurehead of justice, was not I. He was created by you."

It was in this spirit that Dreyfus had studied the court records of his trial *in absentia* before the High Court of Appeal and of the trial of Esterhazy, whom he had never met. Both these trials had been conducted while he was wasting on a rock, forbidden to talk to anyone, slowly losing the ability to express his thoughts and feelings. It had been arduous enough to relearn in these few brief weeks how to live again among human beings and communicate with them. But to master the enormously complicated and bitterly painful facts of his own destiny, to apply objective judgment and to take the measure of his present position and chances was more than could be expected.

As in a dream within a dream, the president of the court-martial showed him the old familiar *bordereau* and asked whether he recognized it. He did not. And then, as if a hand of iron were strangling him, a hoarse cry broke from his throat: "I say again that I am innocent as I said it in 1894. I have endured everything these last five years, Colonel, but once more for the honor of my name and for that of my children, I am innocent, Colonel!"

Even though his beloved wife was present, he listened coolly and to all appearances undisturbed to insinuating questions about his love affairs, true and untrue. He pondered in genuine distress over the hatred that so many of his fellow officers seemed to bear him. He answered all questions precisely and logically. But his own behavior probably had as little influence on the verdict as it had had in making him a flag by which democracy in France lived or died. The key to the trial was General Mercier's ability to extend its scope beyond the area found relevant by the High Court. Protests against limiting the area came from both the Right and the Left. *La Croix* appealed to the court to refuse to hold the trial under such a limitation. "Assuredly no one can want to stifle the truth," *Le Gaulois* wrote. "Such a thing would be monstrous." And Clemenceau proclaimed that "In order to keep the Court from sinking to the lowest level, everybody has to be heard and questioned."

Carrière, the public prosecutor, acceded to the clamor. He declined to follow the Government's suggestion to limit the trial. So the issue was drawn in the courtroom as it had been in the newspapers—Dreyfus or the Army, which was guilty?

Mercier's second tactic was to close the court's doors. He had done it in 1894 at Dreyfus' first trial. Now despite the fact that there was an official sworn statement from the Army that all relevant documents had been delivered to the High Court, and despite the fact that these documents appeared in the public record, Mercier was able to do it again.

At this point, the defense showed a fatal weakness. It did not protest against the exclusion of the public. Thus it implicitly acknowledged that there were secrets involved that could not be made public without danger to the security of the country. The anti-revisionist papers were astonished over the ease of the victory for their side. The mistake was so obvious it seemed to them to be a trap. Beware, they warned in their columns. But it was not a trap. It was the direct result of the disunity between defense counsel. Demange still thought the best trials were those conducted by judges with books rather than by politicians with newspapers. In the abstract, of course, he was quite right. But he, like his famous client, failed to grasp the nature of their case. He favored concessions to the generals and a chance to restore their prestige while Dreyfus was being acquitted. Live and let live was his attitude in a contest to the death.

The browbeating attitude of the court's president, Colonel Jouaust, to Dreyfus and his attorneys contrasted grossly with the deference he showed General Mercier and the witnesses for the prosecution. It shocked the audience and the readers of newspaper reports the world over. He exercised the discretion the military code gave him to give the prosecution every advantage he could. Yet his roughness of voice and manner did not fool the anti-revisionists. They remained wary of him, and they had a right to be. The old colonel was convinced of Dreyfus' innocence. He succeeded in hiding it to the very end, till it came to the vote on the verdict. He voted for acquittal.

Mercier was afraid that Esterhazy would appear and, for what might be paid him, unmask the General Staff and all its lies and forged proofs. Esterhazy, at the beginning of the trial, wrote to the prosecutor

that he had no intention of going to Rennes since the court at Rennes
was bent on acquitting the Jew anyway. However, this was only the
opening shot in what amounted to a campaign to make some money
for himself out of the trial. Apparently the defense would have none
of him and a blackmail of the prosecution was his best hope, for he
besieged the president of the court with letters and, through his attorney, conveyed to Mercier suggestions and threats. To his attorney he
wrote:

Ah, the scoundrels, the ignoble wretches! If you see the nationalists, tell them
that I am without money . . . that Gonse will go straight to jail. . . . Ah, the
beasts. . . . Send me somebody over here, and I will tell him what is going
to happen to them. I may even prove with documents in hand that they are
dead to honor. That will be their end. I shall not die alone, satisfied with a
beautiful funeral. I have two letters with instructions to explain my part in
writing the *bordereau*. I shall be forced to produce them. . . .

Mercier was, however, shrewder than Esterhazy thought a French
general could be. With the help of Bertillon, the handwriting expert,
whose theories were still considered authoritative, however inexplica-
ble, he devised a new version concerning the *bordereau*, one that eliminated Esterhazy from any part in it. Bertillon, who had once told Picquart he was right, the handwriting was Esterhazy's, would now
maintain that it was Dreyfus' altered. Bertillon was not the first scientist to evolve a theory that could convince him of anything he really
wanted to be convinced of.

After the court had heard Dreyfus, the audience was excluded. The
doors were closed to begin the examination of the secret documents.
Colonel Chamoin, who represented both the Ministry of War and the
Ministry of Foreign Affairs (to emphasize that complete agreement
existed between the two ministries) at the trial, emptied the contents
of the secret files before the judges. As he did so, Labori noticed that
Chamoin surreptitiously slipped extra sheets among the documents
from the files. Labori demanded an explanation. Colonel Chamoin
was gravely embarrassed. At first he refused to let Labori see the
papers. Then he declared he would let Labori see them on condition
that he read the first page but not the other two. From the first page it
was clear that this was the now notorious mistranslation by Du Paty
of the coded telegram the Italian military attaché, Panizzardi, had sent

his Government after Dreyfus' arrest. The High Court had exposed Du Paty's machinations and had put the correct translation on the record. In fact the mistranslation was one of the criminal charges now resting against Du Paty. Chamoin only added to everybody's bewilderment when he apologized for having made a mistake. Before coming to court, he said, he had met General Mercier, who gave him a document to look into. He should not have accepted it, of course, he said, and there the apology ended, without a word of explanation as to why he had tried to smuggle the paper in among the secret documents now being offered in evidence.

Court adjourned to consider the matter and the Dreyfusards present at the trial deputized the publisher P. V. Stock to go to the Premier with an urgent demand for the arrest of Chamoin. Premier Waldeck-Rousseau was at pains to explain that he himself was in an awkward situation. Before Stock had had time to arrive from Rennes, the Premier had had a conference on the matter with his Minister of War, Galliffet. Waldeck had insisted that severe action be taken against an officer who, in his capacity as a representative of the Cabinet, had been discovered trying to mislead the court. But General Galliffet was not willing to go farther than to reprimand Chamoin and told the Prime Minister bluntly that if he continued to insist on severer punishment, he, General Galliffet, would immediately tender his resignation and add a public declaration to the effect that he believed in Dreyfus' guilt.

When the court reconvened Chamoin reported that he had, during the recess, communicated his grave error to Minister of War Galliffet and that the minister had accepted his apologies and had told him that Labori should be allowed to read the remaining two pages of the document. In these pages it was shown that several contradictory decipherings of the coded telegram had been made and that the official translation had been of an erroneous or falsified Italian text. Other versions, incriminating Dreyfus even more than Du Paty's mistranslation, were quoted. They were taken from the columns of the nationalist press in the early days of the affair.

Faced with this fantastic mishmash by Labori, General Mercier declared that he had received the material from Du Paty as he was leaving Paris. He knew that it was something about the translation of the Panizzardi telegram but had not read it. But Cuignet, the officer who had discovered the Henry forgery and had been trying to make up for that blunder ever since, said on the witness stand that an officer named

Munier had originally read the telegram in 1894 and told him its text incriminated Dreyfus. Munier later had been found dead in a train.

So the Panizzardi telegram, killed dead at great length and buried at even greater length by the High Court, was back with a vengeance —once more subject to evaluation by a court.

But this was only the overture to the masterly orchestration of confusion and confoundment in which General Mercier played the part of a Toscanini of his day. Mercier was the main witness out of some seventy for the prosecution who were ranged against the defense's twenty. The general, as Reinach described him, had the massive head of an old Caesar. He was unshakable in his self-assurance. He sat at the long, green, baize-covered conference table and faced the judges at arm's length and talked to them and to no one else. He was not a witness, but an old, experienced senior officer addressing his young subalterns, advising and instructing them in fatherly fashion.

Mercier never asked the president for permission to speak. All through the trial he felt free to act as the *spiritus rector,* to comment as he pleased and when he pleased. Even under the pressure of Labori's explosive temperament and powerful aggressiveness, he kept his composure. Reinach wrote:

Not in one instance did Mercier retreat by a single step. Searching questions sometimes drew from him ripostes of peremptory conclusions or flat affirmations, which made discussion impossible. Sometimes he refused to answer altogether or would refuse to be questioned on his opinions. He spoke always in the same haughty tone, dry, commanding, his eyes half closed, without the trace of a tremor on his glabrous face, day by day more sinister, carved with deeper wrinkles like those of a very old woman or of a Spanish archbishop. . . . There were moments when his cynicism had such power and commanded such admiration that one was inclined to believe that crime may perhaps be the originator of some kind of beauty.

Mercier smothered the impact of Captain Freystaetter's testimony backhandedly. The captain, one of the seven judges who had convicted Dreyfus in 1894, testified that the Panizzardi telegram had been instrumental in convincing him of the accused's guilt. Colonel Maurel, the chief justice of that first trial, then was summoned to swear that he had not read the telegram to the judges, but under Freystaetter's persistent questioning he took it back and admitted that perhaps he had.

At this delicate moment Mercier intervened. He produced a letter which Captain Freystaetter had written to a friend shortly after Dreyfus' conviction. In the letter the captain said that his mind had been made up before he withdrew with the other judges to deliberate.

Labori demanded to know why Mercier had presented documents to the court and ordered them kept from the defendant. Didn't the general know this was a violation of the law? Mercier replied loftily that his had not been a formal order but a moral one in the highest sense. To this ambiguity he added—no doubt to make it seem less ambiguous—that he took full responsibility for it, but whether for being moral or for violating the law he did not specify. Had not Mercier promised Hanotaux, then Minister of Foreign Affairs, that he would not proceed against Dreyfus if no other evidence than the *bordereau* could be found? This was a clear admission that the *bordereau* was the first evidence found, and that nothing had been found before it. But the documentary evidence produced subsequently against Dreyfus from the Second Bureau's files all antedated the *bordereau*. How? Why? Labori wanted to know. Why had he admitted to Hanotaux he had only the *bordereau* and how had he managed to find *later* in his own files documents that, on their face, had been put into the files *earlier*? Mercier replied that he had told Hanotaux only that he would not produce documents that might directly involve a foreign power.

Then the general presented to the court a report dated November 1897, written by a Colonel Schneider, military attaché of the Austrian Embassy. The report read:

It can be heard here and there that Dreyfus actually was a traitor. However, I would not come back to this matter had I not heard from third persons repeatedly during this last year that the German and Italian attachés keep saying so. I also refer to the pieces of information published in *Le Temps* regarding the Dreyfus case. These I consider valid with respect to facts, and they assert that Dreyfus was connected with the intelligence offices in Strasbourg and Brussels, and that the German General Staff keep this secret even from their own nationals.

After Mercier's testimony, Colonel Schneider hastened to protest in *Le Figaro*, pointing out that the date of his report had been falsified. He had written it in 1896, when he was still convinced of Dreyfus' guilt, not in 1897, when he was not. But this partial denial did not destroy the effect which the report had on the judges.

Mercier, sitting in front of fellow officers, his juniors in rank, quietly gave a coherent, rounded and fluent account of Dreyfus' guilt. All of Dreyfus' former colleagues distrusted him for being inquisitive, he said. There was a document in the file, dated 1894, written by Panizzardi, in which the attaché said that he possessed plans of railway organization for mobilization. Dreyfus, at that time, said Mercier, had been working on those plans. When Dreyfus was studying explosives, the secret papers on melanite had disappeared. From Dreyfus' notebook at the Ecole Militaire precisely those parts had been missing which referred to details that had fallen into the hands of a foreign power. A report on heavy artillery, which Dreyfus had prepared, disappeared from the War Ministry.

The defense, of course, could disprove many of these charges. For instance, the report on heavy artillery had disappeared when Dreyfus was in prison, those on melanite before he had had any contact with them. Other allegations were irrelevant to the accusation of treason. But the effect on the judges could not be discounted.

Mercier referred to the famous "Scoundrel D——" letter as if it were taken for granted by everyone that the reference was to Dreyfus. It was as if the High Court of Appeal had never existed, and such was the alchemy of his presence that he got away with it. He went into the various reasons Dreyfus might have had for believing at the time when he allegedly wrote the *bordereau* that he was to go off to the maneuvers. It was, of course, his handwriting—Esterhazy had merely lied. But even if if the *bordereau* had not emerged directly from Dreyfus' own pen, he had certainly inspired it.

Mercier's testimony abounded with hints that what he told was but part of the truth, that the whole truth was still too dangerous to France to tell. To the question of a judge whether the *bordereau* in the secret file was not merely a copy, he replied with hints about an "original," and implied that it contained marginalia by the German Emperor. He reminded the judges of the strange, informal and impetuous ways of the Kaiser, who, he said, was in personal contact with secret agents and their activities, no matter how officially it might be denied. Altogether it was a brazen demonstration—few men in high places have ever matched it. Many men in power have lied when they could, but few have dared to lie calmly, effortlessly, almost convivially before a court of law, in the face of such a mountain of incontestable evidence.

Mercier's testimony had been going on for the best part of a day when news came that the police in Paris early that morning had arrested Déroulède and other leaders of his League of Patriots, along with leading royalists and anti-Semites. Guérin himself had succeeded in getting inside his house in the Rue Chabrol, where he had barricaded himself with a few of his faithful.

It seems that Lépine, the Prefect of Police, who had informers in all camps, had received news of a coup. Déroulède had finally yielded to the royalists, at least to the extent of joining forces with them to overthrow the Republic. The matter of the form of the future state was to be settled afterward. The joint committee had fixed the date of the uprising for August 12, the day on which Mercier was to take the witness stand, with the day when the court at Rennes would announce its verdict as an alternative choice. The pretender to the throne had gone on a cruise along the shores of Brittany in order to be near by when the rising flared up. Rennes would be its probable starting point. The Premier believed the subversive leagues would disintegrate if deprived of their leaders. He had obtained the Cabinet's unanimous support for the swoop by the police. It was arranged to hold the plotters for trial before the Senate for an attempt on the safety of the state. To try the "patriots" before a regular jury would have been too much of a gamble.

Except for Guérin, a full bag was made. The anti-Semite leaders seemed prepared for a long siege. The headquarters of the League was stocked with provisions and arms. Galliffet wanted it stormed, but Waldeck abhorred the idea of risking even a single policeman's life in an attempt to capture a few stray bits of human refuse he was sure to get hold of in the end. So Guérin and his fourteen fellow anti-Semites looked down from the balcony and from the windows on the police who kept the building surrounded.

The populace enjoyed the spectacle. People thronged into the Rue Chabrol to see the besieged house, dubbed Fort Chabrol, and listened to the harangues Guérin made from the balcony. The policemen also took the matter lightly. Some of them ostentatiously read *La Libre Parole* in front of the building. It was a mistake on Waldeck's part. Galliffet had been right. The siege lasted long enough to dent the prestige of the Government. Guérin's plan obviously was to hold out until the end of the trial at Rennes. Then he and his associates expected an uprising even though it would be leaderless. In the beginning it seemed only a diversion for Parisians. But it developed into a serious problem. A large-scale demonstration was shaped by the Rightists to liberate Guérin. The police were obliged to give battle. About a hundred people were wounded. After a forty days' siege, Guérin capitulated. He was arrested; his associates were allowed to go home. The Government took no action against the Army officers discovered to be involved in the plot.

William James wrote to Mrs. E. P. Gibbins from Bad Nauheim, Germany:

> The still blacker nightmare of a Dreyfus case hangs over us; and there is little time in the day save for reading *Le Figaro's* full reports of the trial. Like all French happenings, it is as if they were edited expressly for literary purposes. Every witness so-called has a power of statement equal to that of a first-class lawyer, and the various human types that succeed each other, exhibiting their several peculiarities in full blossom, make the thing like a novel. Esterhazy seems to me a fantastic scoundrel—knowing all the secrets, saying what he pleases, mystifying all Europe, leading the whole French Army (except apparently Picquart) by the nose, a regular Shakespearean type of villain, with an insane exuberance of rhetoric and fancy about his vanities and hatreds that literature has never yet equalled. It would seem incredible that the Court Martial should condemn [Dreyfus]. Henry was evidently the spy, employed by Esterhazy, and afterwards Du Paty helped their machinations in order to protect his own record at the original trial—at least this seems the plausible theory. The older generals seem merely to have been passive connivers, stupidly and obstinately holding to the original official mistake rather than surrender under fire. And such is the prestige of caste-opinion, such the solidarity of the professional spirit, that, incredible as it may seem, it is still quite probable that the officers will obey the lead of their superiors and condemn Dreyfus again. . . . Picquart is a real hero—a precious possession for any country. He ought to be made Minister of War, though that would doubtless produce a revolution. I suppose Loubet will pardon Dreyfus immediately (if the court recommends it). Then Dreyfus, and perhaps Loubet, will be assassinated by some anti-Semite, and who knows what will follow?

On August 14 another incident shook the court at Rennes. A man ran into the hall crying that Labori had been shot in the street. Too many mysterious deaths had already occurred in the course of the affair. The news made everyone shudder. Trial was immediately adjourned.

28

LABORI, IN THE COMPANY of Picquart and another friend, had been on his way to court when someone behind them fired a shot. Labori collapsed. As he fell he cried out, "Murderer!"

Picquart and his friend ran after the man who had fired the shot, shouting at passers-by to hold him. In his turn the man kept shouting, "Let me pass, let me pass! I killed a Dreyfusard!" He got away on a boulevard, disappearing into the crowd.

Meanwhile, a man pretending to come to Labori's help grabbed his briefcase and tried to get his dispatch case, too. But the attorney had fallen on it and was too heavy for the man to move. He ran off without it. After their unsuccessful chase, Picquart and his friend returned to Labori. The street was empty. No one had dared help the bleeding attorney. Finally a physician was brought. He discovered that Labori's wound was not dangerous.

The stealing of Labori's briefcase made it plain that the shooting had not been a demented outburst but a deliberate, cold-blooded plot. Anatole France wrote, addressing Labori: "You believed the good Samaritan was coming to you, but it was the infamous Pharisee who, making believe that he came to aid you, stole your papers." And Jaurès wrote: "In 1894, the General Staff suppressed the defense in order to destroy Dreyfus. Now they find it simpler to destroy his defenders."

While Picquart had been waiting at Labori's side General Mercier passed by. He reported that the general had given him a long look of triumph and defiance.

The news soon spread that the bullet had lodged itself in the muscles of Labori's back without doing serious damage. The Catholic *La Croix* produced a limerick, ridiculing the idea that Labori had been wounded at all. The rumors grew wilder when a surgeon who had been a friend of Labori's from childhood came to Rennes and insisted on operating. The local doctor, Reclus, and a medical professor from Paris opposed surgery. Labori himself supported Reclus and, while willing to receive the surgeon as a friend, was not willing to accept his professional advice. The friend was unable to take this rebuff without acrimonious comment.

Opinion now became vocal that Labori had stood in the way of the new line the defense had taken in advocating a compromise with the military and had been shot on that account—by the Dreyfus family, some papers reported, to get him out of the picture; by the Government, other papers said, since the Cabinet was also in favor of a face-saving compromise. Aspersions were cast on the police, suggesting that they had played a part in the shooting in order to pander to the wishes of the Government. Rumor received renewed support when the Dreyfus family tried to substitute for Labori another counsel, Henri Mornard, who had defended Dreyfus before the High Court. Labori protested and threatened a public scandal. On August 22 he was back with the defense. The gunman and his accomplice were never caught. Whether they were local crooks who thought there would be money in a "syndicate" lawyer's briefcase or nationalists who thought there was secret evidence in it was never established.

The president of the court congratulated Labori on his recovery and gave him permission to cross-examine General Mercier. In the meantime, the anti-revisionist press had begun to express disappointment with Mercier. L'Autorité gave him and other generals a warning: "You are in the dock along with Dreyfus." Le Gaulois published an open letter to Mercier: "Your deposition was valiant, loyal, and irresistible. You told a large part of the truth, but did you tell the whole truth? You possess a photostatic copy of the bordereau which you took with you to Rennes: if this is true, confirm it; if it is in error, deny it." The allusion was to the much publicized photostat of the "original" of the bordereau complete with imperial marginalia. Mercier was shrewd enough to know that this forgery was infinitely more valuable as a threat than as a weapon. As a threat it gave off a smokescreen. As a weapon it would have gone off in his face. Du Paty had been arrested for less. Probably the nationalists would not have minded if Mercier had been arrested. It would have been a torch to rise to. But the Caesar-headed general seemed to have no desire to become a torch. He was a wriggler, not a flame.

Labori treated Mercier with a hard hand, but the general slipped out of his grasp like an eel and kept diving into a tangle of ambiguities. He described the days when Dreyfus had been put under arrest. The German Emperor, through his Ambassador, had threatened war, he said. Over the bordereau? Well, of course, you understand that just at this time Tsar Alexander III died, and there was much uncertitude as to his successor's willingness to stand by the French alliance. On account of the *bordereau*? No, of course not. This was a new Tsar he was talking about, and Kaiser Wilhelm was known for his irresponsible, impulsive actions. There was no one around the imperial court or on the German General Staff strong and upright enough to counter the Emperor's vagaries. So those had been days and nights of anxiety. He, Mercier, had kept the Chief of the General Staff on the alert to issue the order for mobilization at a moment's notice. In such a situation legal scruples were not so compelling as in less critical times, and of course you couldn't aggravate things by divulging proofs.

Mercier's wrigglings became point-blank statements when he could put the statements in another mouth. He said the former Minister of War, Charles de Freycinet, had told him of proof that the Jewish syndicate had spent more than thirty-five million francs to save Dreyfus. Labori jumped up as if bitten by a snake. He demanded details. Mercier referred him to Freycinet, who, on being summoned, had no proof and confirmed neither the amount nor the precise source of his information and was willing to back up Mercier only to the extent of guessing that some money had probably been spent to influence foreign countries.

In bringing his testimony to a close, Mercier thrust home the final dagger. "I wish to add one more word," he said softly. "I have come to live to old age to gain the sad experience that everything human is subject to error. If I am an imbecile, as Zola thought me, then I am at least an honest one, son of another honest man. . . . Had the slightest doubt stirred in my mind, I would have been the first to declare before you, and before Captain Dreyfus: 'I erred in good faith and I have come to acknowledge it in all honesty and do all that is humanly possible to right the terrible wrong that was done.'"

Dreyfus jumped to his feet, stung, and stepped up to the general: "This is what you should do! This is your duty!" he cried out.

"Well, no," replied Mercier calmly. "My convictions have not changed at all since 1894. They have only been strengthened by a more thorough study of the files and by the attempts I have seen to prove that guilt is innocence, frustrated in spite of the millions spent in the effort." "Murderer!" a French journalist shouted at him when the general left the stand.

Mathieu Dreyfus sent a message to Joseph Reinach in Paris, expressing his anxiety over the outcome of the trial. The foreign press, in particular the American, no longer expected an acquittal.

William James wrote to Mrs. R. Morse from Bad Nauheim:

> Talk of corruption! We don't know what the word corruption means at home, with our improvised and shifting agencies of crude pecuniary bribery, compared with the solidly entrenched and permanently organized corruptive geniuses of monarchy, nobility, church, Army, that penetrate the very bosom of the higher kind as well as the lower kind of people in all European states (except Switzerland) and sophisticate their motives away from the impulse to straightforward handling of any simple case. *Témoin* the Dreyfus case. But no matter! Of all the forms of mental crudity, that of growing earnest over international comparisons is probably the most childish. Every nation has its ideals which are a dead secret to other nations, and it has to develop in its own way, in touch with them. It can only be judged by itself. If each of us does as well as he can in his own sphere at home, he will do all he can do; that is why I hate to remain so long abroad. . . .

The revisionists urged Premier Waldeck to make a personal appeal to the German Government to acknowledge officially the receipt of the documents enumerated in the *bordereau* together with the exact date of their arrival and the arrival of documents received after Dreyfus' arrest. Waldeck paid a visit to the embassy. His request was sent on to Berlin with the comment that the acquittal of Dreyfus was of great importance to the situation in France and to the Government. But the Germans saw no reason to pull French potatoes out of the fire. The Government then renewed its request, stressing the urgency of the matter. Von Bülow, in his reply, paid his respects to the French Government's fight for the truth, yet declared that he could not go beyond the declaration that he had made in 1898 in the Reichstag, in which he denied that Dreyfus has ever been in German service.

Still the French Government did not give up hope. General Galliffet, the Minister of War, appealed to the Emperor and asked him to contribute to the restoration of an internal peace in France that might even lead to a Franco-German understanding. Galliffet wanted to obtain the Emperor's consent to a hearing of the former military attaché Von Schwarzkoppen before a court in Berlin. The Kaiser scribbled on the request: "It is none of my business. Am I the Emperor of France?" The German Government, nevertheless, issued a statement solemnly repeating its previous declarations, that no German agency whatsoever had stood in any kind of relation to or connection with Dreyfus. This statement was immediately forwarded by the French Minister of Foreign Affairs to the court at Rennes.

Jean Casimir-Périer, President of the Republic at the time of Dreyfus' conviction, refuted Mercier's insinuations (they could hardly be called testimony). Energetically, the former President denied that the German Ambassador had threatened war over the public exposure of any document. Count Münster had protested only against the press for involving the embassy in the Dreyfus case, he said, and the protest had carried no threat at all. Moreover, even this intervention had taken place after Dreyfus was convicted, and not before, as Mercier alleged. Mercier replied only that the date was of no importance, and that this was simply one of countless episodes in a sequence of events.

Paul Bertulus, the *juge d'instruction*, in his testimony again recalled the scene when Major Henry had broken down. This witness, Jaurès wrote, was admirable for his logic, clarity and force of reasoning in asserting Dreyfus' innocence. When he finished, Henry's widow, in mourning, jumped up, shouting at him, "Judas!" But Bertulus was prepared for this scene. He showed the president a letter from a friend received the day before, warning him that Mme. Henry was being brought to the trial for the express purpose of jumping up and insulting him.

In this symphony of confusion and diversions, the defense made no consistent effort to limit the trial to the evidence of treason and of Dreyfus' guilt in it. In Labori's absence Demange missed many opportunities to show up by pertinent questioning lies and absurdities in the testimony. Either he no longer had the talent and energy, or he deliberately refrained in order to hew to his line of saving the military's face. Yet even Labori, after he returned from his encounter with the bullet, did not raise his voice very loud when the trial got involved in endless conjectures over whether Dreyfus could have believed that he was going off to the maneuvers, or whether he could have furnished the secrets which had been in the *bordereau*.

It was, of course, difficult in any case, and in the circumstances of this case practically impossible, to handle a witness like Mercier. Labori wanted him to tell why he had destroyed the commentary he had written out for Du Paty to give to the judges of the first court-martial. Mercier replied that the commentary had been for his personal use only, so he was entitled to dispose of it. But why, then, Labori insisted, had the general communicated it to the court-martial if it was only for his personal use? It had been necessary to inform the court of the origin of the documents, Mercier answered. If so, Labori demanded, why had Mercier destroyed it, and why in particular had he waited until 1897, when new light began to shine on the case, before destroying it? Oh, said Mercier, he hadn't waited. He had ordered it destroyed long before.

Mercier was quite right about this at least. His order had not been obeyed. It had been interpreted by Henry and his associates as an attempt by Mercier to wipe out the traces of his own lawless part in the Dreyfus case. Even so, the question of when it was destroyed did not tell why this had been done. And Mercier never was forced into a corner from which he could not escape except by telling why. One staff officer did give straightforward testimony—Lieutenant Colonel Albert Cordier. He told the court how his doubts were aroused when he learned that the Second Bureau's testimony at the court-martial was that the *bordereau* had reached it in April or May. He knew for a fact that it had come in September. Cordier declared: "I had believed in Captain Dreyfus' guilt. Now I believe in his innocence. I believe in it with absolute conviction."

The trial lasted for thirty-three sessions. One hundred and fifteen witnesses were heard. Mercier and his aide General Roget ruled the trial so completely that when on one occasion they wanted Picquart back on the stand they did not request the president to order it. Roget barked: "Monsieur Picquart to the stand." Out of military habit Picquart obeyed.

As a surprise witness an Austrian named Cernuski was called. He was reputed to be a descendant of the Serbian royal family. He testified that in September 1894 he had seen French military documents on the desk of a German officer. When he questioned the officer on their origin, he replied that he had got them from that "swine of a Jew." General Galliffet did not fail to inform the court officially that Cernuski was a notoriously dubious character who consorted with international gamblers and spies.

Labori waived his right to sum up. The Dreyfus family had asked him to do so. Demange made an astonishing appeal to the humane sentiments of the court. He made it obvious to the judges that he courted their favor. Barrès compared his manner to that of a waiter in a high-class restaurant.

In his summation, the prosecutor made a remarkable suggestion to the judges. Evidence, he pointed out, did not necessarily have to take a particular legal form. In this case the evidence was not in this or that point; it was everywhere as a whole. The law asked them only to announce what their belief was. It did not require them to account for the way they had arrived at this belief.

At the end, the president of the court turned to Dreyfus and asked whether he had anything to say. So pale as to seem bloodless, Dreyfus rose and spoke in his uningratiating way: "I only want to say to the country and to the Army that I am innocent. I have endured five years of horrible martyrdom to save the honor of my name that my children also bear. I am certain that through your honesty and your sense of justice I shall succeed today."

"Is that all you have to say?" asked the president.

"Yes, that is all," replied Dreyfus and sat down.

The court deliberated for two hours, then announced its verdict. By a vote of five to two, Captain Dreyfus was found guilty of high treason.

29

THE COURT HAD TAKEN into consideration what it called "extenuating circumstances." Dreyfus was condemned to a mere ten years in prison. He did not have to suffer an official degradation.

Demange wept aloud; the old lawyer was incapable of informing Dreyfus. The captain awaited the verdict in a side room, and Labori had to shoulder alone the task of breaking the news. Dreyfus immediately requested that his children be brought to him. Lucie had kept their father's fate a secret from them. The children knew only that Papa was on a long voyage and ill. Dreyfus had refrained from meeting the children until they could see him free. But ten years—they would no longer be children by then. If he wanted to see them while they were still his, it would have to be now, in prison. "Please, comfort my wife," he asked Labori, who felt that Dreyfus would not survive this last blow.

"As if the rivers had changed in their course," Zola wrote of the verdict. Wrote Clemenceau:

Extenuating circumstances indeed! The extenuating circumstances belong not to the accused but to the judges who in fact did vote extenuating circumstances for themselves. The vote is nothing but a confession that they struck a deal between discipline and their conscience. . . . The cry for justice, the voice that was suffocated within the walls of the court, will soon fill the world with its clamor. . . . Tomorrow the peoples, stupefied, will ask what remains of the historic traditions that once made us the champions of right and justice for the whole of the earth. A cry will ring out over the world: Where is France? What became of the French? And none but the good soldiers of justice will have a right to answer: present.

The world responded to the verdict with a tempest of indignation. From Russia to America people were shaken by the event. It was incomprehensible to them. French embassies and consulates around the globe had to be protected by strong police forces from protest demonstrations. In Minneapolis the French flag was burned in the street. A movement was launched to boycott the World Exhibition in Paris, scheduled for the coming year. Mass meetings in Chicago and Washington as well as in European capitals urged a boycott of everything French. "France committed the crime of the century," *Harper's New Monthly* wrote, and the rest of the American press commented in a similar vein. "Not Dreyfus but France stands condemned."

Queen Victoria, who had sent the Lord Chief Justice as an observer to the Rennes trial, was shocked by the verdict and made public her hope that the poor martyr would be allowed to appeal to better judges.

Meanwhile people in France by and large received the verdict with satisfaction and the hope that the affair would not play havoc with the pleasures and profits of the World Exhibition. The nationalist and Catholic press were in raptures. "Since 1870 this is our first victory over the foreigner," *Le Gaulois* wrote jubilantly.

But Clemenceau called for action:

France is now a country with no security either for the liberty, the life or the honor of her citizens. A horde ganged up on us, a pretorian guard, a host of monks who have destroyed right, justice and law and have savagely scorched all that forty centuries of human effort has accomplished. A multitude conditioned by monkey tricks, or by the pulpit, permitted this crime, and even encouraged it by its indifference and cowardice. Generals, with nought but surrenders to their names, Jesuits inspired by the spirit of torture, left nothing standing of what France had been but a realm of stupidity and crime.

They denounce us as *sans patrie*. They speak more truly than they realize, for they have taken away our homeland. Now, let us face each other squarely, and see whether we have the guts to reconquer it.

A country that bases its honor on acquitting a criminal and attacking an innocent may call itself republic or monarchy, socialist or imperialist or democratic, may have a parliament, city councils, ministers, judges, hospitals and theaters, all the external façades of civilization; it may construct railroads, conquer territories from defenseless Negroes, make use of electricity, and the telephone, and beat the drums of exhibitions to book up the hotels . . . all this will be but dust in the storms to come. Without firm foundations in thought, without the moral cement of right and justice, no society can prevail.

Premier Waldeck-Rousseau had made no secret of the fact that he would not allow a conviction at Rennes to stand. However, he met with serious objections from Galliffet. The High Court might set aside the verdict and refer the case back to a military court. "But do not forget," the War Minister warned, "that the great majority of the people are anti-Semites. Consequently our position will be this: On the one side—the entire Army and the majority of Frenchmen, and all the agitators. On the other—the Ministry, Dreyfusards and the foreign countries."

Waldeck heeded the warning, at least to the extent of attempting to shorten a protracted legal process and the opportunities for political agitation it would offer. Instead, to show that the Government disapproved of the sentence and rejected it, he wanted to pardon Dreyfus. In this the Minister of War concurred. But under the Constitution it was President Loubet who had the power to pardon and Dreyfus who had the power to accept or reject it. Waldeck wanted the pardon granted immediately to make it not only a pardon, but a gesture of indignation at the court. But Loubet declined to be hurried. So confident had the President been of acquittal that just before the verdict he had urged the country to accept the decision of the Rennes court, no matter what it was. Now he asked Waldeck to give him a week.

Clemenceau was opposed to the whole idea of pardon. It would imply on Dreyfus' part a tacit acknowledgment of his guilt and an overt acknowledgment of his inability to get justice from a French court. The Dreyfusards had been fighting not only for Dreyfus but for law in the French courts.

"Dreyfus may think first of all of Dreyfus," wrote the Tiger at his most tigerish. "That is as it should be. But we think of our country that has succumbed to the imbecile brutality of the iron fist, our country helpless against the enemy. What we want is not the salvation of one individual, but the deliverance of all."

Jaurès felt the same. But Dreyfus, after sustaining himself through to the end of the last awfulness at Rennes, had suffered a mental and physical breakdown. Doctors feared he might not survive the time the High Court would require to act on an appeal and set aside the sentence. Joseph Reinach was strongly in favor of acceptance of the pardon. He, Clemenceau, Jaurès and Mathieu Dreyfus met in conference in the office of Millerand, the Socialist Minister of Commerce. Jaurès, humane as he was, yielded.

"The pardon has the character of partial rehabilitation, an advance payment on the ransom for humanity, anticipation of a total recognition of right and justice," he wrote. Clemenceau was adamant, and Mathieu, that consistently admirable middle-class businessman, remained consistent. He was so deeply affected by Clemenceau's fight for his brother that he refused to try to persuade Alfred to accept a pardon. At this, Clemenceau softened: "If I were his [Mathieu's] brother I would probably accept," he said.

Mathieu went to his brother with a declaration written by Jaurès, to be attached to his acceptance of the pardon:

The government of the Republic gives me back my freedom. It means nothing to me without honor. From today on I shall continue to seek reparation for the atrocious judicial error of which I am still the victim. I want the whole of France to know by force of a final judgment that I am innocent. My heart shall be at peace only when there shall not be a single Frenchman who can impute to me the crime which another committed.

Clemenceau wrote: "A pardon was inevitable. The government had to grant it without delay to wipe out the effects of an unjust sentence. The conscience of the civilized universe had risen in protest against it."

On September 19, 1899, Dreyfus, duly pardoned, left prison. Two days later the Minister of War, General Galliffet, issued an Order of the Day to all commanding generals: "The incident is closed. The military judges, assured of general respect, gave their verdict in full independence. We bowed to it without second thought, as we now do to the act of mercy that the President of the Republic has performed. There shall be no more talk of retaliation against whomsoever. I repeat: The affair is closed."

Galliffet acted on his own, without consulting the Cabinet. Premier Waldeck-Rousseau had had very different plans in mind. He had concluded that the next task of the Government must be to destroy the enemies of the Republic: to extirpate the royalist cadres from the officers' corps; to break the political power of the Church. Moderate as he had been up to the Dreyfus affair, he was now ready to go to the Left for solid support to achieve a stable Republic. Only after a clean-up in the high ranks in the Army and a shattering blow to the Church's influence in politics and a period of education would the country be ready for a rehabilitation of Dreyfus, he felt. Waldeck was greatly angered over Galliffet's action and was tempted to dismiss him immediately. For in his Order of the Day the Minister of War had accepted the sentence of Rennes, expressed unqualified respect for the judges and barred retaliation. However, Waldeck needed General Galliffet for the purge of the Army. He had reserved this painful task for a man the Army respected. Who else could do it more expeditiously, with fewer repercussions?

Zola, who had the foresight of a genius, wrote to Labori: "I am getting convinced that the fight has ended. They will, in a dirty way, grant the same pardon to the honest people and to the bandits." He said that he had lost interest in the affair.

But his warm heart could not withhold sympathy from the innocent who had suffered so much. He wrote to Lucie Dreyfus on that September 19:

Today, Madame, the miracle has been accomplished. Two years of gigantic fighting have brought about the impossible. Our dream has come true, the martyr descended from his cross, the innocent man is free, the husband has returned. Now his sufferings are over, the ache of our heart has vanished, the unbearable thought disturbs no more our sleep. Thus today is the day of a great victory. In silence our hearts unite with yours. There is no woman, no mother alive who would not be moved in her deepest feelings by thinking of this first evening of your reunion while the whole world is with you in love.

Many warmhearted people took pains to write to Dreyfus of the satisfaction they felt in knowing he was out of prison, back home with his family. The great ones among the revisionists also sent messages.

Emile Duclaux wrote that the revisionists had to thank Dreyfus for his support of them. "I mean the courage we drew from what we learned of you and your family, and from your almost superhuman letters, in which suffering almost unimaginable to men had been unable to silence the stoicism and lofty conscience of the soldier." Invitations came from many parts of the world to Dreyfus to take a rest abroad: from the Prince of Monaco; from Lady Stanley, wife of the famed African explorer.

Wrote Picquart:

I am happy to know that you are in the midst of your dear ones, and to think that this dreadful nightmare is over at last. Until your liberty was actually achieved, it seemed to me as if I were in some way linked with your tormentors, and I did not feel easy in my mind until I saw you a free man. What remains to be done is no more than a formality, for you have been vindicated as no one has ever been before—by the voice of the entire world.

Picquart wrote so even though he knew the Dreyfus family had done him grave wrong. They had failed to consult him at all about the pardon and he was intimately involved. However he might try to blink at it, in accepting the pardon Dreyfus had acknowledged his guilt. Thus Picquart was disavowed. He had been left alone to face the hatred and contempt of that Army which was still the only home for his inner being. The pardon freed Dreyfus, but it did not make Picquart right.

30

THE GREAT, RIOTOUS DEBATE of a moral principle had lasted too long. It had become a bore to the population.

The verdict at Rennes was a transparent fraud. The General Staff had been acquitted, but two of the judges—the president of the court who was about to retire from the Army, and a devout Catholic who had put his devotion to the truth above his own church's interpretation of it—had not been hooked. Still, five others had been. But even they had conceded the lugubriousness of their position. What "extenuating circumstances" can mitigate the high treason of an Army officer? Only a court of clowns or Lewis Carroll's mad off-with-his-head Queen could have found any, and done so as the Rennes court did it—by fiat, without pointing out what they were, by simply stating that they existed.

This was not the voice of a court. It was the desperate squeak of men hooked by a crook around their necks and trying to make a protest about it without seeming to. But it acquitted the General Staff, and Dreyfus was pardoned, and the people were bored. "Back to normalcy" was their cry. They accepted the verdict without a qualm. They wanted peace in France for the World Exhibition.

Bored people are likely to become irritable with those who keep on rapping for attention. At the Senate elections in January 1900 there were ninety-nine seats to be filled. The various republican parties won ninety-five of them, but this was true of every republican, no matter which party he represented: if he had been a vocal Dreyfusard, he lost.

So much for the country, but there was still Paris, city of light. The Dreyfusards wanted it to be a white light, not the muddy, ambiguous gray of "normalcy." They grappled furiously with "normalcy" in the Paris municipal elections.

"At this hour," cried Joseph Reinach in a campaign speech, "we are about midway in the intermission between the fourth and the fifth acts of the melodrama, where innocence is to be rewarded and crime punished. . . . So that France's honor should be upheld before the judgment of history, the verdict of Rennes, intrinsically made null and void by the addition of unspecified mitigating circumstances, torn apart by the pardon, must be repealed by a supreme verdict."

The nationalists placarded these words in the streets of Paris with the caption: "Resumption of the Affair." Their press accused Premier Waldeck and the republican parties of the Left of having inspired Reinach's speech. The Jews, they wrote, were out to disrupt once more the peace of the country that had hardly begun to recover. They were only waiting for the "armistice" of the World Exhibition to be over.

The tactics of the nationalists won. Paris rebuffed the republican parties so crushingly as to recall the days of Boulanger.

The Government wanted to end the Dreyfus Affair with a general amnesty for all on both sides. President Loubet had consented to pardon Dreyfus on the understanding that this was what would happen. Waldeck actually hoped to put it through without delay. But it was not so easy—morally, or politically, or legally.

Zola announced he would take up the fight when the retrial of his own case took place. The Government postponed the date of the re-trial indefinitely. Dreyfus appealed to the Premier not to deprive him of an opportunity for legal rehabilitation. He argued that proceedings against Mercier and others might disclose new facts that could serve as a basis for an appeal to the High Court.

Then there was Picquart. The idea of an amnesty embittered him. His innocence was obvious. There could be no doubt about it and he wanted none to exist for the sake of his position among the officers who had been his brothers. Why should he appear before all the world as another Henry, one who had had the gall to refrain from committing suicide? Picquart began to suspect that it had not been an oversight that Dreyfus had neglected to consult him when considering whether to accept a pardon. He wondered: had Dreyfus made a deal with the Government whereby he would be pardoned and pay for it by raising no objections to a general amnesty for all? The Dreyfus family, of course, must have known that Picquart could not accede to such a deal. It would leave him no legal way to restore his honor. Was that why Dreyfus had "forgotten" to inform him when the matter had first come up?

Picquart had never liked Dreyfus. Now he had begun to resent him. No sooner had Alfred been freed than he wrote Picquart a letter of reverent gratitude, asking for a meeting. Picquart never answered.

Debate on the amnesty program dragged on in the committees of both Houses. A long recess was taken for the World Exhibition. Labori had been in the forefront of the move against an amnesty. He strove to get Mathieu to join him. He pointed out that, by accepting a pardon, Alfred had marked his case "closed," and that only in the trials of the lesser figures in the affair could the evidence be developed by which new efforts might be made for legal vindication. But Mathieu refused. He was loyal to Waldeck. The Premier had promised that a way would be found to vindicate Alfred when the atmosphere had cleared, and Mathieu had confidence not only in Waldeck's wisdom but in his good intentions. Even when Waldeck pleaded in the Chamber for an amnesty "only for the guilty," Mathieu still went along with him. Labori was in a rage. The "guilty" who would be amnestied included Picquart. No human imagination, said Labori, could encompass the base ingratitude Dreyfus exhibited when he remained silent in the face of an amnesty that would tacitly brand Picquart guilty.

Labori had never forgiven the Dreyfuses for taking the defense out of his hands at Rennes. He had taken a bullet in his back for them, and then had been asked to sit in silence and listen to his colleague, the aged Demange, carry subservience so far as not even to request the judges to announce with their verdict that Dreyfus was innocent. Demange, to whom the oil of compromise was not an emetic but the wine of life, had told the judges it would suffice if their verdict merely expressed doubts of Dreyfus' guilt, doubts which, under the presumption of innocence, must be resolved in favor of the accused. Labori had written of Dreyfus:

> Personally, he is quite free to prefer his freedom to the establishment of honor, and rest satisfied with the outcome, showing no concern for the interests of others. But by that he becomes an independent and isolated being, not a man bearing the common bondage of humanity and aware of the beauty of social responsibilities, thus feeling solidarity with all his fellow men. So, in spite of the grandeur of the part he has played in the past, he now represents nothing. . . . The Dreyfus Affair has ceased to be a program. From the general point of view the affair is closed.

But it was a Picquart affair now to Labori, and that was not closed. He became convinced that there had been in fact a shady deal under the table between Waldeck and Dreyfus, and he issued an ultimatum: Mathieu must choose between Demange and himself as legal representative.

The controversy elated the nationalists. Their elation drove the wedge deeper into the ranks of the revisionists. Yet for Mathieu the idea of dismissing Demange was disgraceful. The old man had undertaken his brother's defense when no other lawyer of equal reputation was willing to risk it. His unflagging kindness had been a great solace—for long months the only solace in the darkness that followed Alfred's deportation. Mathieu found the situation unbearable. He had given six years of his life to achieve a happy ending for the drama of his brother. He had won that half loaf which, to a businessman, is so much better than none. Now this—the quarrel within the family that was tearing the half loaf into bitter crumbs that could nourish no one and nothing.

Following his pardon, in order to recuperate safe from mob annoyance, Alfred and his family had gone to Switzerland. His stay abroad, aloof from the amnesty debate, had been a subject for acrimonious comment. But Mathieu had refrained from summoning Alfred. Now he felt he had to.

Alfred took the train. The newspapers reported his arrival, but it was a sensation only in their columns. No crowds at the station, none in the streets, no incidents. According to Mathieu, Paris' indifference dismayed Labori. "How? Not a single outcry? Just nothing? This is indeed the end."

In Labori's office Dreyfus and Picquart met at last. Labori insisted that Alfred give over the leadership in a vigorous revisionist campaign to Picquart and himself, and exclude from it other counsel and Mathieu as well. Dreyfus loved Picquart. It had been true in school and it was even truer now: he would have done almost anything to win Picquart's respect. But the choice was cruel. What Demange had been to Mathieu, Mathieu had been to Alfred—multiplied a thousandfold. He would not give up Mathieu.

Labori flew into a temper. He went so far as to voice doubts whether Dreyfus had in fact been innocent and could stand upright before the world, or whether he had not used them to cover up his guilt. He said that Picquart shared his doubts, and Picquart who was sitting there did not deny it. But Dreyfus would not turn his back on his brother. He did not want to dismiss anybody, not Labori, not Demange, least of all Mathieu.

He walked out of the office, an unbending military figure as ever. But before he could reach the outer door, while he was still in the anteroom, he fainted. The pain of the scene had been too much for him. That evening he wrote to Labori that Mathieu would soon be returning to the family business in Mulhouse. "Thus it will be myself— whose sentiments of gratitude and profound admiration for you are known to you—who will exclusively handle my case. Your help in the future vicissitudes is indispensable. I repeat therefore my oral request to you to continue as my counsel."

But Labori insisted that Demange be kicked out too.

Picquart wrote to Premier Waldeck:

It is inadmissible that this situation be prolonged, and that I indefinitely stand without judgment. I demand to be judged. I demand that I be permitted to show publicly that the accusations against me are based on fraud and lies. To grant amnesty to a man unjustly accused means to deprive him of the moral reparation to which he is entitled. . . . The law of amnesty would hit me twice over; it would give me amnesty for a felony that I have not committed, and it would include me in one and the same measure with General Mercier and his accomplices

The Premier had argued for the amnesty on the basis that it "neither judges nor accuses, nor declares innocent nor condemns. It ignores. There are times when one should turn to the future and look not so much to where one expects to see criminals as to the state of things that made those people into criminals." People on both sides of the political front understood the hint. The amnesty was the price to be paid for a large-scale re-republicanization of public life, education and the Army. But to most of the revisionists, ardent republicans though they were, the moral cost continued to seem far too high. They had won a victory. If there were anything less than a forced unconditional surrender of the enemy, the victory would have to be won again and again.

In the legal sense, Waldeck's proposal was not an amnesty at all. Amnesty is a general pardon for convicted persons or for a certain category of them. It relieves of punishment. But there was only one convicted person here—Dreyfus. He had not only been pardoned but was otherwise excluded from the amnesty. The Government was bound by a promise to reserve for him the right to seek vindication by judicial process. The promise was implicit in the Government's proposal to exclude high treason from its amnesty. What the government bill actually provided was a voiding of all legal prosecutions arising from the affair.

In the revisionist camp some were for it. The historian Ernest Lavisse wrote that French national life could not be allowed to lapse permanently into civil war. But Clemenceau stuck to it: "No, we do not disarm. We cannot disarm. If we disarm, tomorrow others would enter the lists for the eternal fight whose honorable burden is carried by the human race: the fight of reason against brute force, of right against injustice."

For Clemenceau, now that Dreyfus and the emotional overtones of his personal misfortune were out of the way, the fight could be shifted to the broad field of political morality. He received support from such an eminent member of the French Academy as Louis Havet, who wrote in reply to Lavisse's appeal to lay down arms: "We have to go on marching straight against the crime until it is punished and until those who endangered France are thrown into the abyss in the implacable light of justice."

Esterhazy would not have been Esterhazy had he not tried to draw advantages for himself from the perplexed situation. He wrote his most dangerous enemy, Clemenceau, and offered himself as a comrade-in-arms, united with the Tiger in hatred of the crimes and hypocrisy of the generals. He proposed a secret alliance. Clemenceau made the letter public immediately with the ironic remark that the publicity might help Esterhazy get some money from the generals to keep him quiet.

Far from being discouraged, Esterhazy turned to the Premier in language more fiery than ever:

It is with profound sorrow that I see myself able to surpass a Gohier, a Clemenceau in their nefarious work. . . . But I warned the imbecile Cavaignac and the hypocrite Boisdeffre . . . [I told them]: "Shall I prove to you that cowardice in this once valiant Army, cowardice in battle, is no longer considered shameful? I am going to tell you of the filthy curishness of Galliffet. . . . Let's get going, as poor Henry used to say." I have refused to do this for 250 pounds sterling; now I will do it free of charge. I am ready for anything. I shall retreat from nothing. I shall go to France to appear before servile judges, to provoke them and to listen to perjured witnesses, to throw the shameful truth in the face of abject soldiers, and thus, in the bottomless mire in which you have plunged me, I shall be the grain of pure sand, the hardened core that makes the rock explode.

He was not thanked for his offer.

Nobody stood in more urgent need of the amnesty than General Mercier and his accomplices. He, as well as the nationalist press, had demanded it as long as it was uncertain whether it would be granted. But once they felt the Government could not retreat from granting it, they made a complete turnabout and described it as a perfidy. They said it had been prepared by Dreyfus, as arch-villain, with Picquart, Reinach and Zola as his henchmen.

Mercier resorted to cunning. He had his name put up for senator in a small constituency in Brittany, royalist and devoutly Catholic. With the full support of the royalists and Catholics, Mercier, the former republican and anti-clerical, was elected.

Waldeck was not without sympathy for the position of the antagonists of the amnesty among the revisionists. He was firmly bent on giving Dreyfus justice. But he was as firmly convinced that any attempt would result in a new defeat until the climate of public opinion underwent a fundamental change. For the same reason he did not yield to Picquart's urgent demands to exclude him from the amnesty. Picquart, he was certain, would be convicted by a military court, and the affair would be back with a vengeance. Waldeck wanted to promote Picquart to full colonel and send him on active service, but Picquart refused to slip back into the Army by the back door. Waldeck was a politician of a high order. The important thing to him was that the affair for so long as it lasted blurred the otherwise sharp dividing line between the Left and the Right. With the affair out of the way he would have a determined majority with which to tackle clericalism and the anti-republican influences in the Army—the two forces that had turned the Dreyfus case into an affair in the first place.

Now Waldeck made two significant moves. He ordered a police search of the offices of *La Croix,* owned by the Assumptionist order. It resulted in discovering 1,800,000 francs in cash, an enormous sum in those times and particularly spectacular for a ragged-edge sheet. Even more suspicious, 1,200,000 francs were in 20-franc bills. This lent strong credence to the belief that the religious orders were financing the anti-revisionist movement. Waldeck's second move was to take promotions in the Army out of the hands of the Army Committee, which was wholly dominated by the royalist and clerical Army cliques, and put them in the province of the Minister of War.

Clemenceau wrote:

We have said time and time again that the Affair was for us no more than an opportunity to show up the evils from which our country has been suffering for too long. Today the showing-up has been done. It is now time for us to draw our conclusions: The priest to his church, the soldier to his duty. The struggle against the influence of the Church and for the republicanization of the Army has been molded into one concept in Waldeck's program.

In the eyes of the republican statesmen, the Church was to blame not only for the reactionary spirit in the officer corps but also for the inefficiency of the Army on the battlefield. Clemenceau kept driving home the moral. It was with him an ever-recurring theme.

Napoleon III, he wrote, preferred to renounce the sorely needed help of Italy against Germany rather than give up custodianship of the Pope in Rome. The Tiger declared:

> The case was never so clear as in 1870 when the obligation to mount guard over the Vatican left us without an ally in the face of a united Germany. France was vanquished, dismembered, but the Church kept her power unimpaired and the good monks continued to furnish us with Chiefs of the Army in the service of the Roman International.
>
> The Franco-German war was the bankruptcy of our military organization. It would appear natural for the French people to condemn unanimously the incompetent generals who brought about the invasion and the dismemberment of France. Nothing of the sort happened. The ensuing civil war permitted the soldiers to return as victors drunk with vengeance instead of coming home with their faces hidden in shame after the saddest of all the capitulations in history. They were praised to the skies, they were objects of adulation, incense strewn before them. They have been the rulers of France since then, and they would never admit that they stood in need of any improvement or reform, or renunciation of their presumptuous ignorance which was the fount of our defeat.

31

IN DECEMBER 1900, a year after the debate began, the decree of amnesty was finally voted. The Dreyfus case seemed to sink surprisingly fast into the rapids of history. The new century had its own history to make.

Dreyfus published his diary of Devil's Island. It was a world success. Joseph Reinach issued the first volume of his documented history of the affair. Zola appeared with his novel, *Truth*; it was intended to be the crown of his life's work, but it didn't turn out that way. Reality surpassed in meaning and design the imagination of the novelist who in real life had been the hero, not the author. Even Esterhazy published the depositions he had made before the French consul in London. Consistent to the end in his inconsistency, he had two different versions of them published.

The books mushroomed, had their day in the sun and then one after another sank into oblivion. The foreign press dropped the case as a news item. The personalities of the drama also began to take their

leave. Bernard Lazare died at thirty-eight. The great old Senatoi
Scheurer did not live to see Dreyfus released. An old friend soon followed him, Grimaux, the famed chemist, deprived by General Billot
of his chair and laboratory. Grimaux had returned to his home town,
St. Hermine, in the Vendée. Catholic bigots there made his life a
misery. Even the small republican circle of the town was divided. In
the end he had a house built for himself in the countryside so that he
might die in peace. Trarieux, whose sober and noble arguments had
left his opponents with no answer to make except that he was a Protestant, died, and so did Emile Duclaux, "the conscience of the Pasteur
Institute."

Zola fell victim to a grotesque accident. He was in the habit of
spending his summers with his wife at Medan, in a house notorious
for its bizarre lack of taste. At the end of September 1902 they returned to Paris, to an apartment in a small hotel. The bedroom was
cold and damp, so they lighted a coal fire in the fireplace. In the middle
of the night Mme. Zola awoke. The air was oppressive. She went into
the next room for a breath of fresh air, then returned. Zola had now
awakened, too. He did not feel very well but persuaded his wife not
to ring the bell to wake up the maid. The couple shared the same bed.
In the morning the maid, worried about their unusual delay in calling
for breakfast, knocked on the door. When there was no answer, she
opened it. Mme. Zola lay on the bed gasping for air. Zola was
stretched out dead on the floor.

Writes F. Hemmings in his biography *Emile Zola*:

> The suddenness of this end aroused immediate suspicion of foul play. Plenty
> of people had been thirsting for Zola's blood since his intervention in the
> Affair. But the explanation was very simple. Certain repairs had been made
> to the chimney [of the apartment] during the summer, and the workmen had
> left a quantity of rubbish in the flue which obstructed the passage of carbon
> monoxide fumes from the glowing ovoids.

Subsequent investigation has revealed no one who would admit
having ordered the repairs and no clue has ever been found to the
identity of the workmen. All that is clear is that Zola died of a typically French detestation of the cold night air, but whether by accident
or design is a question that one side is hardly likely at this late date to
answer to the satisfaction of the other.

The Chief of Paris' police formally asked Dreyfus to stay away from the funeral. He feared incidents. But Dreyfus insisted on paying his last respects to Zola. It was Zola who, when all hope was dying, had raised his personal tragedy into a cause the whole civilized world embraced. No incident marred the funeral.

Clemenceau eulogized Zola's memory in these words:

There have always been people strong enough to resist the most powerful kings, to refuse to bow before them; there have been very few to resist the masses, to stand up alone to the misled multitude. . . . To Zola goes the glory of having given the signal to that peaceful revolt of the spirit which in our tormented France was nothing less than a revolution through the medium of thought. It led to a revolution through action.

Anatole France spoke the funeral oration for Zola's friends and fellow writers:

One is supposed to say over a grave only solemn words of peace and calm. But you know well that peace resides only in justice, and calm only in truth I am not going to betray justice when it commands me to praise what is praiseworthy. I am not going to hide the truth. Why should I be silent? Silence for them, for his slanderers!

When I recall the fight that Zola undertook for truth and justice I cannot keep silent about those who conspired to destroy an innocent man and who felt they were sinking when he was saved. How could I show you Zola otherwise, when he, weak and unarmed, stood up to them? . . .

With the calm and solemnity that a place of death commands, I am going to remind you of the dark days when the government was in the grip of egotism and fear. Some people began to recognize the injustice done but it was supported and defended by so many—open and secret—powers that even the boldest hesitated. Those whose duty it was to speak up kept silent. Their betters, who did not fear for themselves, were fearful of exposing their party to incalculable dangers. The masses, misled by dreadful lies, excited by monstrous aspersions, felt betrayed. . . .

The darkness became more impenetrable. Uneasy silence ruled. This was the moment when Zola wrote to the President of the Republic that poised and frightful letter which unmasked fraud and forgery.

You all know how he was then treated by the criminals, by their defenders who were their associates in crime, by the parties allied to every kind of reaction, and by the misled masses; and you know, you all have seen how innocent souls in their simplicity joined in with the ugly horde of rabble-rousers.

You heard the cries of wrath, and the threats of death that followed Zola to the Palais de Justice, while that long trial took place—that trial which concluded in deliberate ignorance, relying on perjury and on saber-rattling. . . .

In those days heavy with crime, good citizens despaired of the fate of the country, the moral destiny of France. . . . Justice, honor, spirit—all seemed lost.

All was saved. Zola discovered not merely a miscarriage of justice. He exposed the conspiracy of all the forces of violence and suppression that had joined hands to kill social justice, the idea of the Republic and the free spirit in France. His bold words awoke France from her sleep.

The consequences of his act are incalculable. They unfold today in their great potency. They called to life a movement for social justice that cannot be smothered. A new order of things originated in his words, based on a fuller justice, and a deeper insight into the rights of all.

Gentlemen, there is one country only in which such great events could happen. So admirable is the genius of our country! So beautiful is the soul of France which in the century gone by brought the idea of right and justice to Europe and the world. France is the country of reason and of the pondering spirit, the country of just judges and humane philosophers. . . . Zola deserved well of France when he refused to accept the fact that justice was no more in France.

Do not pity him for what he had to endure and suffer. Envy him! He had deserved well of the country, as he had of the world by an immense lifework and a great act. Fate and his courage swept him to the summit; to be, for one instant, the conscience of mankind.

Part Five

VICTORY

32

BROAD-SHOULDERED Mathieu Dreyfus, the generous, dedicated man whose sacrifice had elevated a life that might otherwise have been absorbed by his business to high moral and spiritual planes on which he consorted as a friend with the greatest thinkers, artists and writers of the country—Mathieu never ceased to hunt for evidence that would vindicate his brother. His counsel was now Henri Mornard, who had pleaded for Alfred before the High Court of Appeal. Mathieu came to him untiringly with fresh discoveries. But Mornard was a wise man. The evidence, Mornard told Mathieu, must be at once unassailable and overwhelming. A new defeat would also be the last one.

One of his friends suggested that Mathieu dig into the true reason why the court-martial in Rennes had convicted Alfred. Two officers on that court had voted "Not Guilty." An approach to either or both of them was advised. The chances were they would not mind seeing their lonely stand justified by the High Court of Appeal.

Mathieu began visiting Rennes, meeting acquaintances of the judges, letting them talk, and listening. One of the dissenting judges was a genuinely religious man named Lancrau de Bréon. After his vote for acquittal had become known he had secluded himself to avoid the reproaches of his former friends. He was inaccessible to Mathieu. However, Mathieu heard that an officer named Beauvais, also a judge at the court-martial, had once angrily protested at the Officers Club in Rennes in the following vein: "Jouaust and Bréon voted for acquittal. When I and the rest found him guilty, Jouaust lost his temper and harangued us about convicting an innocent man. Thereupon two of the judges, whom he had convinced, asked Jouaust to put on record that they had changed their minds. But Jouaust refused. He said that according to the law a vote, once cast, cannot be changed. There was one way left at least to lessen the consequences of the verdict, and that was to admit extenuating circumstances. That actually happened, but against my vote. I was for the maximum penalty."

Colonel Jouaust lived in retirement. He had once told friends who inquired about the trial that he was writing his memoirs to make the truth known, but that they would not be published until after his death. Mathieu kept trying to find out who were the two judges who had changed their minds. One after another of the judges had to be eliminated for different reasons. At last only one remained. He, like Jouaust, lived in retirement and was therefore quite free to talk if he wanted to. His name was Maurice Merle. It was said of him in Montpellier, where he lived, that while serving on the court-martial he had been unable to prevent tears from coming to his eyes while listening to Demange's summation. Mercier had noticed it and had sent a message of reprimand.

Mathieu could find no way of approaching Merle. He was on the point of giving up when he met a country doctor, Roger Dumas, a revisionist who enjoyed the thought that he might be instrumental in bringing about a final solution. The doctor was a diplomat. He chose his moment and engaged Merle in conversation about trials in general. To his question whether Merle, in his long career as a military judge, had ever had pangs of conscience over convicting a man, Merle answered "Never." Not even in the Dreyfus case? No, said Merle, there had been absolute certitude there.

This was only the beginning. Whenever Dr. Dumas met Merle he introduced the topic once more. He implored Merle to set his mind at ease on the question of Dreyfus' guilt by telling him on what evidence the judge had cast his vote as he did. Was it the *bordereau*? Esterhazy? Mercier? The secret file? Merle discarded one item after the other. When nothing further seemed left, the doctor exclaimed: "Then, could it be true, after all, that it was that abominable story of the *bordereau* written on thick paper with the notes of the German Emperor in the margin, naming Dreyfus?" Merle became frightened: "Don't talk of that. Anyway, he was guilty. And I have not told you anything." A couple of weeks later they chanced to meet, and the doctor again appealed to his conscience. Finally Merle promised that he would talk if the case were to be investigated.

The doctor asked Mathieu by wire to come to Rennes. Together they concocted a plan. They summed up in a letter their interpretation of Merle's frightened reaction and Dumas then asked him to vouch for this with his signature. Merle became suspicious that Dr. Dumas was an agent of Dreyfus and refused to engage in further conversations.

But it seemed evident that General Mercier had used the same trick on the second court-martial that he had on the first: secret forged documents which the defendant was given no opportunity to inspect. This supposition proved to be true. Mercier had met the second desperate situation by the same desperate means. He was the kind of confident general who might have led his armies to great victories or to complete destruction. On this battlefield it was to be destruction. Jaurès was to use the very same documents as the lever of Dreyfus' vindication.

No one has seen the affair more clearly and presented it with more lucidity and force than Jaurès in his book, *The Proofs*. Jaurès was an old hand at politics. Before joining the last battle he made the rounds among the republicans, sounding them out on what support he might expect. Premier Waldeck, though he disliked diverting his attention from the fight against clericalism, let himself be counted. The Radical Henri Brisson promised his unqualified support. But the rank and file remained reluctant to commit themselves. They feared that the affair still contained enough dynamite to put new vigor into old passions and confound their work against the nationalists. They preferred to wait.

Jaurès planned his offensive carefully. Then he, too, waited—but only for some chance remark to set the battle off. He did not have to wait long. A Moderate criticized the Left for making political capital out of some judicial case. Jaurès hurried to the speakers' stand. Through two straight sessions he told the Chamber in detail how General Mercier's lie about the German Emperor's note had misled the press, the public, the Chamber and the court-martial. It had even survived the affair. It had reappeared on posters at the last elections in an effort to brand the republicans as a party of foreign agents! "Party of

foreign agents indeed," Jaurès cried. "Who but the Right dragged
the German Emperor himself into the Dreyfus case, to make external
affairs subservient to domestic needs?"

The deputies had no very thorough knowledge of the affair. Such
stands as they had taken had been on the strength of arguments that
knitted various facts into a plausible cloak for their prejudices—for
neutrality, or for or against the Republic. Jaurès' tale fascinated them.
A forceful voice and a wealth of thought and emotion emerged from
that bearded, luxuriant-haired politician. Finally, he arrived at
Henry's confession of his forgery and read out General Pellieux's
letter of resignation: "Dupe of people without honor, having lost my
trust in my chiefs who bade me work on forgeries . . ."

At this point, Brisson broke in. "Excuse me for my interruption,"
he said. "If I understood you correctly, General Pellieux's letter carries the date of August 31, 1898."

"Yes," replied Jaurès.

"I was Premier at that time," cried Brisson indignantly, "and I declare that the government of which I was the head had no knowledge
of that letter."

His words had a startling effect. All eyes in the Chamber turned to
Godefroy Cavaignac, Minister of War at that time, who had made
Henry confess. Gnawed by cancer of the liver, Cavaignac, jaundiced,
stubborn and forceful in his narrow fanaticism, faced the storm un-
daunted. "This is a prearranged affair," he shouted, and the performance did show the marks of careful timing. Pellieux, as a matter
of fact, had sent his resignation to the Military Commander of Paris,
General Zurlinden, who had requested him to think it over. Pellieux
had thereupon withdrawn his resignation.

However, it was now out in the open that Pellieux had mentioned
"forgeries" in the plural, though Henry had confessed to but one.
Though the great scene petered out in mutual recriminations, Jaurès
had made his point. His own party moved that an investigation of
the General Staff and the military courts be conducted. The Radicals,
frightened at the prospect of any further airing of the affair in the
Chamber, were inclined to kill the motion. But the Chamber arrived
at a compromise. It passed a resolution that it would not oppose an
investigation if the Minister of War complied with a request to
make one. The request came promptly. Dreyfus presented it to the
Minister of War. He described the alleged note of the Emperor as a

forgery and the testimony of Cernuski, the Austrian of royal Serbian blood, in support of it as perjury.

In spite of Jaurès' exhortation to the republican parties—he told them that they would remain powerless as long as Dreyfus remained a traitor in the eyes of the law—the deputies would not budge from their timorous seat on the fence. "The public followed the prolonged debates absent-mindedly," Reinach wrote. "To their own surprise, they could find no reason to be passionate. It had become possible now to discuss the affair calmly. We may witness in the near future, a broad investigation carried out—and no storms gathering around it." But no deputies gathered around it either.

The Ministry of War conducted an investigation. Unexpectedly, there was wholehearted co-operation from Félix Gribelin, the archivist. He assembled the scattered pieces of evidence of Henry's forgeries. They were in far greater number than anyone had conceived.

A Panizzardi letter had been on file. The haunting initial "D" reappeared in this entirely insignificant message. The initial had originally been not "D" but "P." A routine Henry forgery.

Gribelin readily traced the multitude of undisclosed forgeries as well as the disclosed ones. He was in one man the essence of the wrong side of the Dreyfus issue. He had all the perverted integrity that went into the make-up of the true anti-Dreyfusard. To the last he preserved Henry's memory as a kind of cult. Nothing could have shaken his belief in Dreyfus' guilt. He knew that all the evidence was forged. He himself exposed such forgeries as not even the most convinced Dreyfusards suspected existed. But they made not one dent in that strange psyche bound in its private iron.

To whom or to what does an officer's loyalty belong? Two principal actors of the affair wrestled with the dilemma and came to opposite conclusions. One was Picquart, who believed he owed loyalty to the moral purposes of the institution of the Army. Devoid of the spirit, the institution was to him but a corpse that could command no loyalty. The other was Von Schwarzkoppen, the German military attaché. Not even as late as 1901 was Joseph Reinach, at a friendly meeting in Berlin, able to unseal his lips. In 1917 Von Schwarzkoppen, then a general, was in a Berlin hospital on the brink of death. He began talking French in a delirium. "Frenchmen," his wife heard him cry out in the language of the enemy, "listen to me. Dreyfus is innocent.

It was all just forgery and intrigue. There is nothing whatever against him!" He died the same year.

His memoirs, which completely exonerate Dreyfus and incriminate Esterhazy with respect to the *bordereau,* were not published until 1930. Von Schwarzkoppen had remained loyal to his army although it had made him commit a crime.

The Minister of War forwarded Dreyfus' request for revision, together with the new evidence uncovered by his investigation, to the High Court of Appeal in March 1904. The court, determined to leave no doubt or ambiguity unresolved, ordered a new hearing of the witnesses.

The parade began—a parade of witnesses and documents from the past, from the Rennes of five years before, from the Zola trial of two years before that, from the triumphant trial of Esterhazy, from the first trial of Dreyfus in 1894. A tranquil, muted air greeted the ancients. It all had the aspect of a stale, old, dead-seeming feud. The witnesses were ten years older. Old loyalties were dissolved. Some were disgruntled by premature retirement or involuntary seclusion in the countryside. The political parties they disliked were now firmly in power. One would have thought their minds would change as their bodies had, as their position in life had. But it hadn't happened. With the tenacity of automatons the same witnesses said the same things. Old soldiers never die, the song goes, they merely fade away, and the fading voices droned on—old men, old, old men saying that whatever anybody might prove, they had all been honorable and were still honorable.

The few witnesses who still could argue passionately had a refreshing effect on the judges, the prosecutor, the attorneys, and the representatives of the War Ministry. Cuignet, the officer who had been the first to detect Henry's forgery, was nearly deranged by now with remorse over Henry's suicide. For ten hours he foamed torrentially before the court, heaping accusations: on the justices and the public prosecutor, who, he said, were afraid of the truth; on the previous High Court for having sent his testimony at the first hearing to the Italian Ambassador, who had then declared that the text of the Panizzardi telegram as Cuignet had read it was distorted. He accused the then Minister of Foreign Affairs, Delcassé, of having forged the text, and the Post and Telegraph Administration of having produced the forged text of the telegram to confirm the Foreign Minister's forgery. He accused the present Minister of War, General André, and his aide of having falsified the files to procure new Henry forgeries. In their stolid determination not to leave any allegation, even a mad one, unsettled, the justices summoned the Minister of War, General André, who then sent Colonel Chamoin to testify that each and every document in the files was unaltered and in the same state as it had been in 1899. But, of course, nothing could prove that to Cuignet.

Du Paty was heard for three days straight. He too accused the two ministries of falsifications. The Panizzardi letter with the initial "P" instead of "D" was, according to him, a recent forgery. He did not recognize the ill-famed commentary on Dreyfus that he had passed on to the judges at the first court-martial. He was allowed to bring in his own draft and compare it with the text in the file. He discovered for the first time that General Mercier had altered it in order to incriminate Dreyfus more drastically. Yet he wasn't shaken. He said that he was now definitely convinced of Dreyfus' guilt because of new evidence found by Bertillon.

The court settled itself grimly for an encounter with the bewildering anthropometrist's newest confusion. There was a cut on the right edge of the *bordereau*, Bertillon testified, and exactly the same cut appeared on a letter Dreyfus had written at his home. It showed up in a piece of blotting paper taken from Dreyfus' home when he was arrested. The court decided to summon three experts of great reputation to give Bertillon's testimony the very best attention available. The mathematician Poincaré, Permanent Secretary of the Academy, Darboux, and D'Appel, Dean of the Faculty of Science at the Sorbonne, examined the theory, and the Observatory lent them precision instruments constructed originally for lunar photography. But it took more than these and their lunar instruments to follow Bertillon into his private stratosphere.

Into the midst of the generals and former ministers there popped suddenly plump Mme. Bastian. In the housecleaning that overtook the German Embassy after the Dreyfus Affair, she had been swept out. No more wastebaskets for her now. She was living on relief and she cursed the Jew Dreyfus for it.

The court patiently tackled the final legend. Had there ever existed such a document as the *bordereau* written on thick paper of which the one in the file on a thin sheet was but a copy? If it had ever existed, did it carry on its margin a note written by the German Emperor referring to Dreyfus? And if all this was true, had it been returned to the German Ambassador on threat of war after a photostatic copy of it was made? The court again heard Casimir-Périer, President of the Republic in 1894, and two former Ministers of Foreign Affairs. They testified that no such document had ever entered their conversations with Count Münster, the German Ambassador, that his interventions in the case had been over the hooliganism of the press and had not involved any threat, and that anyway, the conversations had taken place after Dreyfus was condemned.

No one would admit ever having seen even a photostatic copy of the document. General Mercier was questioned. So was the deputy Millevoye, who had quoted its text to a mass meeting. But they all wriggled out. General Mercier testified that he had heard about it from Colonel Stoffel, former French military attaché in Berlin. Stoffel, almost eighty years old now, was summoned; he denied that he had seen the document. He had heard of it, though, from a person as worthy of belief as any justice on the court. However, he refused to name the person. He did not deny that he had dictated the text of the imperial marginalia, but said he had done it from memory so that he could not guarantee its exactness. General Mercier, forced into a corner and perhaps tired, suddenly deposed that he personally had never believed in the existence of the document. The journalists refused to reveal the source of their information, or else named people who had heard of the documents only from others. Paléologue said that he had had it from Henry, who had mentioned it to others, including Esterhazy. Esterhazy had laughed in his face. Maybe that was why Henry had buried this particular forgery. Certainly it could not have been more transparent than those he had preserved.

The investigation came to a close at last and the case was forwarded to a joint session of the three chambers of the High Court of Appeal. Two justices, designated to report on the case, apparently were appalled by the formidable quantity of documents. One declined on grounds of health. Finally a justice, Clément Moras, undertook the task. It was now May 1906. The Government and court delayed until after the elections. The elections marked another crushing victory for the leftist coalition. Nationalists, clericals and anti-Semites were beaten.

But the mills ground on and another working day came to the Palais de Justice. June 18, 1906. The justices of all three chambers of the High Court of Appeal, in ermine-bordered togas, took their seats, Justice Ballot-Beaupré presiding. No exceptional precautionary measures had been taken by the police. There were no throngs to jam the room. There were only the Dreyfus family and a few of the old Dreyfusard guard. For the rest, only lawyers curious about a great legal decision. Manuel Baudouin, representing the state, had on the desk in front of him the bulging manuscript of his plea. He was to take eight sessions to deliver it. He was flanked on one side by Justice Moras, who was to report on the case, on the other side by Mornard, and Demange for Dreyfus. Labori did not even come as an onlooker.

The setting aside of the Rennes sentence was a foregone conclusion. Yet the audience was tense until the end. One question tormented not only those present but the Government as well. Would this court return the case to the military court for a new trial or would it itself announce a final decision? If a military court had to decide again, and decided once more to defy the highest civilian tribunal of the country, the consequences might be disastrous. The Government might be forced to reshape the military organization and jurisdiction completely, even to the point where it might endanger the Army's efficiency and the country's security. It would bring the Dreyfus Affair back into the national mind with a roar. Yes, it was an anxious question.

Mathieu Dreyfus hastened to greet Picquart. He rebuffed the attempt at a *rapprochement* with a nervous gesture. Mathieu returned unhappily to his brother and sister-in-law, who had expected the rebuff and had declined to go out of their way to get it.

The reporting justice stated that from the legal point of view there probably had been no crime at all committed, by Dreyfus or by anyone else. As Picquart himself at one of his hearings had pointed out, the *bordereau* was not a delivery of documents, only a list of documents. There was no proof that these documents, whatever they had been worth, had actually been delivered. But even if they had been, the documents enumerated in the *bordereau* were valueless. Some had been published in military magazines in France or in Germany before the *bordereau* was written, and also the rest were not secret. They were not even confidential. The audience stared. Was everything about this drama unreal? Had it all been a crazy structure of forgeries and lies built on nothing for no reason, a nightmare dreamed during a nightmare?

Mere contact with the enemy, of course, might be punishable. But did not Esterhazy in this exceptional instance tell the truth, that he and his accomplices had sold worthless, even misleading documents as patriotic Frenchmen working against Germans?

For some, in particular for Clemenceau, there was a strange beauty in the fact that the fratricidal battle which for twelve years had ravaged the life of a whole generation had had no material base but had been fought for ideas in the abstract. The Tiger had not shared his friends' disappointment over the fact that Dreyfus in person had proved so inadequate to the part he had been chosen by fate to play. "It is better this way," Clemenceau had said. "At least no one will accuse us of having hurled ourselves into the battle for reasons of personal sympathy."

Henri Mornard, Dreyfus' attorney, unrolled the story of prejudice at work in the case of Dreyfus. Prejudice had dimmed the faculty not only of judgment but of perception. It had distorted reality to fit in with a preconceived unreality. It had made the very paradigms of honest men act dishonestly without the slightest scruple. He went down the list. Bonnefond, general examiner at the Ecole de Guerre, had given Dreyfus a poor mark because he had disliked the idea of a Jew on the General Staff. Lebelin de Dionne, director of the school, had uncovered the unfairness but had refused to revise the marks nevertheless. "The Jew received all the honors that were his due." With this remark he dismissed the case. General Vanson had been assigned to prepare a confidential study tour for the staff probationers. "Watch out," he had been warned by Colonel Bardal, "there is a Jew among the three officers." General Roget had set Dreyfus the task of sketching a logistical plan on assumed facts. Dreyfus had expressed a preference for working out the proposition from actual data. Roget had made a mental note of it. Why? Because Dreyfus was a Jew. D'Aboville had discovered that the writing on the *bordereau* was similar to that of Dreyfus. Sandherr had slapped his hand against his forehead: "How could I have not thought of that?" Even before Dreyfus had known he was accused, he was done for. The mere mention of his name convicted him. Du Paty had imagined that he saw Dreyfus' hand tremble. Proof of guilt. But when Du Paty saw that Dreyfus' hand actually did not tremble it was even greater proof of guilt. Only a crime-hardened hand could have remained steady.

When *La Libre Parole* announced that treason had been committed by a Jew, the public needed no further evidence of guilt. When the real traitor had been discovered, and even when he confessed, the Jews were blamed. They had bought Esterhazy. He was their straw man. Delivery of documents to an agent of a foreign power had been in all previous cases classified by the courts as espionage punishable by a limited term in prison, but in the case of the Jew it had been declared high treason, punishable by lifelong deportation. Devil's Island had been given up as a place of deportation because of its inhuman conditions; it was good enough for Dreyfus. The wives of deportees had the privilege of joining their husbands, but a special order deprived Mme. Dreyfus of this privilege.

So it had gone, but now it had come to an end. On July 12, 1906, the High Court set aside the sentence of the court-martial at Rennes and declared that its verdict of "Guilty" had been erroneous. The court announced that there existed no incriminating evidence of any kind against Dreyfus and that a retrial, since there never had been any facts to try, was unnecessary. The court found that Dreyfus had renounced his right to an indemnity and ordered that its verdict be posted in Paris and Rennes, printed in the official gazette and in another fifty French papers of Dreyfus' choosing, at the expense of the treasury.

President Ballot-Beaupré then elaborated on the reasons for the verdict, a summary unprecedented in its elimination of even the slightest reason for doubt or suspicion. His reading lasted an hour. The case was closed.

The Government without delay undertook the rehabilitation of Dreyfus and of Picquart. It resolved to submit to the Chamber a bill promoting Dreyfus to *chef d'escadron* and conferring on him the distinction of a Knight of the Legion of Honor. Dreyfus, but for the affair, would have been a lieutenant colonel. He was dissatisfied with the promotion and decided to ask for his retirement instead. Picquart was recommended for the rank he would have achieved normally by now—brigadier general.

Next day both Chambers voted the reintegration into the Army of the two officers "to liberate the conscience of France." Only twenty-six deputies voted against. In the Senate, General Mercier rose to protest. He accused the High Court of partiality. A chorus of indignant shouts prevented him from finishing.

The Supreme Council of the Legion of Honor ratified unanimously the Government's proposal to decorate Dreyfus, "an appropriate reparation for a soldier who had endured a martyrdom without parallel."

On July 22, 1906, a military parade took place in a small yard of the Ecole Militaire. It was not made public; only a few friends were invited. Most of the men who had fought hardest for this day received no invitation. Picquart watched from one window, Mme. Dreyfus from another.

Dreyfus arrived at half past one and quietly chatted with a group of officers. A trumpet sounded a call. Two *escadrons de cuirassiers* formed a rectangle. A captain went to escort Dreyfus, who was in full dress. They stepped briskly along the line of *cuirassiers*. Suddenly the blood rushed to Dreyfus' face. For a moment reality dissolved and there came in its place more sharply and clearly than reality itself the frightful degradation that had been visited upon him twelve years before in this very school. His whole body trembled and he almost fainted. No one noticed. He kept on walking mechanically, rigidly, fixed in the manner that was so distressing to those who felt sympathy for him.

Brigadier General Gillain passed before the troops and drew his sword. Dreyfus was led to a position in front of him. Four calls sounded from the trumpet.

"In the name of the President of the Republic, and on the basis of the power conferred on me, Commander Dreyfus, I make you a Knight of the Legion of Honor," the general announced, and touched his sword three times to Dreyfus' shoulders. He pinned the cross on Dreyfus' black dolman and kissed him on both cheeks. "You once served in my division," the general said. "I am glad that I was entrusted with the mission that I have just accomplished."

The last trumpet calls rang out. People cried, "Long live the Army! Long live truth!" The general and Dreyfus stood to attention as the troops marched off to the sound of fanfares. Visitors came to shake hands with Dreyfus. Suddenly a boy ran up to embrace him. It was his son Pierre. Only then did Dreyfus burst into tears.

Alfred mounted into an open carriage flanked by Mathieu and his son. They rode out of the yard. There was a surprise. Two hundred thousand people had gathered spontaneously in the streets. It was a friendly crowd. Happiness radiated on all the faces. Hats were raised to Dreyfus. "Long live Dreyfus! Long live justice!" With one hand he waved greetings and thanks, a smile on his pale face.

AN EPILOGUE

33

IN 1914 CAME the long-dreaded German aggression.

Republicans who proclaimed themselves the heirs of the Great Revolution had headed the Government of France uninterruptedly since the end of the Dreyfus Affair. They were destined to be subjected to a test unprecedented even in France's sorely tried past. Their call to the nation to take up arms and defend the country was answered with equal determination by Catholics, agnostics, Protestants and Jews, "integral" nationalists of the Right, revolutionary syndicalists of the Left.

The Church and the Army stood fast, the first to serve the faith, the second to defend the land. The nation in arms halted with superb courage and sacrifice the first, fateful German onslaught on the Marne. The sympathy of the whole world went out to France; old and new allies armed themselves and worked to ship troops, ammunition and food to help the nation against Imperial Germany.

After three years of war Tsarist Russia and the eastern front collapsed. The Germans hurled all their armies into a final onslaught against France. Morale began to falter and the call went out to an aged statesman, the old Tiger, Georges Clemenceau.

He took over leadership from the generals, forced the Allies to accept a united command, imprisoned and exiled defeatist politicians, imposed his indomitable will on the country, on the Allies and on the enemy. His obsession with nothing less than complete victory, and at any price, infused soldiers and civilians with dedication for a last supreme effort. "I shall fight before Paris," he said. "I shall fight behind Paris. The Germans may take Paris but that will not stop me from carrying on the war. We shall fight on the Loire, we shall fight on the

Garonne, we shall fight even on the Pyrenees. And should we be driven off the Pyrenees, we shall continue the war from the sea. But as for asking for peace: never!"

On November 11, 1918, salvos of guns saluted a Paris mad with joy. Inside the Chamber of Deputies, Clemenceau rose. Erect, impassive, his Mongolian face inscrutable, he held a telegram in his black-gloved right hand. The hand did not tremble; neither did the voice that read the telegram reporting Germany's request for an armistice and willingness to cede Alsace-Lorraine back to France. The "Marseillaise" rang out with a grandeur never before experienced.

The Republic had reconquered France's place in the world.

One year after his rehabilitation Alfred Dreyfus retired from active service to the privacy of home life with his wife Lucie, who had borne the affair with so much dignity.

In 1908 he took part in the ceremony with which Zola's ashes were transferred to the Panthéon. An anti-Semitic journalist named Gregory fired two shots at him, wounding him slightly in the arm. Gregory was subsequently acquitted. The jury treated it as a crime of passion, carried out while Gregory was temporarily of unsound mind. The French are notoriously sympathetic to crimes of passion.

Sarah Bernhardt, the world-famous actress, wrote Dreyfus the following:

You have suffered again, and we have wept again. Yet you should suffer no more, and we cry no more. The flag of truth is placed in the hand of the illustrious dead in the vault. This flag will flutter high above the heads of the howling pack. Suffer no more, dear martyr. Look around you: near and far, and ever farther, you will see that mass of people who love you and defend you from cowardice and lies and oblivion. Among those people is your friend Sarah Bernhardt.

News of the mobilization in 1914 reached Dreyfus in Switzerland. He first served in the northern zone of the fortifications of Paris, then fought in the two bloodiest battles of the war—Chemin des Dames and Verdun. In September 1918 he was promoted to lieutenant colonel and made an officer of the Legion of Honor.

On June 1, 1930, he received a letter from Hanover, Germany. It was signed by Louise von Schwarzkoppen, née Baronne von Wedel. It read:

Much esteemed Monsieur Dreyfus: I am mailing you under separate cover the diary of my late husband, General of the Infantry Max von Schwarzkoppen, published by Colonel Schwertfeger, and called *The Truth About Dreyfus.*

I believe that I do this in the spirit of my husband whose wish has always been to testify in the monstrous trial of which you were the central figure and victim. For reasons that his memoirs clearly indicate, this was impossible for him to do.

After a long illness, Alfred Dreyfus died quietly in bed on July 11, 1935.

Esterhazy survived to an obscure old age in a slum quarter of London. He had a room in a poor boardinghouse. He used to sleep through the day and walk out after sunset. Once a month he called at the post office for a registered letter containing money. No one knew who sent it. He assumed the name of Count Jean de Voilemont. It stands above his grave in the village of Harpenden, England. He died in 1923.

The good Mathieu Dreyfus lost his son and his son-in-law in the First World War. He died in 1930, a heart-broken man.

General Picquart became Minister of War in 1908, in Clemenceau's Cabinet. He was expected to be the architect of the reform of the Army. He is not known to have taken any initiative to that effect. The fate that had first brushed him in Africa and made him take his statement to his lawyer finally overtook him. In January 1914 he fell from his horse, injuring his skull. It did not seem serious. The next day he worked at his desk as usual, but he collapsed in the afternoon and died on January 19.

"What matter the errors of fate and false directions in life?" Jaurès wrote on his death. "A few luminous and fervent hours are enough to give meaning to a lifetime."

A NOTE ON SOURCES

THE DISEASE which afflicted French public opinion appears as the first instance of its kind in history whose full course was documented in print. The press offered not only a day-by-day recording of the mass delusion and its heroic cure, but was also the medium through which the event itself came to pass. The top figures of the Dreyfus Affair were writers; the events themselves, articles in newspapers; the combats, polemics; the weapon, the pen.

Joseph Reinach's monumental chronicle includes an admirable survey of the daily press. The articles of Zola, Clemenceau, Barrès, Jaurès and other leaders were collected and published in book form. Wilhelm Herzog reprinted in chronological order the newspaper articles that made history. This work, and Walter Frank's record of the period, reflect the official German position in detail. Incidentally, the Columbia University master's thesis of Rose A. Halperin contains documentation on American public interest.

Second only to the daily press as a source of information are the ample reservoirs of pamphlet literature. Lesser spirits yielded to the urge to air their consciences, thus contributing to an atmosphere in which lies and truth equally throve. Their words were liberally used, still hot with the passion that inspired them.

The intricate minutiae, however, are disclosed by the records of the court proceedings. The court-martial at Rennes as well as the preceding and subsequent actions of the High Court of Appeal stand out.

The legal analysis of the affair was conducted on a high level by both parties. The case against Dreyfus is impressively presented by Dutrait-Crozon. Not until Von Schwarzkoppen's posthumous book appeared, in 1930, was all doubt of his innocence dispelled in anti-Dreyfusard circles.

On specific points of French modern history, American authors are illuminating: Paul Farmer on the role played by the idea of the French Revolution, and R. F. Byrnes on anti-Semitism.

INDEX

ABOUT THE AUTHOR

NICHOLAS HALASZ *was born in Hungary in 1895. He was educated at the University of Pressburg, in Czechoslovakia, and at the Sorbonne in Paris. In 1941 he moved his home from France to the United States. Mr. Halasz has written extensively in European periodicals on law, philosophy, social psychology and history, and has been a foreign correspondent for newspapers in Hungary, Czechoslovakia, Canada and the United States.*